FINDING HOPE
In Times of Crisis

FINDING HOPE
In Times of Crisis

DON BAKER

INSPIRATIONAL PRESS

NEW YORK

This work was originally published as three volumes.

Depression: Finding Hope and Meaning in Life's Dark Shadow
© 1983 by Don Baker, Emery Nester

Pain's Hidden Purpose
© 1984 by Don Baker

Acceptance
© 1985 by Don Baker

Published in 1992 by
Inspirational Press
A division of LDAP, Inc.
386 Park Avenue South
New York, New York 10016

Inspirational Press is a registered trademark of LDAP, Inc.

Published by arrangement with Multnomah Press

Library of Congress Catalog Card Number: 92-70617

ISBN: 0-88486-058-2

Printed in the United States of America.

Contents

Depression

Finding Hope & Meaning
In Life's Darkest Shadow

To Martha,
who faithfully
supported her husband
in his time of great need,

and

to Mary Ann,
who willingly
shared her husband
in his time of great challenge.

Contents

Foreword

It's a Sunday evening. It's been a beautiful, cool, sunny day in Fullerton. I'm sitting in my favorite spot in our home—a lovely enclosed patio. It's like an indoor garden with lots of plants and two sofas surrounding our favorite old black Franklin stove. A fire has been burning for hours, earlier shared with some dear friends from Waco.

Watching the flames dance from the burning coals, I find myself reflecting for a moment on my past. It is difficult to believe my life was darkened by depression for so long—*fifteen years*.

Depression . . . black as a thousand midnights in a cypress swamp. Loneliness that is indescribable. Confusion regarding God. Frustration with life and circumstances. The feeling that you have been abandoned, that you are worthless. Unloveable. The pain is excruciating.

The roots of depression lie much deeper than our twentieth century living-in-the-fast-lane lifestyle. The very first recorded incident of depression is in Genesis 4. Cain's offering of the fruit from the ground had not been regarded by God. Upon learning that, Cain became angry and depressed. God told Cain, "If you do right, will there not be a lifting up? But if you misbehave, sin is crouching at the door; its intention is toward you, and you must master it" (Genesis 4:7, Berkeley[1]). God's instructions for getting out of the pit emphasized actions of obedience—regardless of feelings.

Did Cain choose to respond to God and do what was right? No. Instead, he had words with his brother Abel and then killed him. Cain chose not to assume any responsibility for his downcast spirit; he did not master his attitudes.

7

Perhaps those few words hold the key that unlocks the door to the black pit of depression. But knowing the responsible way out is sometimes as elusive as a mirage in the desert.

Chuck and I first met Don Baker at a Mount Hermon family conference in the summer of 1979. We immediately fell in love with him and Martha, his wife, and had a grand time during the conference.

One evening Don chose to speak publicly, for the first time, about his own past in the black pit. His vivid imagery immediately brought painful memories to mind. My thoughts returned to the previous spring when Chuck and I had experienced some deep hurts in our Christian service. For the first time in our twenty-four years of ministry, we were both depressed. At the same time. The pain of that experience lasted for nearly four months. But even more vividly, I was reminded of a now distant past when depression had been my own constant companion. So many of the thoughts Don expressed about his depression were feelings I too had shared.

With much emotion I waited until everyone had cleared from Don's presence after the meeting. Then, with my back to those still in the auditorium, I wept with Don. I commended him for his courage to communicate in such a manner and expressed how I had never possessed such courage. His manner of openness had shown me how effectively our lives can minister—providing examples for others in their walk with God through the inevitable change and pain of life.

One of the most beautiful aspects of walking with a sovereign God is His ability to orchestrate the interchange of lives—at just the right moment—to accomplish His own divine plan. The entry of Emery Nester into Don's world during his struggle certainly verified this truth.

Emery had been in the pastorate, and at the time of his meetings with Don, he was a psychologist. Their paths crossed when both were in the pit—hardly a situation providing much hope. I love Emery's persistent pursuit of Don, and his true example of a godly love. He saw Don weekly and spent 100 hours counseling him. Wouldn't it be great if we all had such a claim to friendship?

Even though I wasn't there, I'm confident their time together was marked by a constant attempt to know what was right so they could "do what was right." I'm sure they measured every thought and action against God's Word, though at times their feelings claimed that those truths were lies.

Indeed, insofar as is humanly possible, they came to master their attitudes and finally experience the lifting of their spirits and countenances. They were free. They *are* free.

This book is the result of their pilgrimage, and how privileged we are to be allowed access to that segment of their lives. I know their exposure comes from an intense desire to assist in lifting others from that dismal pit.

If you find the pit your habitat, let me suggest that you read these pages slowly and embellish their words with your own experiences.

Think constantly "what is my responsibility to the circumstances of this day, to the information I have just received?" Then follow through with actions. God instructs us to obey . . . He doesn't say to wait until we *feel* like obeying.

It is my prayer, along with the prayers of Don and Emery, that you will find these insights helpful for you as well as those you love. *Depression* is truly a book of hope and encouragement.

Cynthia Swindoll
Executive Director, Insight for Living

---

[1]*The Modern Language Bible, The New Berkeley Version in Modern English*, copyright 1945, 1959, 1969 by Zondervan Publishing House.

Preface

It is impossible for those who have never been depressed to fully understand the deep, perplexing pain that depression causes.

For four interminable years I appeared healthy, without bandages and without crutches. There were no visible scars, no bleeding, and yet there was the endless, indefinable pain that no doctor's probing fingers could locate—no drug could totally relieve. There was always the pain and along with it the desire for oblivion—an oblivion that would only come in minute snatches of restless sleep.

I seemed to be out of touch with reality. Life was a blur, often out of focus. My life seemed to be nothing but pretense and fantasy. No one really cared, I felt—not even God. The only solution—at times—seemed to be suicide.

To be told that Christians never get depressed only pushed me deeper into my black hole of depression.

The way out of that black hole was a long and painful process—one that required the sensitive and insightful counsel of a friend.

Emery walked with me in my blackness and gradually, but persistently, helped me to unravel the shroud that had forced darkness upon me.

I narrate Part 1 of this book, and Emery discusses depression in Part 2. As we combine our memories and insights, it is our purpose to help you better understand depression and to see that Christians can and do experience it, family and friends can help you through it, and God can use it to enhance and enrich your life.

Don Baker

PART
1

THE PATH OF
EXPERIENCE

Don Baker

"Lord, all my desire is before Thee;
And my sighing is not hidden from Thee.
My heart throbs, my strength fails me;
And the light of my eyes,
even that has gone from me."
Psalm 38:9-10

Chapter 1

Ward 7E

I had visited Ward 7E many times. Its institutional yellow walls and highly polished floors resembled most of the psychiatric wards and mental hospitals where I had gone to minister to members of my congregation.

There's always a certain apprehension that lurks in the shadows of one's mind while walking down those sterile, silent corridors. Behind each door is a different story. I've listened to them all. The criminally insane, the suicidal, the depressed, the alcoholic, the hostile, the addict, and then on many occasions I've tried to talk to those who have forgotten how to respond.

I've never felt comfortable with the mentally ill.

This time, however, my discomfort had been replaced by fear. My apprehension had given way to feelings of impending doom. The very atmosphere was charged with foreboding glimpses of the unpredictable. I was traumatized with humiliation and embarrassment. I was struggling against a creeping hostility waiting to overpower me.

This time I was being led down the silent halls of Ward 7E, not as a pastor but as a patient.

For years I had struggled to understand the unpredictable mood swings that could carry me from peaks of elation to the deep valleys of despair.

I could preach with fervor and power, I could share Christ with enthusiasm and success. I would counsel with meaningful insight and socialize with sheer delight. But without warning, any or all of these positive and delightful emotions would suddenly be forced to give way to feelings of gloom and periods of weakness. I would withdraw, and a form of paranoia would settle in. I would suddenly be overwhelmed with feelings of inadequacy and inferiority. On occasion I toyed with thoughts of self-destruction.

At times I was convinced that my problem was spiritual. I'd pore over the Scriptures, agonize in prayer, go through periods of confession, dig up any and every negative memory that could be found, and cry to God for deliverance.

At other times I was certain that the problem was physical. "I'm working too hard," I'd tell myself, and I'd then proceed to find ways to lighten the load, or even better, escape for days or weeks in an attempt to find relief. I'd had as many diagnoses as I'd had doctors.

The struggle reached its inevitable climax when I found myself too weary to minister, too filled with hostility to love, and too frightened to preach.

One Sunday morning, I collapsed in tears. A dear brother in Christ, one of my deacons, found me convulsed with sobs, unable to rise and unwilling to even try.

In the weeks and months that followed, the bewildering and overpowering bouts with depression finally led me and my family to agree that the only direction left for me was to seek competent psychiatric care.

As I walked through the steel door into Ward 7E, my one thought was that the life I had known was finished. I would never again be able to enjoy the confidence of a congregation who would trust me to shepherd them.

For days I withdrew into a medicated stupor. I resented sharing a room with one patient who was criminally insane and another who walked around like a zombie.

I refused all offers of help. I resisted any intrusions into my silence. I rejected the many opportunities to visit with friends. The only human who could break through the wall was my wife.

The doctors at this point agreed on only one thing: depression—cause or causes unknown. The term was not a new one to me. It was one, however, that I resisted.

I remembered reading Martin Lloyd-Jones's statement regarding depression. "In a sense a depressed person is a contradiction in terms, and he is a very poor recommendation for the Gospel."[1]

Bob George, director of Discipleship Counseling Services in Dallas, Texas, has stated in a Christian periodical, ". . . as children of God, we don't need to be depressed or defeated in life. God has provided us with everything we need for a life of godliness."[2] He went on to say, "When a believer is not experiencing freedom and joy in the Spirit . . . it can only be that he is nearsighted and blind and has forgotten that he has been cleansed from his past sins (2 Peter 1:9). He has forgotten his position in Christ."[3]

Tim LaHaye states in his book that the primary cause of depression is self-pity. Others have flatly stated that depression is a sin.

To be forced to acknowledge that I was depressed was, to say the least, depressing.

I hated the word. It was tantamount to sin. My limited knowledge of its meaning and its universality compounded my gloom with guilt and my frustration with anger.

In an attempt to help me feel the reality of my problem, various members of the hospital staff began gently asking probing questions:

"How do you feel?"

The answer came slowly and with great difficulty. My first response was, "I don't know." Even my feelings had become elusive and indefinable. When I did "feel" something, the words to describe that feeling came with great difficulty. It seemed that my brain had either stopped functioning or at least had slowed to an almost imperceptible pace.

Slowly the words came. Words like,
"Sad"
    "Empty"
        "Alone"
            "Hopeless"
                "Afraid"
                    "Worthless"
                        "Ambivalent"
                            "Rejected"

"Do you sleep well?"

If I'd had the inner energy, I would have laughed. I finally said, "All the time" and "Never." Sleep was no longer the necessary nightly reviving experience—it was nothing more than an escape-mechanism. I would drift off into a fitful slumber when there was work to be done and remain wide-awake during the interminably long hours of the night.

"How do you feel about your job?"

I'm a failure! I had lost touch with reality completely. My pastoral ministry had always been effective. Thousands had come to Christ. My people loved me. My churches had always grown. I have loved the Scriptures and have been in demand as a Bible teacher. My depression (and I was beginning to use the word more frequently) had completely colored, or rather discolored, my perspective on a fruitful and happy ministry.

"Do you eat well?"

"All the time," I answered. One psychiatrist asked me, "If you had three wishes, what would they be?" I could only think of one. "I'd like to get my weight down to a normal 165 pounds." I didn't know at the time whether depression was the cause of my insatiable cravings or whether my bad eating habits were causing my depression. Others, I understand now, react just the opposite. They lose interest in food. Oh, how I wished I could.

"How do you feel about yourself?"

Inadequate! My self-confidence had hit bottom. There was a total loss of self-esteem.

"How do you feel about your family?"

Unworthy! I know they love me, but I don't deserve their love. I was convinced that the many tender expressions of love from Martha, John, and Kathy were all pretense. They couldn't love me—not in the condition I was in.

"How often do you and your wife have sex?"

I couldn't remember. Not only had my interest in sex lessened, but at times I had even feared impotence.

"Are you having difficulty making decisions?"

I could hardly decide how to answer the question. For weeks I struggled with whether or not to resign my pastorate. I would read one verse of Scripture that seemed to tell me to stay and another that suggested just the opposite. I would get different answers each time I prayed.

I never was able to make that decision by myself.

"Do you like to be around people?"

"No!" An emphatic "no." "Please," I said, "just leave me alone."

"Are you often angry?"

With this question I buried my head and began to sob. "Oh yes, and always with the ones I love the most." My wife had felt the sting of unpredicted and uncontrolled anger. My children had begun to cower when I walked by. My deacons, my friends, all of them felt the force of my anger and always without provocation.

"How do you feel when you get angry?"

Guilty! Unforgivably guilty. No one could lift the pall of gloom that settled over me as guilt set in. A thousand *I'm sorry's* made no difference. The changeless promises of God had no effect. I would even feel guilt when there was no cause for it.

"Have you ever thought of suicide?"

Yes. At least once a day. I'm sure that only the grace of God and the graphic memories of seeing so many suicides and struggling with so many shattered lives in the wake of suicide kept me from actually killing myself.

It was a wise and insightful counselor who probed me with those questions and then gently said, "I'm sure, Mr. Baker, that the doctor's original diagnosis is correct. You are deeply depressed—you do need help—you do need to be here—but you'll get better. It will take time, but you'll get better."

Chapter 1, Notes

[1] D. Martin Lloyd-Jones, *Spiritual Depression: Its Causes & Cure* (Grand Rapids: Wm. B. Eerdmans Publishing Co., 1965), p. 11.

[2] Bob George, "There's No Need to Be Depressed," *Moody Monthly*, February 1982, p. 7.

[3] Ibid., p. 10.

". . . my flesh also will abide in hope."
Acts 2:26

Chapter 2

"You'll Get Better"

"You'll get better. It will take time, but you'll get better."
I'll always be grateful for those gentle words—profound in
their simplicity—yet filled with hope. And oh, how I needed hope.

For one brief moment there was a slight glimmer of light in
my black hole of depression. Not much light—not enough to discern direction, nor to illuminate the many unanswered questions.
Not even enough to plot a future, but there was light. It was just
enough to enable me to make out the word—Hope.

I fondled and nurtured that word. I cradled it in every waking
moment. It was the only word that sustained me through the interminable nights punctuated with endless interruptions and the
oftentimes meaningless days filled with frantic activity.

Prior to that bold but simple prophetic pronouncement I had
been left dangling between two contrasting points of view.

One group of doctors was convinced that there was nothing
wrong with me. Another group had agreed that my problems were
so acute and complex that my days of ministry were finished.

Both opinions had devastated me.

But now there was hope, and it was all wrapped up in one
brief but authoritative pronouncement: "You'll get better."

Martha's first visit was extremely difficult for both of us.

Upon my arrival at Ward 7E, I had been searched, bathed, and my clothes had been confiscated. When I objected, they simply stated, "Just routine—you'll get them back when you prove you can be trusted with them."

I was dressed in ill-fitting pajamas, a robe that dragged the floor, and slippers two sizes too large.

I was shaved, my teeth were brushed, but I had lost my comb. I must have looked terribly disheveled. It showed on my wife's face for just one brief moment as she was ushered through that heavy steel door. Her cheerful smile gave way momentarily to a look of stunned surprise. She recovered quickly, but was betrayed by two tears that lingered in her beautiful brown eyes.

Those tears were like mirrors in which I saw revealed the Don Baker I had never seen before. I saw myself stripped of all pride, all accomplishments, and all glory. I saw myself as a derelict who had reached bottom. I felt terribly unworthy of this woman I loved so much.

And yet, as I held her in my arms, I could only think of one thing to say. "I'll get better—it may take time, but I'll get better."

John spent the first Sunday afternoon with me. We played a little pool and watched some television. Just before he left I looked up into my growing son's bewildered face and said, "Don't worry, Son, I'll get better—it may take time, but I'll get better."

Kathy brought me a poem, and, in her own shy but beautiful way, told me how much she loved and admired me. As she was ready to leave, I held my eighth grader in my arms and said it again, "Don't worry, Honey, I'll get better. It may take a little time, but I'll get better."

Even Joey came to see me, and as he searched my face with the inquisitive eyes of a shaggy little poodle, I took his head between my hands and said, "Don't worry, Joey; I'll get better. It may take a little time, but I'll get better."

Over and over again during those uncertain and confusing days, I thanked my Lord for a wise and thoughtful counselor who had taken time to give me hope.

Dr. Leonard Crammer writes about the types of depression in his book, *Up From Depression*.

"Depressions vary in intensity and in duration. Depressions may be mild, moderate, or severe. The general rule is that mild depressions, while distressing, can be overcome rather quickly. Moderate and severe depressions are almost always classified as serious and should be managed with medical help.

"The duration of a depression may be *acute, recurrent, or chronic*. An *acute depression*, no matter what the reason, comes on quickly and may endure only a week, or as long as four months. It can clear up spontaneously without treatment. A *recurrent depression* is an acute episode that reappears at different intervals with normal periods (called remissions) in between. A *chronic depression* arises more gradually and lingers for an indefinite time, even up to two or more years, with ultimate remission."[1]

My bouts with depression seemed to have been graduating from the mild to the moderate and now to the severe.

For nearly four years I had been experiencing depression in all forms. For four years I had been clinging to the slippery sides of that deep, black hole; sometimes falling, then recovering; then falling and again recovering until finally I could hold on no longer. I had plummeted into the deepest recesses of that impenetrable darkness.

But even as the darkness lingered and deepened, there was now one faint glimmer of light flipped on by a wise and gentle counselor whose name has long since been forgotten.

"You'll get better—it may take time, but you'll get better."

Chapter 2. Notes

[1]Leonard Crammer. *Up From Depression* (New York: Simon & Schuster, 1969), p. 25.

"Jesus wept."
John 11:35

Chapter 3

A Distant Grief

*F*or four years I had searched for the cause of my depression. I viewed every experience of loss with great suspicion.

Any loss, whether it be the loss of health, the loss of a job, the loss of a loved one, the loss of self-esteem, or the loss of reputation, can cause one to become depressed.

Job's case is always among the first that comes to mind whenever we consider loss. His loss began with his possessions, swept over his household to claim his family, and finally resulted in the total loss of his health.

When we find him in Job, chapter 2, he is sitting in a pile of ashes, smitten from head to foot with boils, scraping his body with a scrap of pottery.

- He curses the day he was born (3:1)
- He proceeds to describe life as
    "darkness" and "gloom"
                and
    "blackness" and "terror" (3:5)
- He calls it a night without dawn (3:9)
- He wishes he had died at birth (3:11)
- He longs for a death that does not come (3:21)
- He describes his unrelenting agony by stating, "the arrows

27

of the Almighty are within me; their poison my spirit drinks; the terrors of God are arrayed against me" (6:4).
Job had fallen into his black hole.

Martha and I had had numerous "loss" experiences.

We had lost our first son three months after his birth.

As I carefully examined that loss, along with others we held dear, a pattern began to emerge.

In three of the four deaths that occurred early in our marriage, I had deprived myself of the very necessary therapeutic experience of grief.

I conducted the funerals, prayed with the family, and displayed myself as the strong one.

My father, a deacon in the church, died one month after I began my first pastoral ministry in the church of which he was a member. His death occurred at 2:00 A.M. on Saturday. Less than thirty-four hours later, I was preaching from the pulpit and conducting my first communion service.

In assuming the role of pastor I was depriving myself of the greater role of son. I refused to display grief. I rejected my humanness. I buried my grief under a pile of foolish assumptions and suggested to myself that it would be a discredit to my God if I cried.

Twenty-one years later, long after my deep depression set in, I sat watching a rerun of "Rifleman" on television. It was midnight, and I was alone in my little retreat overlooking the Pacific Ocean.

I don't remember the story line except that during the show Chuck Connors had a very moving emotional experience as he was reunited with his long-lost father.

I began to cry. I cried convulsively, continuously, uncontrollably. After nearly an hour, I called Martha long distance in order to hear her voice and to have her pray with me.

At that time the tears were a mystery to us both—just a part of the depression, we thought.

The next evening I recounted the experience to a friend. He asked me to tell him about my father.

As I began to talk, I also began to sob. I began to see that I had been carrying an unfinished transaction of grief that had moved to the subconscious and there had bowed down my soul without my mind even being aware of it.

I conducted my grandmother's funeral. I preached at the funeral for my father-in-law. I have been expected to conduct all the funerals for all of my dear friends. At times I have struggled with this deeply, but silently.

My dear friend, M. L. Custis, a doctor with whom I had shared twenty years of growing experiences, became suddenly and unexpectedly ill of a brain tumor. Within twenty-six days of the first diagnosis he was dead.

M. L. had been a constant source of encouragement to me. He had trusted in me when others could only shake their heads in bewilderment. He had loved me, prayed with me, laughed with me, cried with me.

He gave me my first set of golf clubs and then met me on the course in a vain attempt to occasionally break the spell of my work.

On more than one occasion when I was hospitalized in California, he called long distance from Portland. Our conversations were totally unintelligible. There were no words, only sobs.

At the time of his brief but terminal illness I had been laid aside—exhausted and depressed—again forced to temporarily relinquish my duties.

I was unable to be either his pastor or his friend. His brother, Dwight, conducted his funeral. The service, one of the largest and most precious our church had ever experienced, went on without me.

No amount of explaining has ever completely satisfied my absence to the many who loved him so much. I've never been able to satisfactorily explain it to myself.

Being unable to walk in his death with him and with his dear family again deprived me of the privilege of working through my grief. That bothers me to this day.

Weakness? Quite possibly. There are many, I'm sure, who might feel that I'm not drawing from God's grace or that I'm not displaying pastoral strength. But I have decided it's so much better for me to work through my grief while it's still fresh than to allow it to sift down through the cracks to a subconscious. world from which it is so difficult and painful to dredge up later.

"Iron sharpens iron,
So one man sharpens another."
Proverbs 27:17

Chapter 4

A Walk with a Friend

I had lost touch completely with reality.
> God was not real
> > Life was not real
> > > Love was not real
> > > > My wife was not real
> > > > > My children were not real
> > > > > > Friends were not real
> > > > > > > I was not real

All of life was pretense and fantasy—I thought.

Life was a blur, completely out of focus.

I wrote out my feelings on separate occasions. Once when I was somewhat lucid and again when I was completely submerged in depression. The statements, perceptions, and value judgments came from the same mind, written by the same hand, in the same notebook. The similarity stops there, however. It seems as I read them that they came from totally different persons on different planets, describing different civilizations.

In my black hole I could see nothing with clarity.

I was suspicious of every statement, rejected every advance, and distrusted every motive.

Martha would say, "I love you," and I could not believe her.

33

Father's Day greetings, birthday cards, and even Christmas presents were mere tokens of traditional human responses that carried neither warmth nor meaning.

I walked down the familiar streets of the quiet suburban neighborhood in which I lived. I saw nothing and heard nothing but the inner cries of a depressed spirit.

Each morning as I looked out at the beautiful shaded yard with its orange blossoms, flowering almond trees, and lush green grass, I saw only gray and felt only gloom.

Climbing out of bed was the most difficult task of each new day.

Martha would draw my attention to the birds. "Hear the mourning doves?" she would ask. I heard nothing. It was as if someone had altered my eardrums so that only life's discordant sounds would penetrate.

At other times, sounds were devastating. The invading noises were loud and penetrating. Even in conversation I would put my fingers to my ears and plead for silence. Two sounds—such as music and conversation—descending on me at the same time would cause pain and disorientation.

Martha loves beautiful things. I've often called her "my eyes." So often when we travel I'm engrossed in mental preparation for scheduled messages, but even the beauty she would describe was unrecognizable.

During one of my many trips to the hospital the darkness lifted momentarily. I was sitting in the privacy of my room, looking out of my fourth floor window—seeing nothing.

For a few exciting moments I became aware of a tree—a perfectly formed California hemlock. I studied its magnificent broad boughs, reaching out in all directions to shade a beautifully manicured lawn.

I saw it towering above me like a pyramid, with its stately green tip silhouetted against the bright blue of the sky. I studied the limb ends with their two-ranked needles, green on the top and silver on the bottom, and the pendulous cones like Christmas tree ornaments that often brushed lightly against my window.

The cinnamon-red bark was intriguing. I wanted to reach out

and peel it off, then touch it and smell it.

It was beautiful—it was not just beautiful, it was magnificent!

I wrote a poem—the first that I could ever remember.

> "Today I saw a tree.
> Its stately branches and delicately laced limbs
> > startled me.
> 'Where have you been?' I said.
> > 'Or better yet,
> Where have I been
> > That I should just now begin to see?' "

And then it was gone. The darkness settled in, and I moved back toward my bed to begin again trying to make out the strange shapes and sounds of my own black world.

A depressed person needs desperately to hear himself.

Someone was needed to help me interpret the sights and sounds of that foreign world.

Many times my family tried. I would tell them how I felt, or what I was thinking. But often my feelings were so crazy and my thoughts so bizarre that to attempt to describe them was too threatening for any of us to grapple with.

It was during one of these brooding moments that Emery moved back into my life.

I was in Isla Vista, California, resting and recovering, when he called. I hadn't seen Emery for years. We had driven cross-country together and shared college experiences. He had been a student in my wife's speech class.

Since moving into the ever-busy world of Christian ministry, we had seen each other only on rare occasions.

"This is Emery," he said. I responded with a guarded, "Oh . . ."

"How are you feeling, Don?"

Ignoring his question, I asked, "Who told you I was here?"

"Bob Gillikin," he said.

Emery had a totally disarming manner. A quiet but genuine compassion graces his voice whenever he speaks. His questions are always asked with compelling concern. I felt myself relaxing as we talked.

"May I take you to lunch?" he asked.

"No." The answer was immediate and final. No explanation, no apology—just, "No."

After a few more moments we hung up.

I felt that I had been spared an unwanted intrusion into the privacy of my black hole.

He called again the next day, asked the same question, and received the same reply.

He called again and again until he finally caught me in a moment of deep loneliness. I agreed to have lunch with him.

I had no idea what to expect. Numerous times I was tempted to call and cancel. At other times I looked forward to seeing him with enthusiasm, even excitement.

As we sat across the table from each other, I sensed no distance, no judgmental spirit, I heard no clichés, he shared no profound truths—he just listened without comment.

When he was convinced that I had said all I was going to say, he told me about the time he was depressed. His depression, in many respects, bore a marked resemblance to mine.

He also told me of his wife's nervous breakdown. For years she had been unable to be the wife and mother she had so wanted to be.

He mentioned the time he, too, had felt "thrown away" by a church family to whom he had ministered.

After bringing me up to date and telling me of his continued schooling, his doctor's degree in counseling, and his current counseling practice, he asked, "May I be of help to you, Don?"

"No," I replied. "I'll be all right."

Inwardly my soul was crying out for someone who would listen—someone who could listen without responding—without judging. Someone who could help me translate the meaningless jumble of scrambled thoughts without taking offense or being critical.

I was too closed, too masked, too threatened. I had never really bared my soul to anyone, not even myself. I was so afraid to take it out and look at it that again I slammed the lid shut and guarded it with all the emotional strength I had at my disposal.

Emery then told me a story.

"A man was walking in a wilderness. He became lost and was unable to find his way out. Another man met him. 'Sir, I am lost, can you show me the way out of this wilderness?' 'No,' said the stranger, 'I cannot show you the way out of this wilderness, but maybe if I walk with you, we can find our way out together.' "

There was a long silence as he let those words sift down through the unguarded cracks in my defenses. Finally, from somewhere deep within came a desperate cry for help. "Please, Emery, walk with me."

Each night I went to his home after his counseling schedule was finished. I felt great guilt, intruding on the few sacred moments Emery and Mary Ann had together, but I never sensed that I was an imposition.

My fragile spirit could not have suffered any rejection. Had I been made to feel unwanted or even unexpected, I would have flown, never to return.

Two illusions were shattered during the long hours that followed:

1. *That counselors are unnecessary in the Christian life.*

I had believed this, even ridiculed the counseling profession at times.

Jourard discovered that no man can really know himself until he has been able to verbalize himself to someone he can trust.[1]

King David often employs this therapy in the Psalms as he verbalizes his transient feelings to God.

2. *That if I ever really got in touch with my true self, all I would find would be a hideous monster.*

As I pulled back the curtains and allowed Emery and myself a peek at the inner man, I was both delighted and relieved. Most of my thoughts had no basis in fact whatever—they were just feelings—they were emotions running wild and unchecked. Or they related to some past transaction that had never been satisfactorily completed.

Emery is still my counselor. He still reminds me not to believe everything I think or feel. Occasionally, when the darkness settles in, he is still available to walk with me.

Chapter 4, Notes

[1]Sidney M. Jourard, *The Transparent Self*, 2d ed. (New York: Van Nostrand Reinhold Co., 1971).

*"My loved ones and my friends stand
aloof from my plague;
And my kinsmen stand afar off."*
Psalm 38:11

Chapter 5

Withdrawal

*P*art of the admission procedure included the processing of certain forms and the storage of whatever valuables a person chose to bring to the hospital with him.

I waited in line, oblivious to my surroundings, until a familiar feminine voice said, "Next."

I knew that voice. I knew it well. I had preached to that voice, prayed with that voice, cried with that voice; the voice that had penetrated my silence was the voice of one of my sheep—my "family"—my church members.

In the split micro-second that it takes for two pairs of eyes to meet I wanted to dissolve—to disappear—to die—anything but to be forced to greet one of my own while being ushered through that heavy steel door into Ward 7E.

I watched as disbelief flashed across her face. "Pastor," she said, "what are you doing . . ." and her voice trailed off into nothingness as awareness finally displaced her confusion.

The conversation went nowhere. It never ended. It never really began. There was just this weak greeting—and then nothingness.

We both finished our work quickly and withdrew. I into my deep humiliation and she into her utter disbelief.

What do sheep do when the shepherd is disabled?
Just as they do with anyone else who's ill—
    They pray
        They write
            They call
                They visit
UNLESS—
That someone is mentally ill.

We often say that everyone feels clumsy in the presence of grief. Yet in the presence of mental illness, we're all total cripples.

I have never felt so deserted in all my life. For seven years I had given my time, my energy, my love, and all the abilities I possessed to a wonderful church family. And yet in my deepest need, they were unable to respond.

Unable—not unwilling. Church families are just like human families. It's easy to tend to wounds that are visible and pray for ailments that are definable, but mental illness still carries with it the stigma of the dark ages. The Christian community really hasn't advanced very far when it comes to ministering to the depressed.

The interactions between the depressed and those he loves most are terribly baffling.

As I began to withdraw, first from my wife, then my children, and eventually from my church family, not wanting to impose my unhappiness on them, they began feeling, not compassion, but rejection.

The further I withdrew, the greater was that feeling of rejection.

Prior to being hospitalized, I'd take long drives in the car or long periods of rest away from home. The church would graciously extend periods of time away from my work. I'd often sleep alone.

Whenever I was unable to preach, yet well enough to attend church, I would never go to my own. I longed for anonymity.

As I withdrew, the conclusion of my loved ones was often that I no longer loved them. I no longer cherished their company. I no longer desired their fellowship.

In reality, just the opposite was true. I loved them too much to inflict my darkness upon them. My moods and my responses were so unpredictable I feared that in one weak moment a cherished relationship might be destroyed forever.

In the last meeting that I attended with my board of deacons, I suddenly and unpredictably lashed out at one whom I deeply loved. To this day, I'm sure he does not understand—nor do I.

Another response to my depression was that in some way or other my family or my church felt responsible for the great gloom that had settled upon me. This caused feelings of guilt. Many times when I would retreat into silence, Martha would ask, "What have I done?"

One of my former church members who did write, said, "Please tell us what we did wrong."

Feelings of rejection and feelings of guilt only compounded the problem. They created greater distance. They eventually made communication not only difficult, but at times impossible.

My children were convinced that they and they alone were the authors of every one of my bad moods.

Try as I might, it was impossible to convince my wife, my son, my daughter, and my church that I deeply loved them and that what was happening to me had nothing whatever to do with them.

Yet, those I loved the most continued to stagger between feelings of rejection and guilt. They felt either responsible or not wanted.

These persistent feelings were compounded by the fact that there seemed to be no apparent reason for my depression. When the reason for depression is well-defined and clearly understood, there is little cause for confusion. But my "moments" would come without any advance warning and oftentimes during periods of great happiness.

It is impossible for those who have never been depressed to fully understand the deep, perplexing pain that depression causes.

I appeared healthy, without bandages and without crutches. There were no visible scars, no bleeding, and yet there was that endless, indefinable pain that no doctor's probing finger could locate—no drug could totally relieve. There was always the pain and along with it always the desire for oblivion—an oblivion that would come only in minute snatches of restless sleep.

Some of my most consoling moments came when I sensed I was in the presence of someone who really understood how badly I hurt.

Most of my "comforters" were terribly impatient with me. Many of these felt compelled to finish the slow-moving sentences that I tried to speak. Many found it difficult to slow their pace to mine. Even my steps had become halting. Some told me to "pull myself together" and others could not understand why I could not get up and get moving.

Only one could sit beside me for those seemingly endless moments of silence when nothing would come and nothing needed to.

I looked forward so much to those daily visits.

Martha usually came alone—usually in the early evening—and always brought with her the positive cheer that never ignored my pain but always refused to submit to it.

Just a week after my admission to Ward 7E, I wrote in my diary: "Martha was back this evening. We went out on the lawn for more than an hour—delightful time. Martha is wonderful to talk with. If this is the only plus benefit of this entire experience, it will be well worth it."

A depressed person's family must learn quickly to find its balance on the tightrope between rejection and guilt. In most cases, the family is not the cause of the depression and in most cases the depressed person's withdrawal is not to be viewed as rejection.

If he must withdraw—let him go. Let him move in whatever direction he chooses without encumbering him with guilt. His wanderings will be carefully monitored by the Holy Spirit, and his return will be hastened by the very fact that you respected his moods sufficiently to let him go.

Let him express his ambivalence without giving too much credence to some of his foolish statements. He may say to his children, "I hate you," or to his wife, "I want a divorce." At the moment he makes those statements he may genuinely feel them; but his feelings, remember, are transient and unpredictable and are subject to wide swings that ultimately come back into balance.

Pray positively. Philippians 1:6 provides a positive promise that enables us to constantly thank God in advance for His divine provision. When you pray with a depressed person, your prayer might well include such statements as, "Thank You, Father, for Your presence. Thank You that You're here even if it doesn't feel like it. Thank You that this depression is going to lift and life is going to come into focus again. Thank You, Father."

For you can be assured—it will.

". . . curse God and die!"
Job 2:9

Chapter 6

Death Wish

*M*y first morning in Ward 7E was spent in a suicide-prevention class. It was there I learned that deep, long-lasting, chronic depression often ends in suicide. Suicide is the tenth leading cause of death in America, second for college-age students, and third for adolescents. Suicide now ranks as the fifth largest killer in the fifteen to fifty-five age group.

The typical American suicidal is a white, Protestant male in his forties, employed, and the father of two children.

Dr. Bertram Brown,[1] Director of the National Institute of Mental Health, has stated that of those who have clearly committed suicide, it is found that over 80 percent were definitely depressed. One of the most common things that occurs prior to suicide is depression.

Dr. Whyte singled me out as the newest candidate for his probing series of questions designed to prevent suicide.

"Ever thought of committing suicide?"
"Yes."

"What method would you employ?"
I resisted this question. Not that I had not already decided upon a method, but I had never before divulged it.

47

Hesitantly I answered, "I'd shoot myself."

"With what?"

"A .22 calibre revolver."

"Do you own a .22 calibre revolver?"

"Yes."

"Where do you keep it?"

"In a drawer."

"Is it loaded?"

"No."

"How would you do it?"

"I'd just shoot myself."

"No," he said, "that's not what I mean. In what way would you shoot yourself? Would you place the gun in your mouth—to your head, or point it at your heart? How would you do it?"

The process of verbalizing these prior thoughts was difficult but it was already forcing me into a reality consciousness that I had never allowed myself to consider.

Slowly I answered, "I would shoot myself in the head."

"In what room?"

Again with painful hesitance I answered, "In the bedroom."

"Whose bedroom?"

"My wife's and mine," I said.

"Where in the bedroom?"

"Probably on my side of the bed, next to the window."

"What time of day?"

I was hating him with each new question. He was exposing the deepest recesses of my mind to myself and to that group of men. I wanted to scream at him. I wanted to run from him. But he persisted, "What time of day?"

"Probably in the afternoon—my worst time—when the family is gone."

"Who would be the first to find you?"

I hadn't thought this far. Slowly the vision of a bright-eyed, happy-faced eighth grader, arms full of school books, walking down the street, her best friend by her side, came into focus. I could hear her as she skipped up the steps, slid open the door, and hollered, "Dad, I'm home."

He asked it again, "Who would be the first to find you?"

I lowered my head and said her name—"My daughter—my princess—my Kathy."

Without a pause he asked, "What would her reaction be?"

I tried to imagine her shock, her fright, her disbelief, her frightened attempts to help, her screams, her utter feeling of helplessness and despair. "She'd cry."

"Who would she blame?"

It was not difficult to answer this question. Hundreds of times I've watched different degrees of marital disintegration and numerous times I've seen the aftermath of a crushing suicide experience. Inevitably the living never blame the dead—they blame the living—they blame themselves. Kathy, whose only contribution to my depression had been to continue to love and pray for her daddy—who had written love notes and poems to encourage her daddy—would blame herself.

"Who would be the next to find you?"

By this time—I was pleading with him to stop. "In just a moment," he said. "I think you've had enough. Just answer my last question, 'Who would be next to find you?'"

"John, my son, as he came home from school."

"What would his reaction be?"

"Disbelief," I said. "Disappointment, deep uncontrolled grief that would probably display itself in frustration and anger."

"Sons tend," he said, "to follow the examples of their fathers. I would expect, Mr. Baker, if at some time in your son's life things got too difficult for him, that he would take his life, just as his father had done. Self-destruction often breeds self-destruction," he said.

"The purpose of suicide is usually to destroy the hated self and to end all suffering. In reality, however, suicide is an intensely selfish act, destroying not only the one who takes his life, but planting the seeds of destruction in the lives of all who loved him."

Without my realizing it, these penetrating questions were being used to determine the degree of risk involved in my own suicidal thoughts.

Several strong predictive signs suggested that the risk factor was high and there was the real danger that risk could become reality.

1. I had developed a specific plan with a lethal means which was readily available to me.
2. I had given thought to the possibility almost daily and had even threatened it to others.
3. I was suffering a deep and interpersonal loss and felt cut off from my most important social resources—my family, my home, and my church.
4. My future was bleak. I could see no opportunity for recovery to the ministry.
5. My expectations were unrealistic. I could find no other word than "failure" to describe my present state.
6. I fit the profile—white, Protestant, male in his forties, employed, and the father of two children.

And yet that little trip we had just taken through the door of threat into the room of reality had caused something significant to happen. In just a few minutes' time the word "suicide" had lost its appeal. For what had at one time seemed like a viable means of escape had now taken on the appearance of a monstrous catastrophe.

Dr. Whyte suggested some methods of prevention:

1. It must be recognized that depression may be a fatal illness, terminating in self-destruction.
2. Every expressed death wish must be taken seriously.

I recall the time, one Saturday afternoon, when I was called to the home of a deeply depressed mother. Her husband had deserted her, and her sons were out of control. I found her sitting in the middle of her bed, frantically pulling the trigger of her husband's revolver, unaware that the cylinder had been removed. On numerous occasions she had dropped hints—hints that should have been taken seriously. Her life was spared, but not because of an alert pastor—only because a lethal weapon had been wisely dismantled.

    3. Remove all lethal weapons and drugs.

    4. Expect that even Christians will commit suicide.

A young man in my church received Christ on Sunday, shared an exciting testimony on Wednesday, and shot himself on Thursday. His depression had so fully invaded his life that it took only the slightest discouragement to push him back down into the depths where, in utter despair, he took his life.

    5. Stay with the deeply depressed person until professional help has been secured.

    6. View any significant change in behavior with suspicion. Oftentimes a suicidal person will become relaxed and display normal behavior. The reason may well be that he has made his final decision to die.

Chapter 6, Notes

[1]Bertram Brown, "What You Should Know about Depression," *U.S. News & World Report*, September 9, 1974. Interview copyrighted by *U.S. News & World Report*.

"Why are you in despair, O my soul?
And why are you disturbed within me?"
Psalm 43:5

Chapter 7

"Are You Mentally Ill?"

*F*ollowing the suicide prevention class I was taken into a small conference room where I met the members of the psychiatric staff. Two men and three women. There was not a word of greeting—no smile—not even an indication that I had entered the room.

Everyone seemed preoccupied with reams of paper work piled high on the conference table.

Finally one of the members nodded in the direction of a chair, and I sat down. The silence continued. I shifted uneasily from one side of the chair to the other until one of the staff members picked up a folder, leafed through it quickly, looked up at me, and said,

"Are you Donald Baker?"

"Yes."

"Are you embarrassed to be here?"

"Yes."

"Is your wife embarrassed?"

"Yes."

"Are you mentally ill?"

I lifted my head slightly to look into the impassive eyes of my inquirer. I don't know what I expected to see as I studied her expressionless face.

Maybe I'd hoped that she already had the answer to that question or quite possibly it had been asked only in half-hearted humor. Maybe it was just rhetorical or hypothetical.

I waited for her to continue, but there was only silence. In desperation I looked from one face to the other in the vain hope that someone would come to my rescue. After what seemed an eternity, the question was asked again,

"Mr. Baker, are you mentally ill?"

My response was undoubtedly a classic study in ambivalence.

With great hesitancy I said, "I don't know," and then retreated slightly into, "I hope not." Fearing the inevitable psychological exposure that I had always resisted, I then said firmly and emphatically, "No!" The silence prevailed. No one spoke. Finally I heard a weak, resigned voice originating from somewhere down deep in my soul, utter a halting and barely audible, "Yes."

I felt that I had just confessed to the unpardonable sin. There was some slight relief in my admission but the overpowering emotion was that it was now time for the gavel to fall. My sentence was about to be pronounced. Punishment was now to be imposed.

Instead, my questioner, with a softening look of compassion, said, "How would you like us to be of help to you while you're here?"

With a deep sigh of unexpected relief I answered, "I really don't know." Then through long and ponderable moments I attempted to explain what I had been longing to hear for nearly four years. "Please," I said, "just tell me how to get out of this black hole I'm in. Please. Please."

Without the slightest hesitancy she answered, "We will. Don't worry, we will. It may take a little time, but we will.

"But first," she continued, "we must determine why you're in this black hole of yours.

"Depression," she went on to explain, "has a cause. It's not the result of some mysterious visitation of the gods. It's an illness that is the result of certain biologic or social forces that in some complex way are acting detrimentally to your health.

"We must find those forces. They may be internal, they may be external. They may be physical, they may be mental. They may be real or they may be imagined, but we must find them and when we do, we will recognize them and so will you.

"Then, Mr. Baker," she said, "you will get better."

I had been searching for the cause of my depression for years.

At first I became almost psychoanalytical. I called it "My Trip to the Womb." I tried to recall all of the early incidents that could possibly have had negative impact.

I remembered hearing of my mother's initial rejection of me at birth. My parents had lost twin girls at ages one and two. These daughters had been replaced by two sons. When I was born my mother was desperately hoping that I would be a girl. At birth, I'm told, she refused to see me—for a full minute or two. This incident had apparently caused little damage to my fragile psyche, since it had often been told as one of the family's longstanding jokes—and I had enjoyed telling it as much as anyone.

I strained to recall the many experiences of discipline in my early life. Both my father and mother had been involved in numerous instances of corporal punishment. These had apparently not traumatized me, for I could recall many more times when I should have been spanked but wasn't.

I walked through the halls of my first and second grade classrooms. I revisited the old homeplaces. There were twenty-three of them. Yes, we moved a lot and possibly the absence of a place to put down my roots had affected me; but when I was growing up, it seemed that many families moved a lot. I never remember resisting or regretting those moves. They seemed to be always exciting to me.

Had I married the wrong girl, chosen the wrong profession, moved to the wrong church? No, none of these could be given much credence. I give God far more credit than this. A sovereign God had delightfully superintended all the major decisions of my life; and time coupled with years of affirming experience had confirmed that these major choices had been the right ones.

Was my family depressive? Some of them, yes—others, no.

Our family had grown up with a work ethic, however, which had made us all terribly conscientious, even compulsive. This work ethic has always been one of the prime suspects in my attempts to determine the cause of my depression.

One psychiatrist went so far as to suggest that my father had been terribly cruel in imposing such a demanding work ethic upon his children.

Twice during extended hospital stays I was given the Minnesota Multiphasic Personality Inventory, a battery of questions that determine one's psychological makeup. In each instance it had indicated some wide gaps between my goals and my physical, intellectual, and emotional abilities to achieve them.

I have always set high goals for my life. I have always wanted to be Number One. I've worked harder, stayed up later, studied longer, in an effort to gain that superiority in my profession. Carnal as it may sound, I've always wanted to be the greatest. "Sanctified ambition," I called it.

At the same time that I had these aspirations, I lacked the robust health, self-discipline, and keen intellect necessary to achieve such goals.

This frustrated me terribly.

I had fully expected that my pastoral experience was going to launch me into heights of meteoric accomplishment.

As this goal became more elusive and my attempts to reach it more demanding, I found myself mentally retreating into a rather strange and forbidding world. I began feeling depressed.

I never reached that goal. Others who did began appearing as competitors, even enemies. I deeply resented their successes.

Attempting to achieve success can be terribly depressing in the ministry. A carnal goal can only be accomplished with carnal methods. Carnal methods meant dependence upon human strategy, programing, manipulating, and physical energies—none of which I had in sufficient amounts.

One of my members reminded me one day that "there are only three persons in the Godhead and you are not one of them." My actions had very subtly denied this reality, however, and oftentimes I had suggested by my demeanor that I was all-wise, all-powerful, and ever-present.

What a delightful day it was when I learned that only God is adequate for ministry.

And such confidence we have through Christ toward God. Not that we are adequate in ourselves to consider anything as coming from ourselves, but our adequacy is from God (2 Corinthians 3:4-5).

As I was attempting to unravel the complex implications of success and faithfulness, I came into the possession of a series of cassette tapes used to record a teaching session by Dr. Ray Stedman. The passage being studied was 2 Corinthians 2-6. These discussions later formed the basis for his book entitled *Authentic Christianity*—a must for anyone who desires to serve God effectively.

I'll be eternally in the debt of Dr. Stedman, because the fresh biblical concepts in these oft-neglected passages changed my life and ministry.

They helped considerably to bring this conflict into focus.

There's a fine line between compulsion and sanctified ambition. It has taken years to discover it, and maintaining a balance is oftentimes like walking a tightrope.

The scriptural requirement for a good steward is faithfulness, not success. Faithfulness *is* success, regardless of how it may appear in the eyes of this world.

These truths released me, freed me, and enabled me to place my confidence where it belonged and in so doing caused me to leave the outcome of my efforts where they belonged—with God.

*"I was dumb and silent,
I refrained even from good;
And my sorrow grew worse.
My heart was hot within me;
While I was musing the fire burned; . . . "*
Psalm 39:2, 3

Chapter 8

Group Therapy

*B*ut I was still depressed.

A strange mixture of feelings prevailed whenever I found myself scheduled for group therapy in Ward 7E.

I looked forward to the therapy sessions with a restrained excitement, combined with a feeling of frightening apprehension.

Excited over the prospect that some question might be asked, or some statement might be made, that would cast light down into my black hole . . . apprehensive with the fear that someone would strip away one or more of the many masks I had accumulated during my years of public life.

One counselor, David, could probe our minds with the superb skill of a surgeon. More than once I watched him as he began a particularly brutal line of questioning. After long minutes of emotional pain, he was able to help one of us gain an insight that ultimately became a source of slight relief.

Most of the people in my group were young, just released from active military service, and had been involved with drugs. Many of the users had become addicted to drugs or were helpless alcoholics. Vietnam was the recent tour of duty for a good number of them.

Their struggles were immense. Mine seemed terribly mild by

comparison.

One young man had returned from Vietnam a psychological cripple. His mood swings would take him from the extremes of deep depression to acts of insane violence.

He had accidentally killed some Vietnamese children.

The counselor had been working with him for months, trying to help him gain release from the overpowering sense of guilt that bound him. David finally persuaded him to verbally relive those tragic moments in "Nam." We listened spellbound as he painted a grim word picture of the scene that smoldered in his mind.

When finally he had said it all and had left us mentally staring at the lifeless corpses of innocent children, he began to cry. The convulsive sobs that followed wracked his entire body.

No one moved to comfort him. No attempt was made to quiet him; we all sat mute and still.

Finally, as his crying began to subside, David said quietly, "And you feel that you need to be punished for what you did?" The young veteran began nodding his head and saying, "Yes, yes . . . I need to be punished. Yes, yes."

To my utter amazement, David moved from his chair, picked up a wooden ruler, and said, "Hold out your hands." As the ex-soldier obeyed, the therapist began beating his hands and his forearms mercilessly.

I expected just token punishment—a symbolic beating. But David didn't stop, and we recoiled as we saw that ruler come down again and again on hands that began reddening and swelling with each successive blow.

After what seemed an eternity, the beating ended. The tears gone, the look of pain had eased. Our counselor took that grown man in his arms and held him close as a father would his son, all the time repeating, "It's all right. It's all right. It's over. It's over."

The rest of us then crowded close and held that Vietnam veteran until he began to relax. He looked at the therapist and then at the rest of us and began to sob in relief, uttering over and over again, "Thank you, thank you."

Diane was another therapist I encountered who was skilled at helping her subjects find relief.

I respected her for her confrontive abilities which drew all of us out of our protective shells. But at the same time I resented the verbal manner in which she dealt with patients.

Her language, to me, was unbearable. The gutter talk, the four-letter words, the explicit phrases that passed from client to therapist and back again, cut through me like a knife. I was so conscious of this foreign language that it took me days to penetrate beyond it, to see and hear the meaningful transactions that were taking place in the lives of many group members.

She occasionally worked with me, but seldom did we have a significant exchange. I did learn, however. In fact, one of the most profound insights I gained was a result of her group therapy session.

I wrote in my diary, "Diane is trying to get me to be a more aggressive person. She is not succeeding." As I reflected on those words, a little light came on; and I added, "I cannot be aggressive until I become angry, then hostility takes over and eventually I am completely immersed in guilt."

This was a pattern of life for me. Somehow I had gained the impression that confrontation, directness, and even argumentation were not Christian.

I had never learned to rationally express disagreement or displeasure.

Whenever I encountered a disagreeable experience in the hospital, I suppressed it until eventually I could suppress it no longer. And it would then burst from within in the form of hostility.

Punishment of my children was usually done in anger. This was probably one of my greatest sources of guilt.

I would allow anger to seethe until its source was no longer definable. This floating anger would then lash out unpredictably in any or every direction and usually land on unsuspecting—even innocent—victims.

The ensuing guilt would devastate me. No matter how many times the victim would offer forgiveness, I could never forgive myself.

Feelings of guilt are quite often the cause of depression.

None of us can break God's rules, society's rules, or even our own set of rules, without feeling the pain of guilt.

Guilt is a subjective human response to what is viewed to be sin. It is one of God's ingenious tools designed to painfully penetrate the soul of humanity in order to drive humanity to the only adequate provision for sin, which is Jesus Christ.

David in Psalm 32 gives us a classic description of depression resulting from human guilt. He describes the physical and emotional responses by saying,

> When I kept silent about my sin, my
>   body wasted away
> Through my groaning all day long.
> For day and night Thy hand was
>   heavy upon me;
> My vitality was drained away as with
>   the fever heat of summer (Psalm 32:3-4).

This was how I felt when my responses were ugly and un-Christian. The ugly words that spewed from my mouth left me drained of all vitality as I floundered in my black hole.

My problem was not just anger, with its subsequent guilt, or hostility. It was also a problem in communication. I had never learned to disagree agreeably.

I began forcing myself to learn to respond to every question and to question every response. I struggled for clarification. Often I would repeat another's statement before responding, to be sure its meaning was clear.

I would not allow myself to brood over ambiguity. I repeatedly asked for meaning whenever meaning was hidden or uncertain.

I began working to express disagreement before disagreement could deteriorate into hostility.

Learning to share myself at the appropriate time and in the appropriate manner meant that I was to become more bold, more direct, more confrontive and sometimes even more blunt.

My first attempts at this were very clumsy. It's not easy to learn ". . . to speak the truth in love" (Ephesians 4:15). Oftentimes

I moved to the extremes of cruelty and insensitivity. But I found it necessary to carefully analyze all feelings as well as all responses before I wrapped words around them.

Some of my feelings today are just as irrational and senseless. But in verbalizing them I literally defuse them and ultimately render those emotional time-bombs harmless before they are allowed to scatter verbal debris in all directions.

This insight, though it offered no immediate relief, was to later become profound and meaningful, especially in the pulpit.

Many times I have "vented" from the pulpit, overreacting to some trivial, unimportant event, not realizing that my reaction was not to the stated event at all. It was often to some unresolved inner conflict of my own that had needed careful attention.

To be able to carry only one package at a time into the pulpit—one truth—without being forced to juggle it with undetected emotions, has turned preaching into a pleasurable, non-threatening experience.

This insight did not show me the way out of my black hole, but I'm convinced that it has often kept me from falling back in.

"My tears have been my food day and night,
While they say to me all day long,
'Where is your God?' "
Psalm 42:3

Chapter 9

Has God Deserted Me?

*O*ne of my early callers was a well-meaning Christian who made weekly visits to Ward 7E.

I tried to avoid him; nevertheless, he recognized me, called me by name, and then tried vainly to stammer some words that wouldn't betray his shock at finding a Christian minister in a psychiatric ward.

Before leaving, he asked if he could pray with me. Included in his prayer were the words, "Father, forgive this man for whatever sin has brought him here. . . ."

There were other words included in his prayer, I'm sure, but none penetrated, for suddenly my mind had absorbed all it could hold.

After he left, I buried my head in a pillow and sobbed until there were no tears left in me. "Please, Father," I cried, "tell me what I need to do! Please, Father, just tell me something."

But the heavens were silent—or so it seemed.

For hours each day I would ponder such questions as:

"Where is God?"

"Why doesn't He answer me?"

"Has God really deserted me?"

My theology rejected the last possibility, but my life seemingly had nothing to show for His abiding presence.

My Bible kept saying to me that God is a changeless God, and yet it seemed that without explanation He suddenly had become terribly indifferent.

This God of mine, who had promised never to leave or forsake, appeared now to be playing some cruel form of hide and seek. No matter how diligently I sought Him, He was nowhere to be found.

This God whom I had loved and served had promised to keep His ears ever open to my cries. When I prayed, however, it seemed that He had now become stone deaf.

My Bible, always a source of strength, had little to say to me. When it did speak, the words were soon lost in the pall of gloom and forgetfulness that had settled down over my mind.

Time and again I would leaf through its pages, seeking a promise or an explanation, only to close its covers in disappointment.

Martha brought me a book by Andrew Murray, one of my favorite authors, entitled *Abiding in Christ*. The cover picture was that of an earnest Christian kneeling beside a chair, apparently agonizing in prayer.

I studied the picture for a few moments and then threw the book across the room in disgust.

In later years that same book became a treasure, but often I have recalled that moment with bewilderment, wondering what emotion triggered such a violent response.

Was I expressing a momentary disbelief in prayer?

Was that picture calling on me to expend levels of energy which I no longer possessed?

Was the whole concept of "abiding" saying something to me that I wasn't ready to hear?

I have never known for sure just why I threw that little book with such force—except that possibly the word *abide* had never been one of the more important words in my theological system. The word really had very little meaning—relational significance for sure, but its experiential meanings were vague and elusive.

To "abide" had always meant something similar to "stop," to

"rest," to "be still," to "be quiet."

Whenever I would read a verse like Psalm 46:10, "Be still (cease striving) and know that I am God," I would never stop to ponder its meaning.

Christian ministry, to me, was never characterized by words like *rest, stop, quiet,* or *stillness.* If that was what abiding meant, I didn't have time to waste on such an exercise.

For twenty years I had grown accustomed to a ministry of action—a ministry that made insistent demands on both time and energy. I was convinced that I should be in my study before the men of my church began their work day. I prided myself on being the last to turn out my light at night.

In three pastorates I gave my entire work day to counseling and visitation—six days each week. After the family would retire, I would slip over to my office to spend the quiet hours of the night in study, returning home at about four in the morning.

This schedule worked well until some of the local police officers came to Christ. Those officers who worked the night shift would drive by, see my light on, stop, and come in for counseling.

I was accustomed to a Christianity that gave obvious active meaning to every moment. Anything less suggested a flaw in my commitment.

Friends would encourage me to slow down. Doctors would warn me to change my lifestyle.

Encounters with God were always on the run. Prayers were telegraphed.

My study of Scripture was impersonal. Every new concept was assimilated with my people in mind and remembered only to be incorporated into a future sermon.

For a fast-paced Christian like myself, the word "abide" had little meaning.

Now that my whole world had stopped its violent, wrenching pace—I was bewildered.

Like Elijah (1 Kings 19:10-12) I felt that I had been exceptionally zealous for the Lord. I had worked diligently at tearing down the "false altars" to the "false gods." I was accustomed to the "great and strong winds" and the "rending of the mountains" and the "fire" and the "earthquakes," but a total stranger to the "still small voice."

There comes a time in every Christian's life when the only thing he can do is "abide."

My time had come and I did not know how to do it.

It took weeks for an active mind to slow to the pace of an exhausted body. When it did, however, I was pleasantly surprised.

God was still speaking—

God was still present—

His Spirit had not flown—

His power had not diminished.

I had stopped. God had not. In the quietness God had unique methods available to say things to me—some things I had never taken time to hear before.

Through the lips of friends, on little get well cards, in seemingly insignificant events, God kept whispering sweet somethings to my heart.

I finally opened my Bible again. During the last few weeks in Ward 7E, I spent every private moment studying just four chapters (chapters 13-16) in the Gospel of John. I would have gone farther, but I found it impossible to do so. There was just too much. My Lord had said so much in that Upper Room that I had never really heard before. It was as if I were hearing it for the first time. And it was to me—to me alone—not to my people—just to me. A very private, very wonderful little seminar was being conducted in that little cubicle. The emptiness and loneliness would disappear for a brief time each day.

I found to my amazement that God even loved the inactive. What a revelation! What a delight to just abide.

I found to my amazement that God not only loved me in my inactivity, but He had things to say that could never be heard and understood on the run.

There are times today that I long to return to the stillness of that little room and the joy of that refreshing experience.

My God had not deserted me—just redirected me and then settled down with me to teach me things about our relationship that could never be learned on the spiritual battlefields of life.

". . . he can deal gently with the ignorant and misguided, since he himself also is beset with weakness."
Hebrews 5:2

Chapter 10

My Fellow Sufferers

*T*o admit to my fellow patients that I was a minister was terribly embarrassing. I was always grateful to those staff members and patients who didn't probe with the ever-present question, "What do you do for a living?" These were few, however.

Most of these strangers in this other world were very inquisitive. After asking my name, the next question usually was an inquiry into my profession.

I tried desperately to remain detached, withdrawn, and, if possible, anonymous. Of course, I couldn't.

One of my two roommates was the first to know. He was the son of a Bible college professor. But his teenage years had been wasted due to the continual use of drugs and his mind crippled by the abusive chemicals he had injected into his body. Before his admission to Ward 7E, he had been arrested on charges of rape, assault with a deadly weapon, and kidnapping, all accomplished in a twenty-four hour spree of terror. His terror was now confined to our room, where his obscene language and actions escaped the nurses' attention.

I had never bunked with a criminally insane person in my life; likewise, he'd never roomed with a Baptist preacher.

He was assigned to escort me to the lab shortly after my arri-

71

val. As we walked down those long, sterile corridors I noticed a look of disdain whenever our eyes met. I finally turned to him and asked, "Why are you looking at me that way?"

"That's the way you're looking at me," he answered.

That was my first rebuke. It was appropriate and timely. I'm thankful now that it came on my first day. I had really never given the subject much thought, but I'm sure that I regarded inmates in mental institutions as "lesser beings." I was inclined to look beyond their personhood and see only their problem.

Fred, another patient, and I met while folding sheets in the laundry room. Fred was twenty-seven, the father of two children. He and his wife were separated.

He had been arrested for drunkenness and indecent exposure and admitted with delirium tremens. His daily nourishment consisted of "bennies" and a half gallon of whiskey.

After telling me his story he asked, "Hey, what do you do for a living?" I was silent for a long time, worried that my answer would create distance between us. Finally I answered him, slowly and reluctantly. "I'm a minister," I said.

His response was immediate and animated. He dropped the sheet he was folding, grabbed my hand, shook it wildly, and said, "Damn, that's great. I've never talked to a preacher before. Tell me, what's it like? What do you do? How does it feel? Do you think I could ever become a Christian?" He never once asked me why I was there.

Bill, who later became a dear friend, was an alcoholic who was in for rehabilitation. His drinking had begun at a housewarming. He and his wife had just finished building a beautiful home in the suburbs. They decided that it would be impolite to invite guests without having liquor available. He prepared a drink for his wife— her first. When she later died from the effects of alcohol, his life disintegrated. He not only was alone and an alcoholic, but also thought himself a murderer. His guilt had driven him to numerous suicide attempts.

Alcoholics have a world of their own, and they cannot believe that there are those who do not drink.

In therapy sessions with alcoholics, the psychiatrist turned to me and asked, "How long have you been an alcoholic?"

"I've never drunk," I told him.

The entire group laughed incredulously. The doctor got up from his chair, walked over to me, and said, "You're a damn liar, and the sooner you admit that to yourself the better off you'll be." To this day, I still doubt that he believes me.

Bill gave me my first lecture on alcoholism and then took both Martha and me to the Alcoholics Anonymous meetings. I had never realized the complexity or the severity of this problem. These men became close friends after I had learned to relax with them. In later weeks most of my spare time was spent in counseling them. They appointed me as their chaplain and asked me to serve as a member of the board of directors for their Halfway House.

Bill gave his life to the Lord and went from the hospital to Bible school to study the Scriptures. He entered his new world very clumsily but with great delight.

He stopped at our home following an afternoon session in class. All four of us were at home. He came into our living room in tight-fitting jeans, western shirt, and boots. He tossed his wide-brimmed hat on the chair and announced, "Hot damn, I just had the greatest time of my life. I just learned about the *crucification.*"

Some of the staff members often displayed more hostility than the patients.

I had been instructed to take my medication with food. Pill-taking time required standing in line in front of one of the nurses' "cages" and then swallowing the pills in her presence. When Sheila, a staff nurse, handed me my pills without my snack, I asked her, "Do you really want me to take these on an empty stomach?" She looked at me and snapped, "Have you got someplace else to put them?" I then retreated into my silent world to brood and to mentally create verbal replies designed to devastate her. None of those ingenious retorts was ever delivered. They just sank down into the pit of my stomach and churned.

Chuck, a male nurse, pulled me from my cot on the third morning and said, "OK, Baker, it's time to get up and out. Time to play some softball." With that, he took me to the locked clothes closet, retrieved my street clothes, and told me to put them on.

I wrote in my diary, "It's surprising what a little thing like clothes can mean when you've been denied them, and when they suggested going outside, I felt like turning handsprings.

"But softball? Me—an old man—weak, depressed, playing softball with all those young fellows," I thought.

I complained to Chuck, the male nurse, and spent long minutes describing my health history, my exhaustion, my reluctance. He listened attentively and patiently. After I had finished, he calmly took my hand and said, "OK, now let's go play softball."

Oh, how I hated it at first. Then the need for exercise came into focus. I became aware of the greater opportunity to get better acquainted with the men. It was on the softball field that I accomplished the impossible. I got Harry, my other roommate, who never spoke, never responded, to smile at me.

On my third day at softball I hit a double and then fell from exhaustion before I could reach second base. But oh, what this did for my ego as my new friends cheered me on.

One of the most memorable remarks came from Norm, another staff person who recognized me and had known of my ministry. He played on one of the church softball teams and remembered me from one of the games I had attended.

He took me aside and said, "It took great courage to do what you did!" Those simple words sustained me during those long weeks.

My fellow sufferers became my close friends—a camaraderie developed—much like that acquired in military service.

I find myself to this day defending the unfortunate, the alcoholics, and some of the criminals, and often seeking opportunities to move alongside them.

A call came recently from the psychiatric ward of Portland's Veterans Hospital. I visited a stranger in deep depression who had beaten his wife and children and then attempted suicide. I tried vainly to build a bridge between us. He remained detached and silent until I said, "I think I know how you feel. I've been right where you are—depressed, angry, suicidal. I, too, have served time in a psychiatric ward of a veterans hospital."

With that he looked up in astonishment and said, "You . . . a preacher? I don't believe it." After convincing him, he began to weep. He stood up and threw his arms around me and cried like a baby.

Before I left, he prayed to receive Jesus Christ as his Savior.

*"Are you bound to a wife? Do not
seek to be released."*
1 Corinthians 7:27

Chapter 11

The Family

"*I* think I'd like to have a divorce."

"I don't care what happens to you."

"I don't care what happens to the family."

"I don't care what happens to the church."

It seems impossible that I should speak those words—yet I did. I barely remember them. Martha recalls them vividly.

Those words, common to many, were so foreign to us. Most couples think them at some time, many speak them, some actually mean them.

When I spoke them, they came unexpectedly from somewhere deep in my black world and exploded with powerfully destructive force upon my wife.

Her world was so shattered, so disrupted, and so tentative that she sought counsel from a doctor, a psychiatrist, and from Emery.

During those few hours with Emery she pulled our twenty-three-year marriage out of her memory, studied it carefully, and decided it was worth saving. The love had been genuine, the commitment real, and the memories cherished.

It was primarily because of her refusal to honor my foolish talk that we persisted in working through that very difficult time.

77

We had met, fallen in love, and married while still in college—she from Indiana, a speech teacher. I, from Oregon, a preacher-boy.

The moment I saw her I fell deeply in love with her. She was all my dreams wrapped up in one person. Flashing brown eyes, long black hair, beautiful features, a petite figure, a sense of determined purpose, strength of character, a love for the Lord, keen intellect, and a desire to marry only a man with whom she could become a soul mate.

I left our first casual meeting, went back to the dorm, knelt beside the bed, and thanked the Lord that He had finally introduced me to my wife.

We were married nine months later.

I often marveled at the faith of a woman whose father was one of the greatest Bible teachers I had ever known and who would marry a preacher whom she had never heard speak.

Ours has been a happy and exciting marriage. We have never known boredom. Living by faith is always an adventure. Each new day is fresh with surprises.

We have always enjoyed happy and fruitful ministries. Our churches have grown, our relationships with our people have always been secure and precious.

We've traveled through much of the world, loving and being loved by a delightful missionary family.

She shares the ministry with me—speaks, counsels, laughs, weeps, and prays with whoever needs her.

Martha is the most accessible person I have ever known—always available to anyone regardless of who they are or what they might need.

I have watched her, perfectly at ease with a railroad bum as she tenderly bandaged his lacerated leg. I have seen her equally composed as she chatted with the President of the United States.

She is a great mother. I never abdicated my role as a parent in favor of the ministry, but there have been many times when she has been forced to be both mother and father and has always performed ably.

Our marriage, like most, however, has had its struggles.

Marriage is designed by God to be part of the perfecting process, and sometimes that perfecting can be terribly painful. At times it has been painful to us.

Our expectations have always been high. We have both refused to settle for mediocrity. Both of us are perfectionists, creative, capable, and competent people, demanding much of ourselves and of each other. There are times, I'm sure, when we subconsciously have even felt in competition with each other.

Our schedules are horrendous. She maintains a career as a speech pathologist, teaches Bible classes, speaks for women's groups, disciples young believers, counsels the hurting, maintains a home, and accompanies me to most of my pastoral engagements. For weeks we may go nonstop, ending each day too tired to talk and sometimes too weary to even pray.

Quite often we're forced to send verbal telegrams to each other or go for long periods of time without really finishing a communicative transaction.

Often I'm gone, and she assumes much of my load as well as her own.

I am not an easy man to live with. Much of the time, even when I'm with her, I'm absent. My mind is busily working through counseling sessions, administrative problems, or preparing messages.

Vacations are cherished times. It's then we laugh and love, walk and talk, and virtually get reacquainted.

To help us bring our marriage back into focus the staff of Ward 7E scheduled a family conference.

I was terrified.

I was certain that I was about to be exposed as the incompetent fraud I felt myself to be. My appraisal of my role as a father, our relationship as a couple, our parenting, was all spelled out in one word: failure. In my darkness I could see nothing that looked good.

The family came, all of them—Martha, John, and Kathy—poised, polite, and beautifully groomed.

The large room with its high windows and bare walls was anything but inviting. The long, wide table forced us to sit uncomfortably far apart. Two staff people whispered to each other, studied a sheaf of papers for a few moments, and then proceeded nervously and very clumsily to penetrate our secret little world.

It was obvious from the beginning that we were somewhat different from the usual clients. There was no alcohol or drug problem. Neither of the children had ever run away from home. No one was scarred from any brutal family beating. The children were not dropouts or truants. The language was not crude or uncaring.

The questions were ill-prepared. We all felt awkward, and yet every question was answered ably and honestly. John and Kathy withheld nothing. Facts as well as feelings were laid out on the table for careful analysis.

"Do your parents love each other?" they were asked.

"Yes," they answered.

"Do they love you?"

"Yes," again.

"Do you love them?"

"Yes," without hesitation.

"Do they ever argue?"

"Yes."

"A lot?"

"More than I want them to," answered John.

"How does that make you feel?"

"We don't like it."

"Does your dad like to have fun?"

"Not much. He's working all the time."

"Do you like your family?"

Both answered "Yes" and seemed surprised that such a question should ever be raised.

It was concluded that our family was normal, happy, loving, open, and unusually close.

I was somewhat surprised. That was not the appraisal from deep within my black hole. It didn't quite fit with the miserable images that I had been conjuring up—but it was delightful to hear.

Through all of its ups and downs our marriage had never been brought into question. We never once doubted the fact that God had uniquely designed us for each other—until I let loose of those strange and shattering words that had been given birth somewhere deep in the blackness.

Depression speaks a totally foreign language at times. As it gropes for meaning, it looks at anything and everything that might be its cause and sometimes draws some very foolish conclusions.

At times I'm sure I felt that our marriage was the cause, and divorce was the cure. That thought was one of the many elusive straws I clutched at. I'm so grateful that both God and Martha always kept pushing it beyond my reach and held it there until the darkness finally lifted.

". . . to keep me from exalting myself,
there was given me a thorn in the flesh,
a messenger of Satan to buffet me—to
keep me from exalting myself!"
2 Corinthians 12:7

Chapter 12

Physical, Emotional, or Both?

*T*he medical doctor who examined me upon my admission to Ward 7E questioned me carefully. He mentioned his suspicion that hypoglycemia might be playing a part in my illness.

Hypoglycemia, or low blood sugar, has been related to a long list of symptoms and often acts as a catalyst in bringing emotional disturbances to the surface.

The list includes fatigue, anxiety, depression, and tension. It also includes sweating, weakness, tremor, lightheadedness, unexplained hunger, headache, blurred vision, confusion, incoherent speech, wide mood swings, sudden outbursts of temper, forgetfulness, insomnia, and much, much more.

Low blood sugar sounds like the body needs more sugar. Just the opposite is true, however. What it means is that the body has an intolerance to sugar and other similar carbohydrates because of an oversupply of insulin. The excessive insulin drives the blood sugar down. As the sugar falls rapidly, sometimes below safe levels, the above list of symptoms often occurs.

Rapidly falling blood sugar can affect both the mind and the body. The brain is fueled by glucose and when the fuel supply of glucose, or sugar, is low, the person may notice an inability to think clearly or to concentrate. One can become emotionally upset.

Depression, anxiety, paranoia, or any number of emotional responses may occur.

A heated medical debate has continued for years. The focal point of this debate is whether hypoglycemia is a very common or very rare disease.

In my first pastorate I experienced a rapid and unexpected weight gain—sixty-five pounds in less than one year. Whenever I would diet—and it was always a crash diet—I would experience a wide range of frightening symptoms, from migraine headaches to fainting spells.

The first time I ever heard the word *hypoglycemia* was from the lips of a doctor who treated me after church one Sunday morning following a mysterious "collapse."

He said, "You know, Reverend Baker, your symptoms sound like you may have hypoglycemia. What you need to do, whenever you feel weak, is eat a candy bar." I did, and I continued to feel weak. I continued to eat candy bars, and I ballooned. My weight went unchecked and out of control, and with the weight gain came all of the negative feelings toward self a person can have when any part of his life is out of control.

I hated myself.

Yet, no matter what diet I chose, it was impossible to maintain it over any period of time without becoming ill.

For long periods I would live on amphetamines (they were prescribed freely then) until I could tolerate them no longer. To help me sleep, doctors would then prescribe seconal. For years I ping-ponged it between "uppers" and "downers," trying vainly to curb my appetite and then calm down sufficiently to sleep.

The inevitable collapse occurred nearly four years before Ward 7E and the lingering exhaustion and depression made it almost impossible for me to do my work.

I received a long-distance telephone call from another long-time doctor friend, Dr. Richard Saloum, who invited me to come see him. Dr. Saloum had spent five years as staff physician at Dammasch State Hospital and had found numerous patients struggling with emotional symptoms that were related to physical problems.

After extensive tests, he confirmed the diagnosis of hypoglycemia which had been suspected years earlier.

The intense relief that I felt was immediate. Just hearing that the wide, unpredictable, and indefinable mood swings might be related to physical factors brought me added hope.

To hear a doctor confirm that weight loss for a hypoglycemic is an impossibility without a special diet was more than encouraging.

Then came discouragement—I could find no other doctor who agreed with that diagnosis. I noticed that whenever I remained with Richie's prescribed regimen, I felt better; but since no one accepted it, I fell back into my old habits and felt worse.

Numerous times during these four baffling years, I lapsed into unconsciousness, and on three occasions was taken by ambulance to a hospital. There was never a conclusive diagnosis.

I shuffled down the long hall of Ward 7E in a state of restrained hopefulness. That doctor had actually said that he suspected hypoglycemia. Most of the doctors and psychiatrists I had seen since Richie's diagnosis had not accepted the part it could have played in my struggle.

I was immediately placed on a six-meal per day regimen containing high-protein, low-calorie food with vitamin supplements. This diet was maintained during my entire stay in Ward 7E. For ten weeks I ate on schedule and only the appropriate foods. For ten weeks I watched my weight drop daily, regularly, and predictably. I saw it move right down to that figure that I had expressed earlier as only an impossible dream.

With the weight loss came a corresponding rise in self-esteem.

My mood swings became less severe.

The depression began to lift.

The black hole turned somewhat gray.

I found myself praying more, studying more,
thinking more lucidly.

One weekend I was given a pass to go home to my family.

Saturday night we indulged ourselves in the Baker tradition—popcorn and lots of it. Sunday we went to the Tropicana, a local restaurant, and ate ice cream. Later that day, I ate a candy bar.

On Monday I wrote in my diary:

"Super low! Depressed, weak, nervous, disoriented."

The unit chaplain suggested that I was grieving.

I concluded that if it was grief, it was caused by an overwhelming sense of failure.

It was not until Tuesday evening that the light came on. I wrote in my diary, "If I have hypoglycemia, then why don't I act like it? I'm convinced that my low was related to my bad eating habits over the weekend. I can't accept hypoglycemia as a condition I have and then ignore the effects of excessive carbohydrates—ice-cream, popcorn, etc."

Weeks after my release from Ward 7E, I received an application for renewal of my pilot's license. Two questions were asked: (1) Have you ever had a nervous breakdown? (2) Have you ever been declared insane?

I didn't know how to answer either of them.

I took the application to the head of the Psychiatric Division and laid it on his desk. "Doctor," I asked, "you're the only one who can answer these two questions. Tell me, what was your final decision as to my problem?"

He picked up my chart, reviewed it briefly, and said, "Don Baker, you have not had a nervous breakdown, nor were you insane. In the ten weeks you were a patient here, we proved to our satisfaction that you do have reactive hypoglycemia."

I have lived with that information for ten years now. Conclusions about depression that include hypoglycemia as a factor are accepted by some and rejected by others. In my situation, I allow for its influences.

It necessitates a dietary regimen that is extremely difficult for me to maintain.

It is aggravated by the large doses of stress that one is forced to take along with the ministry.

Often I eat what I'm not supposed to, and, just as often, I pay the consequences.

In looking back, I believe that my struggle was partly related to this physical area. This doesn't minimize the lessons I was learning in other areas of my life. Yet its discovery provided clues, new clues, for my way out.

It has been a source of contention in discussions with others. It's frustrating, and difficult, when people disagree with me about hypoglycemia's part in my depression.

The sole reason for my depression? No. One factor cannot be isolated from all the others. But physical problems are often interrelated with other battles. With this in mind, I made some corrections, and I profited as a result.

"Do not forsake me, O LORD;
O my God, do not be far from me!"
Psalm 38:21

Chapter 13

My Career Is Over . . .

*M*y church family had been very patient. The leaves of absence, the periods of time spent in the hospitals, and now an extended time in Ward 7E, however, had taken their toll.

Sheep need a shepherd. My church was no exception. The attendance had begun to drop off, the sharp edge of excitement was gone, and the people were almost as bewildered as I.

The chairman of the board had announced, for want of a better diagnosis, that I had had a nervous breakdown.

It seemed in the best interests of the church for me to resign. Each day I would struggle with that decision. In the mornings I would waken with the conviction that today some "sign" from heaven or some divine pronouncement would simplify the decision-making process.

Martha and I would discuss it for long periods of time, but when I would ask, "What should I do?" she would always answer with "that has to be your decision."

Bud McRae, chairman of the board, visited me one evening, and all we talked about was whether or not I should continue.

I finally asked him, "Bud, let's pretend we're in a board meeting, and the members are seated again around that long table. I'm going to poll them by name, one by one, and you are going to tell me how you think they would vote."

I drew their names from my memory and began asking the question, "Do you believe that our pastor should resign?" "Marvin," "Melvin," "Bud," and so on until each member had voted in the manner that had been previously discussed. Only one voted, "No." All the others had stated an unqualified, "Yes." I was stunned. I felt so secure, so convinced that they still wanted me, but I had been wrong. My board overwhelmingly believed that I should go.

Never before had any member or group of members in any of my churches even suggested that my work was finished. I felt the blood drain from my face. My hands renewed their shaking. Beads of perspiration popped out on my forehead as the enormity of that judgment began to penetrate.

"But where will I go?" "What will I do?" Many times I had counseled with the unemployed, prayed confidently with them, and assured them, "Don't worry, God will provide."

Suddenly, I was unemployed—for the first time in over thirty years. In fact, I had started earning my own way in the fifth grade and had not, since then, been without an income.

Martha had returned to school and had secured a master's degree in speech pathology and was already in demand in the county school system. But I couldn't depend on Martha to support me. That was not the way it was supposed to be.

I think for a few brief moments the "man of faith," the "spiritual leader," the "pastor," must have displayed panic, for it was then Bud said, "Pastor, don't worry, we have already decided to pay your salary for six more weeks."

I fell silent. "Six weeks," I thought. "Six weeks, with a boy in college and a girl preparing for high school and a home to pay for and a car," and I began thinking through that long list of commitments. Finally I turned to Bud and said, "Thank you, Bud. You have been a big help to me. I'll write my resignation tomorrow."

I wrote it—painfully—and then called the church secretary to type it and mail it through the channels.

When the call was completed, I slowly placed the receiver back into place, shuffled back to my room, and cried.

I felt empty
I felt deserted
I felt unwanted
I felt thrown away

The church was more than justified in its action, but still that action was totally unexpected.

As I thought through all the implications of resignation, I wavered between staying and going. "I'm sure that a majority of the people want me to stay," I thought. "If I could just take my case to the people, they would reverse that decision." I listed the names of close friends I could call, and I began thinking through devious methods to gain the support of a majority.

But then the consequences of such action began to pass through my mind. I had often said that I would never allow a church to "split" because of me.

I am obsessed with the necessity for a visible, tangible, demonstrable unity with the Body. It is one distinguishing mark that sets the church apart from all other organizations or institutions. The church is the only place on earth where the potential for peace is to be found.

Our church had already been divided too many times. I could not and would not be the cause for another fracture.

I let my resignation stand and took the full responsibility for that decision.

I stated to the church that "due to continuing poor health and an unpredictable future, I feel it is necessary for me to tender my resignation."

As I signed that letter, I was sure that all my previous fears were now confirmed—"A life of normalcy is forever threatened. No church would ever call a man to be its pastor who had spent time in a psychiatric hospital." Those words were written in my diary shortly after my admission; now I was convinced that my ministry was finished.

*"O God, Thou art my God;
I shall seek Thee earnestly;
My soul thirsts for Thee,
my flesh yearns for Thee,
In a dry and weary land
where there is no water."*
Psalm 63:1

Chapter 14

Starting Again

A s I left the hospital, there was no fanfare and no welcoming party. That really was the way I wanted it. In fact, I left without even saying goodbye to the staff or to my many new friends.

I returned home with many helpful insights.

I had

a new compassion for the hurting,
a new strategy in counseling,
a new insight into communication.

I had some memories that would last a lifetime.
I had a confirmed diagnosis,

and I could recognize blood sugar episodes,
and knew what to do about them.

I was more calm, more confident.

I was free of the stress of pastoring.
It was Friday and I had no need to prepare sermons
for Sunday.

Yet, I was still weak; I was still confused; and I was still depressed.

The black hole wasn't completely black anymore, but it was still dark enough to make it difficult to see any future or even interpret the present.

And, of course, I was unemployed.

For the first time in my life I began leafing through the classifieds. I even prepared a resumé, but I didn't have the slightest idea where to send it.

I timidly called some friends and asked if they knew of anything. I drove from city to city, just dreaming about possibilities, but not really knowing how to make meaningful contacts.

It was then I heard of an opening in a Christian school. The president was a long-time friend. I was excited as I dialed his number, but dismayed when his secretary told me he was busy. It was much later when I received a call from his assistant. Trying to ask for a job was one of the most difficult things I had ever done. The sentences were clumsy. My responses seemed incoherent. I'm not even sure that he fully understood the purpose of my call.

He did say, however, "If there is any opening, we'll call you." He took my phone number, my address, and hung up. He never called again.

I took my family to a number of different churches without ever feeling at home. It seemed that I was permanently and indelibly marked. Those who knew me were terribly condescending. Some of my pastor friends would meet me at the door and after an embarrassed greeting would turn away quickly, not knowing how to act or what to say.

There were a few, and oh, how precious they were, who seemed to genuinely care. Their presence was like a cool breeze on a parched desert. They not only provided much-needed fellowship, but they bolstered a shattered ego.

What was I going to do? I really wasn't strong enough to do much of anything. But as the weeks and months dragged by, I was feeling not only economic pressure but also the great and insistent desire to be busy again in the Lord's work.

After checking out numerous opportunities, I knew there was only one thing in life for me, and that was the pastorate.

I needed to be alone. I needed to pray. I needed to fast. I needed to seek God's face. I needed to know beyond any doubt that God was still there and that He knew I was still here. The heavens had been silent for too long. I had to hear from God.

My friend and neighbor, Arnie Blesse, loaned me his cabin at Hume Lake. I took only enough food to keep my blood sugar under control and left home for an indefinite period of time.

It was almost impossible for me, yet I climbed to the top of a nearby hill and stood beside a wooden cross where hundreds of young people had given their lives to God.

As I stood there, I began to weep. I realized that God's call to me to preach had not been rescinded. He had not changed His mind. There had been no new directions given, no new commands ordered. I was never told how long when my Lord pointed in the direction of His harvest field. I only knew that all of the present uncertainties had come from some strange source other than my sovereign God. He was not the author of my confusion. I didn't know who was, but I was certain He wasn't.

I knelt beside that cross as others had done and began to pray. It was the longest, most lucid prayer I had prayed in months.

"Oh Father," I said, "I love You and I know You love me—even when my feelings tell me otherwise. I still don't know all that's happening in my life or why, but I do trust You. I do know You have a plan and even though I may never fully understand it, I still trust You.

"Please, Father, let me pastor a church again. I'm not interested in its size or its location. Just give me a dozen people to pastor. I'll earn my own living, if necessary. Please, Father, let me be a shepherd again.

"If there has ever been any doubt about my commitment, Father, I want you to know I'm Yours. I'll do whatever You want."

As I knelt on that mountaintop, I took a stake and drove it into the ground—a strange procedure for me—and then said, "Father, I'm driving this stake as a sign that here, at this place, I've committed my life anew, and it's Yours for as long as You want to use it."

I walked slowly down the mountainside, not feeling much different, except that I had made a statement, not out of necessity or fear, not even out of my anxiety, but out of an overwhelming, lucid desire to be used of God in any way He chose to use me.

*"Be of sober spirit, be on the alert.
Your adversary, the devil, prowls about
like a roaring lion, seeking someone to devour."*
1 Peter 5:8

Chapter 15

My Final Foe

As I sat in that mountain cabin, reflecting upon the reasons for my lingering depression, I asked myself again, "Was Satan in any way connected with my depression?" This question was asked in various forms time and again during my four years of groping in the darkness. Many were convinced he was. I dismissed them all casually and sometimes even carelessly. I rejected the possibility.

The works of Satan had been relegated to textbooks and history. I preached about him occasionally and truly believed in his existence, but never gave him more than just a passing thought.

My first real introduction to the world of the occult came in Haiti in 1965 when I was introduced to Olipha. His story staggered the imagination.

Olipha had kept his little Haitian village completely under his spell for more than fifty years. Men, women, and children both feared and worshiped him. His word was law. His power was real.

Then it happened. Jesus Christ moved into Olipha's family. His brother became a Christian. Shortly after his conversion he confronted Olipha with the message of salvation. Olipha's response to his younger brother was swift and frightening. He pointed his bony finger at this brand new believer and said, "Within three weeks you will die!"

His brother's response was simply, "Olipha, I am no longer afraid of you—'for greater is He that is in me than he that is in you.' "

Twenty-one days later, to the day, Olipha, the sixty-seven-year-old Haitian witch doctor, bowed his head in the presence of his younger brother, still very much alive, and surrendered his life to Jesus Christ.

Olipha, a preacher of the gospel, stirred my heart with his ringing testimony. I had seen a twentieth-century demonstration of divine power in a classic, clear-cut victory over Satan.

Evidences of satanic activity were abundant. Voodoo, witchcraft, sorcery, animal and even human sacrifice were commonplace. Wherever Satan's power was displayed, however, God's power was proven to be greater.

I returned to my church with a new respect for my enemy. Yet, as I looked for him, it seemed that he was nowhere to be found. There were occasional glib references to him, numerous scriptural indications of his activity, but no real evidence of his presence. It seemed, then, Satan was either in hiding or his activity was far too sophisticated for detection.

In recent years, however, the very doors of hell have been opened, and the masks have been torn from Satan's face. In just a few short years the world has witnessed an open frontal assault by our enemy and his demons that is unparalleled in human history. Satan's blitzkrieg has been successful.

I began studying Scripture very carefully to determine whether or not there might just possibly be some relationship between Satan and my depression.

After all, it had been during a series of sermons on Ephesians 6:10-20 that I had first collapsed—and it had been just a few days after my first personal encounter with a Satanist that I slipped into my black hole.

That was a frightening experience. It happened as I was walking to my room at a conference center where I had been invited to teach for a week.

Standing in my path was a handsome young man, twenty-seven years of age, dressed in army fatigues.

"Is your name Baker, or Barker?" he asked.

"Yes," I replied, "my name is Baker."

"I've been told to talk to you," he said.

His manner was strange and threatening. His voice was flat and colorless. His eyes looked cold and empty. I felt fear as I looked at him.

He came into my room with me, and I asked him to be seated. He said, "No, I'll stand." Then he said, "I must tell you something, but I cannot look at you; and you cannot look at my face." With that he turned to the wall, pressed his head against the wallboard, and began reciting the most bizarre story I had ever heard.

He had been a worshiper and priest of Satan for seventeen years. His devotion to the evil one had taken him all over the country and had involved him in every occult practice known to man. Every twenty-two days he was visited by a demon and driven to unspeakable acts of evil. He hated God. He hated Christ. He hated talking to me, but he was compelled.

During the time that he was describing his life, a very strange thing was happening to me. I could not stay awake. I was listening to the most awesome story I had ever heard: sordid, ugly, and frightening. There were descriptions of orgies, confessions of vile practices, admissions of guilt, and, through it all, I wanted to sleep.

I felt drugged and used every method I knew to remain alert. I pinched, bit, kicked myself. I prayed constantly just to be able to stay awake.

After two hours he suddenly turned on me, his eyes filled with hate, and screamed, "Aren't you afraid of me? Don't you know I can kill you?"

With supernatural calmness I looked into that enraged face and said, "No, you can't, for greater is Christ Who is in me than Satan who is in you" (1 John 4:4).

Instantly he screamed, a hideous high-pitched scream, threw up his arms, and fell to the floor. In uncontrolled rage he began pounding his head on the concrete floor, uttering noises horrible beyond description.

I looked around vainly for help. I called, but no one came. I was alone—alone with a demoniac. Face to face with the enemy for the first time.

"O God, what do I do?" I cried. I knelt beside that writhing human form, placed one hand between his forehead and the concrete and the other on his back. As I stroked his head and shoulders I prayed, "Lord Jesus, deliver this man from Satan." I continued to pray, all the time shielding his head from the floor. "In the name of Jesus, Lord of heaven—Lord of all—I command you, Satan, to come out of this man's body."

If there was a precise formula, I didn't know what it was. I did know that Jesus' name always rang the death knell to the demons in the Scriptures.

After what seemed an eternity, his body began to relax. He stopped jabbering and foaming. I urged him to speak the name, Lord Jesus—Lord Jesus. Each time I said that name he looked at me with pleading eyes and then grabbed his throat and his tongue to indicate that he could not speak.

As I knelt beside him, clutching his body to mine, I prayed again, "Lord Jesus, release this man's tongue, that he may speak Your name." Finally, it happened. His lips began forming words. "Say it," I urged. "Say His name. Say Lord Jesus."

"I can't," he cried.

I prayed again.

Finally he lifted his head, summoned the little strength he had left, and cried, "Lord Jesus."

With those words he slumped to the floor, unconscious.

I covered him with a blanket, rubbed his head, massaged his shoulders and back, and waited for him to revive.

His first words after opening his eyes were, "Lord Jesus." He then raised up, moved to the side of my bed, knelt there, and gave his life to Jesus Christ.

It was just two weeks after my encounter that I lay helpless on my office floor.

I sobbed convulsively as they loaded me into the ambulance and continued crying for days. Every new voice—every soft word—would start me crying all over again.

Since my release from Ward 7E, I had read every book available, every Scripture passage that was written, on the subject of Satan.

If there had been any fault after my Satanist friend's deliverance, it was that of self-glorification. I loved to tell that story. I delighted in the admiring responses. I quickly took the praise to myself. I truly underrated the power of the enemy. Pride engulfed me—and nearly destroyed me.

As I was putting together the pieces of the puzzle, I wrote on a sheet of paper:

"Millions are being influenced, oppressed, and enslaved by the occult. The world is reeling as its prince has begun unleashing his fury in preparation for the final deception (2 Thessalonians 2:9-12).

"The church is feeling his blows. Christians everywhere are falling. I fell, emotionally wounded, bewildered, disoriented, confused, depressed—a casualty of Satan's onslaught."

As I wrote those last few words in the silence of that mountain cabin, I suddenly became aware that my paper was nearly drowned with my tears. I began to sob, and I said aloud, "Oh, God, is this what happened to me?"

I moved from the table to the couch, weeping and praying and asking forgiveness. I had underrated my enemy. I had ignored the pleas of Scripture. I tried to fight this great battle without my armor. I had taken God's glory to myself and even claimed a victory in which I had only been a bystander. "O Lord, did I really ignore You? Forget You? O Father, forgive me, forgive me."

I continued to kneel by that couch long after the tears had dried and the prayer was finished.

I noticed as I remained there that things felt different. Nothing ecstatic or noisy. Nothing high-powered or sensational. I just felt different.

As I examined that feeling, I became aware of strength in my limbs, of objects before my eyes. I saw, I felt, I heard. Was it possible? Was the cloud finally gone? Had my world come alive again?

I stood and moved carefully at first. The feeling, the sensations, the awareness, the strength—was it real? Was it back to stay? I began thanking and praising God, singing and laughing.

I put on my shoes and ran down the hillside—more falling than running from Arnie's cabin to where carpenters were building a new dining hall. One of my deacons was there. I shouted to him, "Jerry, I'm all right! Thank you for praying." He looked bewildered and unbelieving. He needed time; but eventually he, too, would rejoice at the reality of what had finally come full circle.

I continued to walk with vigor for the full three miles around the lake. I sang. I cried. I laughed. I prayed. I quoted Scripture. I talked to the birds, I talked to the trees.

To this day I'm grateful no one saw me. I would have been shipped back to Ward 7E for sure.

Three days were spent testing and trying this new view of the world, no longer from within a black hole, but now from a mountain peak where I could see anything, everything, clearly and distinctly. My depression was finally gone with all its multiple causes and multiple effects . . . it was gone.

Upon arriving home, I called my family together and told them nothing—only that God had been working. "I won't explain it for at least three days. In the meantime," I said, "just watch me and listen to me, and see for yourself that I am different."

With that, I went to the garage, cranked up the lawn mower, and proceeded briskly to mow first the front yard and then the back. I edged the lawn, raked up the grass, put away the tools, and strode past three astonished human beings. They had been watching me from the window all the time I had been working, fearful that at any moment they would be forced to come out and pick me up. As I walked back into the house, they asked if I was all right. When I answered, "Yes," they asked me to tell them what was happening. "Not yet," I said. "Let's wait and you watch, then I'll tell you."

I couldn't keep it for three days. We were only into the second when we all gathered in the living room and I told them the story.

We prayed, we laughed, and we cried. Martha has often stated that this final step was the most dramatic and instantaneous healing she had ever seen. The missing pieces of the puzzling struggle had been found.

It was some time before we were able to make any announcements, but finally we told it—to anyone and everyone who would listen: "Dad is finally out of his black hole." "Dad's depression is gone."

*"He brought me up out of the pit
of destruction, out of the miry clay;
And He set my feet upon a rock
making my footsteps firm."*
Psalm 40:2

Chapter 16

Back to Work

Someone pounded loudly on my door. It was just hours following my "deliverance." As I answered, I was given a phone number. Someone had called long distance. I was to return the call as soon as possible.

My good friend, Dr. Norman Lewis, from Portland, Oregon, was on the other end of the line. He explained, "Don, we have a missionary conference scheduled in just a few weeks here at Hinson. In our missionary committee meeting last night it was decided that I should call you and ask you to be our keynote speaker and moderator. Are you free to come and spend an entire week with us?"

"Am I free?" I said. "I've never been freer."

"Would you like to pray about it first?" he asked.

"Norm," I said, "I've been praying for a whole year. Certainly, I'll come. I'd be delighted to be with you."

I didn't know at the time that Hinson was without a pastor. All it meant to me was at least one week's opportunity again to minister.

I arrived in Portland as the guest of Western Conservative Baptist Seminary. The guest room was filled with flowers, large cans of assorted nuts, and a basket of fresh fruit. On the table was a warm greeting from my dear friend, Dr. Earl Radmacher.

Hinson is a church with 100 years of history, filled with tradition and memories. Some of the greatest have served as its pastors. Its honored place among Conservative Baptists had been earned and well deserved.

And it had no pastor.

In recent years the church had been embarrassed by scandal and fractured by division. Its pastors had struggled long and hard to bring about changes they thought would bring it back to life. Its membership had declined, its attendance was down, and so was its morale.

It was peopled, however, by some of the most faithful and loyal Christians I have ever known. They had refused to give in to discouragement. They were convinced that their church had a future as well as a past.

As I walked through that week with them, I enjoyed every moment—recapturing old friendships, sensing God's presence, experiencing His power.

We were praying for an exorbitant Faith Promise goal. We reached it that Sunday. On Sunday evening scores of young people came forward to give their lives to God.

I couldn't have been happier.

During the week, one after another came and asked if I'd stay. Dr. Walter Johnson was the first. With tears in his eyes he said, "Reverend Baker, I think God wants you to be our pastor." Kermit Miller, Frances Peters, and many others said they just felt compelled to ask me if I would be available.

I found it extremely difficult to suppress the wonder and the amazement at what I was hearing and feeling. "Could it be possible . . . ?" "No, not Hinson, not after where I'd been," I thought to myself.

Two members of the pulpit committee visited with me. They both asked numerous questions. We chatted and we prayed.

The deacons asked me if I could stay over and meet with them. I didn't tell them I had nothing else to do; however, most of them knew.

As we met together it became increasingly obvious that God

was doing something—in me—and in them. It seemed that in spite of what they knew they wanted me to be their shepherd.

They asked, "If you become our pastor, what will be your program?" Without a moment's hesitation I said, "I haven't the slightest idea," and I meant it. I had finally learned that churches, like people, are all different, with personalities of their own. It's impossible to superimpose one church's program on another. "But God knows," I continued. "The Holy Spirit will lead us. It may take time, but He will show us."

In that meeting I told them about my depression and about Ward 7E. I wanted no surprises. They deserved to know the worst. I asked them to call the chief psychiatrist and discuss my stay in the hospital and learn for themselves what had happened.

I explained that I was depressive and with that background plus a blood sugar problem I could possibly give way again if I became exhausted or was placed under too great stress.

All of this was discussed openly and freely with the whole church. Dr. M. L. Custis, my friend and champion, fielded numerous questions. An entire congregation listened and reacted to my emotional struggles.

Then they voted to ask me to be their pastor.

I never questioned for one moment that this was the will of the sovereign God. Martha, John, and Kathy had the same exciting assurance.

When Dick Wahlstrom called to give me the news that the church had voted to ask me to be their pastor, my answer was immediate and positive.

I'm well into my ninth year at Hinson now. No ministry has been more fulfilling or more fruitful. In these years we have all watched pastor and people relax, begin to love each other, and enjoy a totally unthreatened relationship.

In nine years nearly 2500 new members have been added—more than 1,000 by baptism. Attendance has tripled, giving has increased five times. World evangelization is a goal of the entire church family, with nearly 100 of our own young people either in foreign service or presently preparing. The church has moved out in the direction of the poor, the helpless, and the needy. We have given birth to two new congregations, each experiencing more than 300 in attendance.

Laughingly, many have said, "God took a dead man, married him to a dead church, and brought about a resurrection of both."

Soberly, I have said many times, "I am so honored to have the privilege of pastoring a church at a time in which God has chosen to bless."

How does one evaluate this entire experience?

I have stopped trying.

I am content today to marvel at a God who loves to take the weak things of this world and use them to display His great strength. He has had no weaker vessel than this one through which to do His work.

What have I learned from this experience?

New insights continue to come into focus daily. I see my God, my self, my family, my Bible, my congregation, and my ministry much more clearly than ever before.

I learned that I am depressive—not always depressed, but depressive, and find it necessary to continually medicate to control my unpredictable mood swings.

I learned that I'm part of a great company of depressive people. The word *depressed* strikes a more responsive chord when I speak it publicly than any other single emotional illness.

One doctor told me that 15 percent of the world's people inherit a tendency toward depression and are helpless when it strikes.

Whenever I speak of my depression, scores of Christian people whisper their thanks and acknowledge their own struggle.

I learned afresh the great value of constant exposure to the Word of God. Lies do not find their origin in God. "God is not a God of confusion" (1 Corinthians 14:33). "In Him [God] there is no darkness at all" (1 John 1:5). The negative thinking that prevails in the black hole of depression can only be countered by the positive Truth of God. In my lucid moments the best defense I could find was to move back into Scripture and allow God to speak.

I learned not to believe everything my feelings tell me.

Feelings need to be understood and sometimes even honored. Feelings, however, are fickle and often determined by physical

conditions or external circumstances. I *felt* condemned. I *felt* unloved. I *felt* unwanted. Those feelings were real but they were not
valid.

My relationship with God was just as secure and genuine during my darkest hour as it had been on my brightest day.

Romans 8:1 kept coming back to me and whispering over and
over again a simple truth that my emotions attempted to reject—
"There is therefore now no condemnation for those who are in
Christ Jesus."

Even though I was unaware of what was happening, my ten
weeks in Ward 7E had been weeks of unconscious ministry.

The Holy Spirit, though not perceived, had been at work.

Men were constantly coming to me for counsel. I had been
selected by a group of twelve alcoholics to be their chaplain.

Men were saved in Ward 7E.

The unconscious fragrance of a new-covenant relationship
was being wafted through those corridors from the life of a Christian who "felt" that the Holy Spirit had long since deserted him.

I learned not to believe everything Satan tells me.

The deceiver, who is constantly at work accusing the breth-
ren (Revelation 12:10), is always attempting to overload our
spiritual circuits with guilt. These constant overloads often result
in total power failure.

One way to distinguish whether our feelings of guilt are false
accusations from Satan or true convictions from the Holy Spirit is
that Satan's accusations are general and nonspecific. They take the
form of constant reminders that we are not worthy or that God
could never love such as you and me.

In sharp contrast to this, however, is the convicting work of
the Holy Spirit. The Spirit of God is specific and always points His
finger right at the actual instance of sin. He is not the author of confusion, but very carefully convinces of a specific act that needs to
be confessed and forsaken.

When guilt comes and persistent searching fails to determine
a just cause for that guilt—write it off as another lie from the father
of lies, the devil himself.

I learned not to believe everything man tells me.

When man says, "Depression is a sin," don't believe it. Depression is oftentimes caused by sin, but depression in itself is not a sin. When they say, "Christians don't get depressed," don't believe it.

Moses, Elijah, David, Jeremiah, Jonah, Paul, and even Jesus in His humanness all displayed the symptoms of depression. David even referred to his soul as a "cast soul"—a "soul in despair" as he encountered the pains of depression.

Norman Wright has said that in many cases depression is a healthy response. Depression is a normal reaction to what is happening to a person psychologically and physically. Depression is a scream, a message that some area of life has been neglected. A person should listen to depression, for it's telling him something that he needs to know. [1]

Depression, though its message is often confused, is not telling him, however, that God has deserted him or that God's forgiveness is no longer his.

The screams of depression should never be allowed to drown out the whisperings of God's assurance of His love for us and His presence with us.

What was the cause of my depression?

I do not know.

I've told it like it happened. This story is true.

To attribute it all to Satan gives him more credit than he's due.

To blame it all on the physical discounts all the confused notions and feelings that were a very real part of me.

To blame it on pride, ambition, self-glory, seems reasonable but still incomplete.

It was probably all of these—and possibly even more.

What I do know is that a gracious God took His loving hand and placed it on the psyche of a very self-sufficient child, brought him to his knees, and caused him to be totally dependent on His adequacy for the remainder of his lifetime.

Why have I told you my story?

I have shared a painful part of my past with you in the hope that you who stand beside a person trapped in his own black hole might understand, be patient, loving, and especially careful not to be judgmental or indifferent.

And my desire for you who suffer in this darkest shadow of life is that you will be able to identify with some part of it and find hope. Remember—you will get better.

Chapter 16, Notes

[1]Norman Wright, *An Answer to Depression* (Eugene, Ore.: Harvest House, 1976), p. 18.

PART 2

THE ROAD TO UNDERSTANDING

Emery Nester

Chapter 17

Walking with Don Baker

A phone caller told me about Don's withdrawal. Alone in an Isla Vista beach apartment, he sat with curtains drawn and emotions broken down. Bob Gillikin, my brother-in-law, had called to see if I might get in touch with Don—and help him.

Fifteen years had gone by since Don and I had been together. Similar desires and pursuits had thrust us into each other's worlds. We were both early members of Evangel Baptist Church in Portland. Both attended the same undergraduate university. Both aspired to the pastorate. And both of us did become pastors in the same fellowship of Oregon churches. But in spite of all of those shared experiences that might have provided the tight bonds of a close relationship, the friendship had been casual. Something less than genuine.

And now this casual acquaintance was to be the basis of a counselor-counselee relationship. I questioned the success of such an idea. How could I help Don deeply when our past association had been so shallow?

This was not the only jeopardy we faced. From the very first time I met him and began to know of him, I had felt alienated from Don. Early in our ministries, I saw him and a particular group of ministers in our denomination as snobs who were aloof from me. I did not feel wanted or liked by them.

These negative thoughts about Don didn't arise simply from his responses to me.

My own inadequacies and my early struggles to accept who I was led me to compare with others. I compared myself with Don and his seeming place of prominence. This put further distance between us.

There were many things in my own life I was just now beginning to work through.

I was a dropout from high school. I had a severe speech disorder. I had spent most of my adolescence in the armed forces and experienced an unusual early social life. I had many personal doubts about ever being a successful pastor although this was the desire of my heart.

All of these negative concepts of self became the filter through which I interpreted Don's and my relationship. I did not realize that Don shared similar negative feelings about himself.

When I heard that Don was in Isla Vista in this sad condition, old tapes began to play. My first thought was, "It's finally caught up with him. His problems have gotten the best of him."

But he was a servant of God—laid aside and hurting. I sensed a concern and a responsibility. I had heard this man was being used by God in some unusual ways, so I stepped into the role of helper, determined to get to know him and be involved intimately with him.

After Don and I entered our therapy relationship, my attitude toward him began to change. After approximately 100 hours spent together, his attitude toward himself had changed. He was a different person.

I saw him originally as a trembling, helpless person, desperately wanting to be free from depression. He made some commitments to me and took therapy seriously. He promptly kept every appointment. He discussed inner feelings, distorted thinking, and anything else that might be related to his emotional illness. He opened up to my suggestions. And he worked hard to get well.

As therapy progressed, I saw Don in a new way.

He was human after all. I laughed with him, cried with him,

and felt some of his hurt. I learned something of his heart, the things a person can only learn when walking alongside a wandering, searching soul.

He would talk of contemporary thoughts and struggles. He missed his family. There were fears concerning how he would make a living. There were struggles relating to his church family from which he had been ruthlessly pulled away. Many personal problems from long ago surfaced.

I became a big ear for Don. And he opened up his inner life to me. During that process, we both changed. And I began to know this person I previously labeled "aloof."

As we neared the end of our counseling journey, I felt Don had become a real person.

He exhibited a quality of humanness that was fresh to his personality. Sensitivity to his own and others' feelings had deepened. He now distinguished what it meant to be an effective servant. He understood more about succeeding in his work without falling into the pit of depression again.

A final sign marked the end of his therapy with me. And that was the sign of our true Christian friendship. Here was a man I loved and respected, and one who loved and respected me.

What I wish to say at this point is not easy to talk about. Yet these thoughts complete the story of my feelings about Don.

Don has graciously stated that he owes his ministry in part to me and my help during his darkest hour. And now he significantly ministers to me each week.

Two years ago Don became my pastor. I now experience the way God uses him. Our church is bound together in love and unity. From week to week, people respond to the invitation of the Savior and experience new life. Hearts are warmed and lives stabilized in the context of faithful biblical preaching.

Don has also become a model to all of us in his openness and honesty as a human being.

The ancient Zaddik order of rabbis in Poland became touchable and accepted things naively and at face value. Their humanness enabled them to find an unbelievable acceptance into people's hearts and lives. In much the same way, Don models humanness and down-to-earthness and has found a place in the lives of count-less multitudes.

If having some part in this man's continuing ministry had been my only service to the Savior, it would be enough. Based upon this fact, my life could never be in vain.

Section 1

The General Nature of Depression

Chapter 18

Types of Depression

*D*epression has many faces.

It can be the experience of a youth who has learned that he must succeed to please his parents. But he does not live up to his parent's expectations and he feels rejected, unable to please. He gradually withdraws, sinks into a depression, and ceases trying. He sleeps much, eats poorly, and may contemplate taking his life.

Depression can be an unwanted intruder into the life of a middle-aged man. Although well-trained academically, he has no control over his life experiences. He suffers a life-disabling disease that takes the sharp edge from his thinking. He loses his job to a younger man and learns he is unemployable. It is too late to retrain. Life opportunity seems to have completely slipped from his grasp. He has nothing to do, no place to go, and no way to support his wife. These circumstances and losses cause him to slip into a deep trough of despair and hopelessness. There is no way out of the corner.

Depression is a common problem of the aged. The typical retired older person is a widow living at poverty level. During earlier life, she experienced depression from time to time. Now she is alone. Her life seems to be without meaning. Her friends are mostly gone. She is neglected, moved from place to place, and no longer included in family social activities. Such typical experiences of the aged contribute to withdrawal, lack of concern for self, and severe mental disorders which include depression.

As we can see, the types of depression cannot and should not be lumped together under one category. Depression cannot and should not be stereotyped from one individual's experience.

There are several kinds of mood disorders.

One disorder may be characterized as circular with wide swings. Margie will from time to time slip into a deep, prolonged depression with no seeming cause. Her depression continues unending for months. Gradually, however, she feels better and moves to a place of elation and hyperactivity almost as disabling as her deep depression. Over many months and years, she repeats the process again and again.

Another disorder might be like Jeff's experience. He simply feels like a failure with no control or ability to help himself. He sinks into a deep, stable, depressed condition.

Different times of life seem to make some more vulnerable to depression. The later years are particularly rough.

Certain personality types exhibit a proneness to depression. It is much easier for an individual who is perfectionistic with a sensitive conscience to get depressed than it is for a person who possesses a carefree approach to life.

Depressive conditions even appear to occur more often in some families than in others, though usually not in an immediate family. This would be true of such disorders as manic-depressive psychoses that appear to have genetic bases. Usually this disorder can be found in several members of a family tree.

Depression knows no timetable for our lives. It may occur during any period of life. We will discuss the susceptible period of the middle years under the heading *Involutional Melancholia*. But as we have already said, another period of life when many confront depression is old age. During these years, personality characteristics are accentuated; our defenses are often much weaker. A tendency toward depression in earlier life will often lead to serious depression during old age.

One personality type leads all others in its candidacy for depression: the obsessive-compulsive. His overly conscientious character displays itself in an excessive concern with conformity and adherence to standards of conscience. He is markedly inhibited and overly dutiful. This sensitivity of the perfectionist often results in depression when he feels he has fallen short of certain standards. Because the obsessive-compulsive blocks the expression of his anger, he may be more prone to turn it inward on himself and therefore become depressed.

Four types of depression give insight about some general causes for the malady. Understanding the dynamics of each one sketches in a little more of the diagnosis outline with which a counselor works.

REACTIVE DEPRESSION (DEPRESSION CAUSED BY ENVIRONMENT OR CIRCUMSTANCES)

Susan has been married for thirteen years. Although her marriage has not been perfect, she considers it satisfactory. She deeply loves John, her husband.

One day John indicates he wants a divorce. There has been no quarrel or other precipitating event. Efforts to change his mind, to dissuade him from this decision, fail. And John moves out and begins divorce proceedings.

Susan feels deserted. She has not worked outside the home since she married John. She doesn't know what to do. Inwardly she is angry with him for deserting her but dares not show this overtly. She becomes deeply depressed.

Environmental circumstances are by far the most significant and important causes of depression today. Some counselors who have spent their entire lives treating depression have found that every one of their counselee's problems were related to the counselee's environment.

Reactive depression is a reaction to a significant loss. The loss is perceived as unpleasant, harmful, or devastating. Examples include losing a spouse, a job, a reputation, or meaning in life. Coupled with the particular loss is an unrecognized anger. This anger is subsequently turned inward. In this position, the depressed person has made himself the object of his own anger and feels "down." Anxiety naturally follows and joins the feelings of depression.

INVOLUTIONAL MELANCHOLIA
(DEPRESSION OF THE MIDDLE YEARS)

Thelma is a woman in her early fifties. She has been a homemaker for twenty-eight years. Her children have married and have established homes of their own. Thelma tried returning to school but felt unable to compete with younger students. Her marriage has been mediocre, and in many ways she feels trapped by it.

Her husband shows very little interest in her. Affection is gone. Communication is poor. It seems that hopes for life held earlier in her experience are unrealistic. She no longer dreams. Harsh reality pushes her toward the conclusion that there will probably be nothing else in life for her.

In the midst of these circumstances, Thelma sinks into a depression that is much like a stupor. She exhibits little reaction to anything. Mornings are more severe than other times of the day. She is plagued with guilt feelings. She suffers severe weight loss. She would probably be diagnosed as suffering from involutional melancholia.

Involutional melancholia is a depressive disorder that occurs during the middle years of life. The onset does not directly relate to a life experience. Instead it stems from a general feeling of discontent about a person's circumstances in life and a belief that what is left of life is not worthwhile. Such an evaluation is not based on thoughts that are within the depressed's ready reach. These thoughts are either at the periphery of consciousness or are fully repressed. Only severe depression remains in full consciousness.

Men also struggle with the themes of love and relationships into the middle years. But a man's profession and its demands to keep in step threaten and disturb him more. This professional threat can become an obsession, and a man eventually finds himself unable to make decisions. Paralyzed in this state of indecisiveness, he resents having to depend on others. Everything seems to be slipping away. All is about to be lost. The resulting severe depression takes hold when an individual can no longer see a way out. Worry, anxiety, agitation, and sleeplessness are a man's common bedfellows in this condition.

PSYCHOTIC DEPRESSION

Consider a situation in which a teenager makes a meager but realistic attempt to take her life. She is trying to hurt her mother who has been too harsh and strict. The daughter survives, but the mother, who is distraught and feeling guilty, loses contact with reality. She is convinced that her daughter is dead. Her daughter appears to be alive, but this is only a trick of the doctors. She thinks her daughter's eyes are really propped open with tiny toothpicks. This severely depressed woman would be diagnosed as a psychotic depressive.

A psychotic depression is a reaction to a severely disturbing life event. It impairs the ability to test reality and to function in normal ways. In this sense, it is an acute form of depression which may last for a long time.

In a psychotic depression, the individual considers his depression justified and so he desires to maintain it. A drastic change in his appreciation and approach to life occurs.

MANIC-DEPRESSIVE PSYCHOSIS

Arthur is a man in his late thirties. He is a professional with a good position and an adequate income. Twice in his earlier adult life he has been deeply depressed, although there are no identifiable reasons for the disorder.

His latest encounter with depression began after a rather lengthy period of hyperactivity. This period included not being able to sleep well, excessive talking, and an over-elated state. During this time he would go to the home of neighbors at 5:00 A.M. and awaken them. A period of relative normalcy followed the manic period and gradually gave way to a deep depressive condition which continued for many months.

Manic-depressive psychosis lists as a severe type of depression and a major emotional illness in today's society. A sufferer's mood can swing from the depths of depression to the pinnacles of elation. These wide mood swings may disappear from the manic depressive's life only to reappear at a later time. The result is an inconsistent life of normalcy interrupted by unpredictable highs and lows. Remission that seems complete dissolves into a reoccurrence. Because no related environmental event can be seen as the trigger for this type of depression, some consider manic-depressive psychosis to have a genetic or biological basis.

Manic-depressive conditions often respond well to drug therapy.

The chapters that follow share practical insights related to the mood disorders. The next chapter considers depression and its relationship to how we see ourselves.

Chapter 19

Self-Concept and Depression

A counselor on the hospital staff gently probed Don with this question. "How do you feel *about yourself?*"

A description of his own condition formed in Don's mind: "Inadequate! My self-confidence has hit bottom. There is a total loss of self-esteem. . . . I'm a failure."

A visit to the hospital by Don's wife brought more of those thoughts into his consciousness. "I saw myself stripped of all pride, all accomplishments, and all glory. I saw myself as a derelict who had reached bottom. I felt terribly unworthy of this woman I loved so much."

Depression has a way of making a person feel insignificant, unworthy, and of very little value.

In the midst of a battle with depression it is difficult to realistically evaluate ourselves. We see only the negative, the flawed. We have a negative self-concept. Observing this correlation, many attribute depression to negative self-concepts or "negative self-images."

In this chapter we will see what self-concept is and show how it relates to depression.

Let me hold up a caution flag here for our thinking about self-concept and depression. Although negative self-concepts seem to accompany depression, they do not cause depression. Here is a clearer statement: A positive self-concept will fortify us against depression.

Each life experience affects the way we see ourselves, our self-concepts. But if our self-concepts are more positive than negative, the losses we encounter—such as those feelings that bombard us in a depression—will not totally devastate us. We will absorb the negative experiences instead of them absorbing us.

WHAT IS SELF-CONCEPT?

We see ourselves in countless ways. Each of these is a concept of self.

Using myself as an illustration, I see myself as a man, a Christian, a husband, and a father. I am a teacher, a past runner hoping to get into running again, a bicyclist, and an owner of German automobiles. I have pastored churches. I am a psychologist and also somewhat of a maverick.

These are just a few of the concepts of self that make up "me." All of our concepts of self are shaped by our experiences in the world.

Concepts of self differ in importance and clarity. Being a Christian is certainly more central and important to me than being seen as an owner of German automobiles. Being a Christian is the most important relationship in my life. We can see, then, that certain concepts of self rank higher than others—they are more crucial.

In much the same way, some concepts of myself are clearer than others. I see myself as a Christian. I have no doubts in my thinking about this. Christ redeemed me, and I stand in grace. To say, "I am a good Christian," however, differs from my claim to be a Christian. And it is not nearly as clear as the previous statement.

When we organize perceptually all of our concepts of self— all of the ways in which we see ourselves—we have formulated a self-concept. We do this unconsciously.

Picture a line extending from left to right. Each of our concepts of self is attached to this line, the most negative being ranked furthest left on the line and the most positive the furthest right. A dividing line in the middle separates the negative from the positive. If we have more concepts of self on the left or negative side, our self-concept will be negative. More concepts of self on the positive side means a more positive self-concept.

How Does a Self-Concept Begin?

Self-concept begins shortly after birth. It's difficult to determine how we see ourselves at this point. We can at least say we have vague and hazy concepts of self.

Very early in our lives, people who are significant to us respond to our needs. When we are hungry, our crying brings mother with a bottle. The discomfort felt from needing a diaper change may or may not bring a quick response from a parent.

As little children we need to feel secure—to develop trust that though mother is out of sight, she has not deserted us. We also need to be touched, handled, held. (Without human skin contact, infants will simply wither away, becoming victims of a condition known as marasmus.)

We begin to judge our worth from these early responses. If these needs are neglected or ignored, we develop negative feelings about ourselves and see ourselves as worthless. But the opposite is also true. If significant people respond to and interact with us in positive ways, we will form positive concepts of self and see ourselves as worthwhile.

We organize these concepts of self into our own distinctive self-concept and continue to shape it as we mature.

Two Truths About Self-Concepts

Two characteristics are true for all self-concepts.

First, a person's self-concept is stable. Once it has been organized, it does not easily change. We have an inner need to preserve self-concept—to entrench and fortify the self that is. This is true whether the way we see ourselves is positive or not. And so our stable, positive or negative self-concept colors what we see in every situation. We interpret events according to the quality of this self-concept.

We see this process in the behavior of a husband who feels inadequate. Interpreting his wife's general friendliness as flirtation, he preserves his self-concept of inadequacy by over-interpreting his wife's congeniality. (Many couples have relationship difficulties because one or both have poor self-concepts.)

Likewise, a spouse with a more positive self-concept would interpret his wife's friendliness as charming behavior. She is seen as outgoing, gracious, and one who likes people. His interpretation tends to confirm his own positive self-concept. He has an adequate spouse.

The second characteristic of self-concept may seem to contradict the first. Instead, it compliments it.

Although it is stable, self-concept has a characteristic fluidity about it. This means that no self-concept is forever fixed and unchangeably set in concrete. The constancy of our self-concept in interacting with our environments does not prevent slight movements or changes in how we see ourselves.

CHANGING SELF-CONCEPT

Change. The word sounds harsh, almost like the clamor of metal being hammered, of steel being bent. It is a hard, slow, and difficult process. But many people who come for counseling want to change. They want to change their self-concepts.

Effecting a change in self-concept in a series of counseling sessions is not possible.

Many counselees expect a counselor to tell them a few things that will magically change their self-concepts. Such magic cannot be worked with a few special words or a snap of the fingers. When we examine our own responses to statements we don't actually feel are true about ourselves, the result is *not* instant belief and an attitude change. The result is disbelief in the form of embarrassment or speechlessness.

Some suggest that understanding what the grace of God has accomplished for us will give us positive self-concepts.

This thought is nice, and it is a "spiritual" thought. It does sound theological and logical. The only problem is that it doesn't work that simply. Countless Christians who understand their position in Christ and deeply appreciate the grace of God are yet shy and experience predominately negative feelings about themselves.

Looking at Don Baker's story, we remember that he did experience God's grace in a fresh way. In the silence of his depression, he discovered to his amazement that God loved the inactive. He even loved Don Baker. And he hadn't deserted Don. But this realization alone did not pull him from the grip of his depression.

It is possible that the experience of feeling loved and accepted by the counselor may change how a person sees himself. Indeed, working in a relationship with a loving and acceptant therapist may be the first time a person has ever experienced understanding and genuine caring. This may change him some . . . but ever so slightly.

How, then, can we change our self-concept?

We must have experiences that contrast with how we presently see ourselves. Such experiences take place as we interact with the environment. This is a process. It is not simply a matter of thinking differently.

Suppose we see ourselves as poor academic achievers. We must pass a class, complete a degree, or leap over some other kind of academic hurdle in our lives if we are ever to feel that we can achieve. Or think about parenting. If we are ever to see ourselves as good fathers, we must experience ourselves being good fathers.

WHAT DOES SELF-CONCEPT HAVE TO DO WITH DEPRESSION

First, we must understand that self-concept becomes the screen through which we interpret what is going on around us.

I have already stated that my own negative self-concept became the screen through which I interpreted my relationship with Don Baker. It colored my view of our friendship and gave me negative feelings.

To illustrate further, let's use personal loss as the event being interpreted. If our self-concepts are generally negative, we will interpret loss in negative ways that relate to our feelings of worthlessness. Loss will only confirm how we already feel about ourselves. If I lose my job and already feel like a loser, the loss only confirms negative feelings about self. The concept of being a loser will deepen and encourage depression.

If, on the other hand, I see myself in more positive ways, I will not interpret a loss or failure in negative ways. The loss will be integrated effectively into my total self-concept, a self-concept that is a rich reservoir filled with positive ways of seeing myself. I can even give a positive interpretation to the loss or failure. In this way a positive self-concept becomes a guardian against certain types of depression.

The Word of God clearly suggests the importance of a positive self-concept. In Matthew 22:39, the writer relates self-love and neighbor love. The ability to do both is connected. Paul states in Romans 12:3 that we should think realistically of ourselves and practice self-acceptance.

We have said that self-concept is the interpreter of events as they relate to us and thus a determinant of how we feel about ourselves. This is important for the depressed person. (It is also important for the non-depressed person!)

In terms of self-concept and depression, a second step is needed to help us out of our dark holes. We need to change our negative self-concepts to positive self-concepts through positive experiences in our world. We must help fill that self-concept reservoir with positive ways of seeing self.

During Don's hospital stay, he ministered to others—he pastored. Even when he didn't feel worthy of being known as a pastor, he entered into significant, supportive experiences with others. And a group of men struggling with alcoholism adopted him as their chaplain. This confirmed Don in some of his abilities once again and in the way he saw himself. We all need, and should seek, these positive kinds of experiences for ourselves.

It is important that parents, teachers, ministers, and others involved in human relationships place value on the importance of a person's self-concept. We should work toward helping people have experiences that will result in positive self-concept.

This is not the simple cure for depression. But feelings of worthlessness and uselessness find their source in negative self-concepts. And these are associated with depression.

Chapter 20

The Feelings That Won't Go Away

"How do you feel?"

Elusive, indefinable feelings skittered through Don Baker's mind during his depression. Unable to pinpoint any feeling that dominated his outlook, he answered the therapist's question with a volley of emotions that pelted him at different times.

"Sad. Empty. Alone. Hopeless. Afraid. Worthless. Ambivalent. Rejected."

Reading the moving narrative of Don's depression leaves us with our own ragged feelings of guilt, embarrassment, worthlessness, confusion, and hopelessness.

Feelings command universal interest and importance. Yet we neglect their influence in our own lives. We will expand our thinking about feelings using part of Don's story, but we must first understand a few basic concepts about them.

BASIC CONCEPTS ABOUT FEELINGS

1. Feelings—right or wrong?

Richard works the night shift at a canning operation. The economy is down. Demand for canned fish is low. The factory cuts its hours back. And Richard is laid off. He feels an emptiness

135

creeping into his thoughts. And he feels down.

Is that feeling right or wrong?

Feelings are neither right nor wrong. They are simply there. What I do with a feeling makes it right or wrong. This is true of any and all feelings I might have. It is a fundamental concept. There is no sin in feelings.

2. Feelings—irrational and subjective.

Betty and Jim invite their neighbors to dinner. Their neighbors graciously decline, but they do so on the very day Jim loses a major sale at work.

Meanwhile, Betty receives a telephone call from the school. Son Jimmy twisted a few of the conduct rules, and he has subsequently been asked to leave school for the day.

When Jim pulls into the driveway, Betty meets him and they exchange the glum news. Wistfully looking across the lawn, the couple wonders about their neighborhood. They feel the community doesn't like them. An irrational and subjective feeling at best.

Feelings are irrational and subjective. We may or may not know or be able to find the basis for them. They can distort our reality. Indeed, they often do! We must seek to understand the nature of our feeling world.

3. Feelings—vital and necessary.

What would "going home" mean apart from those nostalgic feelings about warm memories in familiar places, gentle thoughts of days gone by, and deepened love that stirs for family and friends? Can you imagine hearing Handel's "Hallelujah Chorus" near the end of *The Messiah* and not feeling the surge of deeply set emotion as the audience rises to its feet in unrehearsed awe? How about the absence of that tender protectiveness, that sweet cherishing of life in a parent's heart when he cradles his helpless infant closely at night? What would life be like without that feeling?

Feelings are vital and necessary in our makeup as human beings. Feelings in our lives can bring quality to existence. With little or no feeling, life would be bland and possibly lack meaning. Without the accompanying provisions of joy and peace, salvation would be considerably less enjoyable and practical in this drab world of pain.

4. Feelings—if they are denied.

Gene saw the rebuff from his father coming. He had made the decision to protect the family interests with a sheltered investment of their shared monies. But the investment had gone sour and the money was lost. In front of the families, Gene's father dressed him up one side and down the other, describing him as an "incompetent fool." Gene listened quietly, not arguing.

Now, months later, he still seethes inside. Though he never expressed his anger or even admitted that his father had made him angry, Gene senses the temperature of his hostile feelings rising daily. But he is not aware of the reason for his anger. Initially he had denied it even existed.

If denial of feelings becomes part of a lifestyle, we leave ourselves vulnerable and exposed to the ravages of emotional illness. Feelings of anxiety and anger, when repressed or denied, will move us toward neurotic illness. Inability to adequately deal with these conditions causes less effective functioning. We become unable to deal realistically with our inner lives and therefore less able to grow in genuine qualities of humanness.

5. Feelings—"You shouldn't feel them."

Sally is a frustrated single woman. Incurably full of life until her thirtieth birthday, she had taken delight in her career and cared little for planning much further in advance than the next weekend. Having or not having a husband did not seem to matter to her.

But the birthday that had taken away Sally's twenties had also brought the future into clearer view. And the last few years had increased her apprehension of what a life alone in an apartment would be like without a companion. Her friends had urged, "As a Christian, you shouldn't feel that way." But she did.

When we respond to another person by saying "you shouldn't feel that way," or "why do you feel that way?", we don't help them grow. (I have found it helpful in therapy to drop these statements from my repertoire of responses.) When addressed with these remarks, people naturally respond defensively.

6. Feelings—Learn to feel them.

People need to be taught to feel things. We need to learn to call our feelings by name—to identify them.

Partial or selective feelings as a style can encourage emotional illness. Only when we allow ourselves to experience honestly the full range of our feelings—and then deal effectively with them—will we move to a place of better mental health. With these practices incorporated into our lifestyle, we will begin to insulate ourselves from the possibility of emotional illness.

HANDLING PROBLEMS AND FEELINGS

Humans often cope by "defending" their egos. Many types of defenses exist.

Denial is one defense. Being unable or unwilling to face possible death during a life-threatening disease is often handled by a denial of the entire condition. We defend ourselves from death and its reality in this way.

Repression is another defense that reduces levels of anxiety. We push unwanted and painful experiences into lower levels of awareness where we can forget them and not feel as much hurt. Severe forms of repression produce amnesia, a form of selective or total forgetfulness.

Or consider projection. With this defense we put blame on a person other than ourselves for something we are surely responsible for. All of these maneuvers protect our egos.

These defensive practices, when not overused, are normal and necessary for our psychological survival. When we become too defensive, however, there is danger of developing a neurotic lifestyle. In this context, neurosis simply implies subjective psychological pain or discomfort beyond what is considered normal for a person's present condition. This pain leads to relatively immature behavior. Such neurotic lifestyles seem to be linked to depression.

A person may survive a lifetime with strong defenses and yet have an underlying neurosis that makes life less productive. On the other hand, a physical condition or combination of physical conditions may cause a person's defense system to be less effective. The psyche, or self, is exposed. Problems and feelings surface. Dealing with the problems underlying an individual's neurosis then becomes crucial.

This is often true with a disorder such as hypoglycemia.

Such an illness will weaken the defense system and make ego defenses less efficient. Those neuroses underlying a person's lifestyle will come to the surface. At this point, a person suddenly comes face to face with most, if not every problem he has ever struggled with.

In Don's illness, hypoglycemia activated his neurosis. It forced him to face many old and new issues in his life. This process of neuroses being forced to the surface through weakened defenses is uniquely true for many who suffer "emotional breakdowns."

Without his struggle with hypoglycemia, Don might not have faced many of the feelings and problem areas of his life that emerged during his depression. Some of these areas were incidental and miniscule. In his feeling life, however, they were giants, magnified all out of proportion.

Active psychological problems loomed on the horizon of Don's experience. Formerly out of sight and undetected, these problems robbed him of an efficient lifestyle even when his defenses were intact. But then they became alive, vivid, and tormenting. Some feelings associated with the new conditions could be trusted; others were gross exaggerations. Don had to experience, examine, and deal with each of them the best he could.

Today Don allows himself to feel. He can laugh and cry. He yet experiences anger. We who sit at his feet do know him to be truly human. We know his physical and emotional frailty. He is a weak human vessel through whom God's strength is made perfect.

Can we dare allow ourselves to feel? Dare we be truly human vessels? The "fruit of the Spirit is love, joy, peace, ..."—human feelings.

Section 2

Helping and Being Helped

Chapter 21

The Helping Family

*B*arbara stared at the darkened ceiling. As she lay in bed, she thought about her husband, Robert, sleeping beside her. It had been three months since he had admitted to her that he was depressed. He had lost weight and missed several days at work. He didn't even play golf on the weekends anymore.

Robert turned fitfully, mumbling a few unintelligible phrases. Barbara wondered if he would wake up and wander into the living room as he had done so many nights before. No. He still slept. That was good. They had talked seriously about help through counseling a few weeks ago, but he had resisted with the plea for "a little more time to straighten things out myself." She began praying little thought prayers, hoping her anxious feelings would die down. Should she encourage him to see a counselor or wait for him to decide? Was he getting better, or worse? Was she part of the reason for his depression? She didn't know what to think . . . or do.

No one can be seriously depressed without the immediate family being involved. Depression impacts the lives of those who live with the emotionally disturbed person. Close friends and associates may even feel the impact from the discouraged, hopeless outlook of the individual trapped in this state of mind.

AM I TO BLAME?

When a member of my family gets depressed, I may experience many feelings that will cause me to ask myself a whole new set of questions. I may ask, "How have I caused or contributed to this depression?" Pangs of guilt may condemn me. I see the depressed person and feel I am responsible, in some way, for his suffering.

But we must realize this: Depression is the specific result of an individual's own inner dynamics or his physical condition working in concert with those same inner dynamics to cause the emotional ailment. Viewed this way, it is the depressed person's responsibility.

On the other hand, few become depressed totally apart from their family condition. This does not mean that a family member must bear total responsibility or be seen as a major part of the cause of the suffering. But there are types of lifestyles in a family that can contribute in a general way to depression.

Certain kinds of family events or interaction can bring one to a place of seeming hopelessness.

Losses such as death can steal away hope within a family. Continued berating of a family member, such as a mother's ongoing contempt for her gangly daughter, crushes the spirit about the future. Simple non-acceptance as seen in an avoidance pattern sensed by the aging grandparent withers a person's aspirations about himself. These things may relate to the depression of one or more family members. Even in an occasional depression which has physical causes, the family can be involved in the negative environment with which the depressed person interacts.

As a family or a family member we can have a more positive response to depression than misplaced guilt. We might consider the severe depression of a family member as an occasion to evaluate our family structure and how it impacts each person. Loving families who support their members in healthy ways usually experience emotional health. Acceptance and understanding for each person will reduce the incidence of depression.

But no family is perfect. And when a member of our family

experiences depression, there is really no reason for any member to saddle himself with a burden of guilt. At this point it would be wise for the family to spend time in family therapy with a compassionate counselor.

Don's family opened up to counseling sessions for insight. Martha, his wife, and his children, John and Kathy, all got involved. In the end, they received the reward of knowing that their family was "normal, happy, loving, open, and unusually close." This was an assuring word in a troubled time.

A FAMILY'S IMPATIENCE, A SUFFERER'S MANIPULATION

One feeling common to parents, spouses, and siblings of the depressed is that of impatience. When will it ever end? How long will it take him to pull himself out of this?

We can be terribly impatient because of the pain of the depressed person. We feel so helpless as we see our loved one suffer. Why can't he just cheer up? It is hard for those who are not depressed to understand why someone who is depressed can't simply "turn it off."

We are impatient because of the inconvenience we feel.

Our own life routines are interrupted. The style of living we know has been radically altered because of the attention we must now direct to the sufferer. We find our self-styled encouragements make no difference. It is easy to find ourselves longing for a routine of normalcy again and becoming frustrated, even angry, when the condition seems to never end.

Another aspect of the dynamics of depression important to the family concerns the depressed person himself. The depressed person often manipulates others. He or she may think "if only he becomes aware of how severely depressed I really am, he will reverse the decision that has left me so down. Then I will no longer be depressed."

I have known depressed people who I am convinced are actually getting mileage from their depression. Sometimes a husband will use his depression to keep his wife from following through with divorce plans. He uses depression to gain control over another person—his wife.

Manipulation will sometimes work for a brief time to the advantage of the depressed person. Soon, however, he will find a new, fresh, and startling anger from the person he has manipulated. And the sufferer will end up more depressed than ever.

Family members should be aware of such manipulative tactics and gently, but firmly, resist them. In this way we help by not involving ourselves in a whole new set of unhealthy dynamics.

HOW CAN FAMILIES HELP?

There are specific ways family members can help the depressed person. We will list some below.

1. As previously stated, be patient. Both with the person and with the speed of his recovery.

There is nothing more difficult than "trying not to be depressed." The person can't just "snap out of it." Recovery from any type of emotional illness is a slow, arduous process, with many "ups and downs." The treatment is not like that for physical illness and often can't be corrected with the passing of just a few weeks.

Depression can linger for months. How well I remember the slow progress of my wife Mary Ann. For awhile she would make gains, and we would be greatly encouraged. Then she would once again sink into a despairing state, and we would both be sure she would never recover. This process went on for more than a year.

It is important for a helping family to understand that there will be many periods of gain with intervening lapses.

If we could only evaluate accurately, we would see that the sufferer has not really slipped to a previous low level. Rather, the "up and down" process is gradually moving him to a higher mood level. He is improving. My suffering family member will ultimately be free from the feelings that now impair him.

2. Be willing to listen when the depressed person wishes to talk. Listening in these circumstances includes the following important characteristics.

First, the individual should not be coerced into talking. He should talk only if he wishes to talk. And he should decide how long he will talk. Otherwise he may not feel accepted or regarded as a person in his own right.

I remember Don's comment about his wife's visits. "Only one could sit beside me for those seemingly endless moments of silence when nothing would come and nothing needed to." She was a good listener.

Second, we must try to really listen. We need to be comfortable in the depressed person's world and try to understand it as best we can. He will share things that may be nonsensical to our understanding of life and the events before us. But they are very real to him. And he needs acceptance in the world where he is struggling.

It is not necessary to become the sufferer's therapist at this point. Advice-giving usually isn't helpful, particularly in the form of quoting Scripture or laying spiritual "trips" on the person. He is already confused and feels guilty. We can be helpful if we convey that we really hear him, and that we are honestly trying to understand him.

Hear him! Walk with him! Share his feeling and world! But always remember that the hurting person must ultimately bear the responsibility of working out his difficulty himself.

3. Continue the family schedule and routine as long as the structure is reasonable and healthy.

Meals should be at normal times. Times for rising and retiring should remain generally as they have been. Keep up family recreation. Include the depressed member—if he is willing—in social events that are part of family activities.

There may be a tendency for the depressed person to want to sleep continuously or withdraw from eating meals or other family activities. Normal family expectations and familiar patterns will encourage the depressed to "stay involved." A stable, normal home atmosphere helps the family as well as the person who is "down."

4. Encourage the depressed to be involved in some new activity. Help him choose things he has always wanted to do but for which he has never had time.

One person I remember had always wanted to take up sailing. He acquired a small sailboat, maintained it, and spent hours sailing in the harbor. Both the time occupied, as well as the contact with nature and the sea, were helpful activities during his depression. Photography would have somewhat the same impact upon a person. It is time-consuming, puts one in touch with nature and beauty, and preserves select portions of the total experience.

Remember these suggestions about a new activity for the depressed.

Aim for an activity that is available, geographically and financially. It should be interesting. It best serves if it is time-consuming. It should be within the capabilities of the individual. Gardening, painting, photography, or an aerobic sport such as running or swimming are often activities that fit the above criteria.

5. I have suggested that family members are not helpful if they try to become therapists. This needs some emphasis and elaboration.

Too many of us want to figure out "why" a person is depressed.

Even if we could accurately determine the cause, what help would this be? Knowing the causes does not guarantee recovery. As a novice, most therapeutic efforts on our part are actually a hindrance to progress and impede recovery for the person we are concerned about.

Let me repeat. Don't try to be the therapist! Be stingy with advice. Offer encouragement by "walking with the person." Listen deeply. Be a big ear!

Learn to listen even with the "pores of your skin." Open your entire self to hear. In doing this we exercise the gift of encouragement and instill hope. We become true paracletes, true helpers alongside of one who suffers.

6. I have assumed that the family of a seriously disturbed person would encourage and assist in finding professional help for their situation. Sometimes this is not the case.

Too many Christians fear a stigma related to seeking out someone who provides psychotherapy. The psychotherapist simply enables another to sort out his feelings and thoughts. We have all experienced uncertainties and even anxieties when we think about "going for counseling." Don shared his embarrassment over this in Part 1. He also shared his present enthusiastic views toward counseling.

My personal observation as a counselor may be important at this point for the reader who needs encouragement to seek help.

I am a professional psychotherapist. I see people in therapy as a very special group when I compare them with the general population. I spend the significant part of every day, week after week, with them. I listen. I try to feel with them. In some ways, I participate in their struggles.

These valued people are not crazy! Indeed, they are a group of those who have sensed a need to grow. They learn to apply spiritual and psychological principles that enable them to grow. They are open enough to seek the help of another in order to be free and productive persons. These attitudes are not always present in the person who is not involved in counseling.

These statements should help to cure the "leper-like status" many associate with counseling. Both the depressed person and his family members need the cure.

Help should be sought as soon as it is apparent that the depressed person is not effectively handling his condition. This is especially true if the condition is obviously worsening. Routine work becomes difficult—he can't pull himself up—life's picture darkens: delay at this point will only lengthen the time of recovery.

GUIDELINES FOR SEEKING A COUNSELOR

A therapist should have adequate training. This usually means academic work to the doctoral level and supervised training in clinical settings.

In addition to professional competence, Christian counselors have an understanding of a believer's unique place in the world as a child of God. Without this understanding, the counselor will have "blind spots" in working with the believer. Problems can be spiritual, as well as psychological, or a combination of both.

A therapist who lacks a biblical understanding of guilt, as opposed to feelings of guilt, would never be able to walk with a person lacking assurance of salvation. Let me explain. Guilt is theological and objective. We never feel it. Feelings of guilt are more psychological and certainly subjective. If we believed we were without God's salvation every time we felt guilty, assurance would be elusive. On the other hand, knowing biblical means of handling feelings of guilt—confession and restoration to fellowship—provides a means that enables us to keep moving and not be overwhelmed by a sense of sinfulness.

Psychology without an adequate theology will be as ineffective as theology without an adequate psychology. Both are needs for a therapist who is to be effective in the life of a Christian.

The counselor needs to be relational and empathic. If one cannot relate effectively to the therapist, little progress occurs. Satisfied clients often pass along the word about the ease of relating to certain therapists, aiding those seeking an effective counselor.

When medical or physical problems exist, one might consider a psychiatrist as the choice of therapists. A psychiatrist is a physician with special training in mental disorders. If a psychiatrist is not involved, the therapist of choice should be willing to work with a physician if a biological base for an emotional disorder seems probable.

7. Sometimes properly prescribed medication is a great help in handling mood disorders.

Don openly acknowledges his use of medication. For many Christians, however, this is a practice fraught with misunderstanding and anxiety.

I am not a physician. As a psychologist, however, I would urge Christians to carefully examine their attitudes relating to biochemical treatment.

For some kinds of depression, medication can make the difference between a person's continuing to function or becoming totally disabled.

In this chapter, we have attempted to give suggestions to those who want to help a close family member suffering with depression. In the next chapter, we will discuss ways a hurting person can help himself.

Chapter 22

Helping Yourself

Robert rolled onto his side. He looked at his watch. Two a.m. He had awakened at the same time every morning these past few months.

The next four hours would be agony. Lying awake. Frustration from not being able to sleep. But relief that at least he did not have to face the day . . . yet. And then promptly and harshly at six, the snapping on of the alarm. Feigning sleep, he would pull the covers close while Barbara got out of bed. And another day would have arrived to demand his participation.

That was hours away, though.

At the moment he listened to Barbara's soft inhaling and exhaling. He was glad she was asleep, because she had told him about lying awake late at night, worrying about his depression.

Robert reflected about his condition. He knew that staying in bed when he was down wasn't the answer. Neither was hiding from his friends. He thought there must be something he could actively do to cause the depressing thoughts to lift. His mind told him there was. But what was it?

No set of specific rules helps each person who is depressed or who suffers from some other emotional disorder. The following things often give support through easing the pain and making the condition more bearable. In some cases, these actions are significant helps in the healing process. However, their impact varies not only because of differences in the basis for each illness but also because of differences in the personalities of those experiencing the illness.

We can improve our poor mood levels by:
1. Developing good aerobic exercise program
2. Maintaining a healthy diet
3. Always hoping for improvement
4. Finding meaning in the depression experience
5. Getting in touch with feelings—especially anger

AEROBIC EXERCISE

I remember a man coming for counseling who had been depressed for many months. Combined with his psychotherapy, I encouraged him to get into a daily running program. His condition was severe enough that he was willing to do anything to get better. Within a few months he was running four miles a day and it seemed he literally ran out of his depression.

Getting into a regular exercise program may be one of the most difficult things we ever attempt while we are depressed. Our lack of energy in a depression makes sleeping or inactivity much more desirable and inviting.

For those who are able to persist, however, exercise becomes one of the most effective means of self-help.

Many physiologists feel that aerobic activities—those that stimulate the cardiovascular system and increase our heartbeat to at least 130 beats a minute—activate natural antidepressants that ward off depression within our systems. In time, improved conditioning of our bodies also causes us to feel more positive about ourselves.

Exercise is a friend to the depressed individual.

The exercise should involve kinds of activities that produce aerobic conditions. Jogging, bicycling, and swimming are examples. These exercises are especially helpful for the depressed individual when done daily. Running and biking will also put an individual in the out-of-doors and in natural areas that are not only beautiful but therapeutic.

Though benefits often come early in the program, we experience the full value only in time as exercise becomes more of a lifestyle.

DIET

Eating properly is another means of self-help. A proper diet should include many fresh fruits and vegetables, whole grain cereals, and significant reductions of red meat and sugar.

Many specialists feel there is a relationship between what we eat and our emotional health. The intent of this book does not include examining this relationship. If there are doubts or questions about the effects of diet upon a person's emotional condition, consult a physician or dietician.

AN OPTIMISTIC OUTLOOK

Developing an attitude of hope when depressed is far from easy. But it is very helpful when possible. Feelings of despair and hopelessness dog the depressed person. It's very easy to think about giving up.

Don's early lifeline to which he held tenaciously was "you will get better." This statement from someone in the hospital gave him support and encouragement. When depressed, being optimistic and having hope are very important. This hope is not groundless because most people ultimately get better in spite of the help they do or don't receive.

An early researcher, Eysenk, found that a significant number of those who are mentally ill will make improvement without help from anyone. What a helpful, hopeful thought! This is consistent with my belief that there are regenerative powers in every human organism that move us toward healing and health. It is particularly true for those of us in whom the Spirit of God dwells.

No physician or psychotherapist ever heals a person. We only provide the conditions under which the healing will take place naturally. Some of these conditions involve the counselor sharing himself, practicing acceptance and empathy, and encouraging openness. But he can never heal.

Yet hope develops in the counseling process. For some depressed persons, the hoped-for improvement would never come without outside help. (Eysenk also found that only part of his research population improved without help.)

We learn during counseling to alter our styles of life and thinking to become more effective. As we gain insight about ourselves, we mature and learn to handle pressure better. We break the recurring cycle of depression as this learning takes place. All of these realizations and steps build our hopes.

When we look at the other side of the coin, we realize that hope must undergird the healing process and the counseling experience.

Counseling is a process. We build new resources and learn about ourselves slowly, in small increments. Lack of visible progress can dull our determination and author despairing thoughts unless we broaden perspectives to include our overall improvement. Hope bargains for the time we need while this happens. Having to bring the painful past and present depression into clear focus—a necessary part of healing—makes hope an even more important ingredient. Remember. You will get better.

FINDING MEANING IN DEPRESSION

I remember well a concept Don and I considered during his therapy. A writer we both had read talked about the "pregnant moment . . ."—that moment when an event or events take on meaning. Any experience in a period of time has meaning for us. This is especially true for Christians.

When depressed, anxious, phobic, or in any other state of emotional imbalance, we can seize the opportunity to learn more about self. If we can do this, experiencing an emotional difficulty may be a rare, insightful time to learn what God is doing in us.

Every experience in time can be "pregnant" with meaning, not only for now but in eternity. We can experience our weakness and the need for God, and obtain a clearer understanding of the suffering of others. We can even get more in touch with our strengths as well as our vulnerabilities.

GETTING IN TOUCH WITH FEELINGS— ESPECIALLY ANGER

Trying to get in touch with many of our feelings when depressed is usually not necessary. Feelings are there and can ravage the individual.

One feeling is different, though. In depression, we often turn anger inward. This process is sometimes described by individuals who say "when angry, I stuff it," or "I just swallow my anger."

We experience relief from our inverted anger when we finally feel it—get in touch with it—and learn how to handle it less destructively. Anger felt is no longer anger turned inward and directed against self. And this will cause a decrease in the depression. It is not easy to be depressed and angry at the same time.

Let me illustrate. Rejection by a loved one commonly causes reactive depression. Anger is certainly present in us when this form of depression settles in. There are feelings of worthlessness and scorn that result from turning our anger inward. The idea of "getting in touch with anger" means to simply feel the anger that is really there. Admit it! "I am really angry with her!" There is no need to be hostile or berate the one who spurns us. But we should feel the anger rather than turn it inward.

These suggestions are certainly not depression cure-alls, nor are they substitutes for the avenue of counseling when it is needed. They may, however, significantly aid in the healing process of a depressed or otherwise emotionally ill individual.

Chapter 23

Helping Your Children Be Non-Depressive

*A*pproximately 50 percent of the people who come to me for counseling related to depression have not reached their thirtieth birthday.

This seems strange. Surely childhood, adolescence, and early adulthood are more carefree times than middle and old age. Yet this is not evident when we look at the age categories for depressed people.

Some describe the generation of young adults at this period in our century as the generation of depressives.

I want to suggest ways parents can move a new generation away from depression as a lifestyle. We can avoid mistakes in child rearing that may prevent depressive qualities from appearing later in our children's adult lives.

LEARNED HELPLESSNESS

Seligman has given us a relatively new approach to the dynamics of depression. He calls it "learned helplessness."

Basically, learned helplessness describes the experience we know as depression. It is a condition an individual finds himself in when he believes that his person and actions do not make a difference. As a result, he gives up, puts forth no more effort, learns to be helpless, and becomes depressed. Only when he experiences his actions making a difference will he no longer be depressed.

My generation may be partly responsible for the depressive characteristics of the present generation. We may have eased the demands of life for them so that they learned to be helpless.

We remember well the struggles of those difficult years of economic chaos—the era of the 1930s when so many of us and our families struggled just to help pay for food and a roof over our heads. As we bore children later, many of us chose to not let our young people struggle as we did. We gave them everything they needed and wanted without their doing anything for it. "Getting without doing" did not teach them that their actions made a difference.

Our parents reared us differently.

We struggled, worked, and accomplished. My parents contributed nothing to my support or education after I reached the age of sixteen. The last money I received from my family after I was seventeen was a $100 wedding gift. I have been responsible for providing funds for my college, seminary, and graduate work. I have paid for every automobile I have owned, every house I have lived in as my own, every suit of clothing I have worn, and every vacation I have ever taken. Though my life was difficult I have seen that my actions have "made a difference." I have invested effort into what I have received.

I had often felt I would have appreciated help. And I helped my children as they grew up. But perhaps we do our children a favor when we don't give them everything. When they struggle and accomplish they learn that there is a true relationship between the effort they put forth and what they get in return. In these ways they learn that their actions do make a difference. We may be effectively helping them avoid a depressive lifestyle characterized by learned helplessness.

ANGER TURNED INWARD

In reactive depression, we sense loss and the consequent

anger about that loss is turned inward and dumped on self. Having made ourselves the object of our anger, we feel down. This is similar to what we feel like when another person is severely angry at us. Except we are now that angry person.

Let's talk about "anger turned inward" as a model we give our children. As Christian parents, we may overvalue tranquility, practice "peace at any price," and feel that anger itself is sin. Many of us would do anything in our power to not be angry or show anger outwardly.

Such behavior either directly or indirectly teaches our children to handle anger by repression (not allowing ourselves to feel anger) or denial ("Who me? I'm not angry!"). We may be helping them to become depressives in this way.

Anger as an emotion is not sin. Learning to experience anger without becoming aggressive is more realistic than repressing it or denying it. As Christian parents, we need to allow ourselves to feel angry and resolve it without sinning. We then become effective models for our children. We need to teach our children to keep anger where they can deal with it satisfactorily—up front, in full consciousness, where they are aware of it.

When dad is angry with mother because dinner is consistently late, he allows himself to be angry and says, "I am really angry that I am unable to keep myself on a realistic evening work schedule because meals do not seem to be on time. It is difficult for me to understand why this must be true night after night. Could you help me with this?"

Or perhaps mother is really angry with dad because he constantly leaves things lying around and the house seems messy and cluttered. Mother allows herself to be angry and says, "I spend much of my time every day trying to keep the house straight and orderly. I get terribly frustrated and angry when I have to go back over the house again and again. Too much of my time is spent this way. Won't you help me?"

In each of these examples, the parent allowed himself to be angry. They described their feelings accurately without personally blaming the other and requested help from the other with their problem. Children will pick up on this kind of modeling.

ADEQUATE, CONSISTENT DISCIPLINE

Realistic, adequate, and consistent discipline plays an important part in our children becoming optimistic, happy adults.

By realistic I mean a disciplinary action that is tied closely to the misbehavior. Adequate means discipline that is appropriate for the misbehavior. By consistent we emphasize that the child should be aware of the gravity of the situation and know what to expect every time the misbehavior takes place.

When we ignore realistic, consistent training of our children, we encourage depressive lifestyles. Remember Seligman? Responding appropriately to our children's misbehavior or inadequate behavior helps them feel their actions do make a difference.

Healthy discipline does not call for excessive, unrestrained force. If we over-discipline, we can put an intolerable burden upon the child.

Look at the discipline of the Lord in contrast to this. Scripture teaches that God's discipline of His children is always in grace. It is never as much as we deserve. His actions toward our behavior have discipline in mind, not punishment. The difference between discipline and punishment is that the former is well thought out, never a reaction, and always has an ultimate purpose that involves our development.

Do we as parents practice these positive characteristics of discipline?

I recently heard of a father who was exasperated because his little son wet the bed. In his anger, the father wrapped the child's head in the wet sheet, upended him, and put him head first into the toilet.

That is not discipline. That is nothing more than undiluted child abuse. It is severe and inappropriate punishment. These kinds of child rearing methods will surely create a depressive lifestyle for the child in later life. The child will end up feeling unloved, unimportant, and dehumanized. Such treatment does not consider the human dignity of a little child.

How can we help a child know that his actions do make a difference?

What are some guidelines for developing principles of excellent, consistent, and reasonable discipline?

Rudolph Dreikur's concepts of logical consequences help us here. As parents, we can set up reasonable consequences of misbehavior and firmly, clearly, and lovingly tell the child what will happen if the misbehavior occurs again. The consequences need to be directly related to the child's misbehavior. When the misbehavior occurs, the consequence is allowed or made to happen—with no exceptions.

Five-year-old Johnny makes it a habit to leave the table after his father offers thanks. He gets up from the table, plays elsewhere, and no amount of persuading will get him to return to the table during the normal course of the meal. Just before the family finishes dinner, however, Johnny returns to the table and slowly eats his food. The family cannot finish the meal in normal fashion. Johnny's actions thoroughly frustrate each family member.

A popular method of dealing with this problem involves threatening to spank the boy. In reality, this reaction reinforces his attention-getting behavior, teaches him how hostile others can be, and perhaps convinces him that a parent can beat up on five-year-olds.

What would reasonable, consistent discipline be in this example? The parent should get down on Johnny's level and look directly into his eyes. Without anger, the parent should say something like "Johnny, we want you to eat dinner with the family. If you don't want to, however, you don't have to. If you choose not to eat with us, you will have to wait until breakfast to eat again. There will be no snack. You make the choice!"

If Johnny doesn't remain at the table, let him go. But he will not eat until morning in spite of his arguing and crying. He will not die of starvation if he waits until morning. In all likelihood, he will be a full-time participant during the next meal.

The principles in this illustration can be applied to every act of misbehavior. Notice. The consequence, not eating until the next meal, is directly related to the misbehavior, leaving the dinner table. The consequence was simply allowed to happen. Johnny couldn't come back to the table.

Johnny certainly had the ability to change his behavior. Expectations were not confusing nor was his behavior change impossible. And he was clearly and firmly informed of the consequences of his actions.

Consistent, reasonable discipline rather than punishment that is reactive and inconsistent will help our children develop non-depressive lifestyles. They will know clearly what is expected of them. And they will learn the results of their actions.

ALLOWING CHILDREN TO BE IMPERFECT

The Fremonts wanted their son Glenn to do well and handle himself successfully in life. Demanding and perfectionistic, they reared Glenn in such a way that he demands much of himself, is very concerned about failure, and even has a higher I.Q. score than most of his peers. Glenn should become a successful and happy adult. Agree?

Some recent research indicates, however, that children like Glenn have the highest incidence of emotional problems in our society.

If we teach our children that failure is always inappropriate, if we communicate that producing as much as is humanly possible without ever failing is always best, or if we leave the feeling that only top performance is acceptable—we build into them a structure for a depressive lifestyle devoid of human and hopeful qualities. Such children will grow up to be "uptight," perfectionistic adults.

We must accept children in their failures and teach them to see these experiences as valuable in their overall development. We must show them that our love is constant and unconditional. We need to help eliminate anxieties they have about their performance in order that they may be free to do their best creatively in directions of their own interests and choosing.

Boys who show interest in automobile mechanics should be encouraged to tinker, explore, and work on old cars. They may become automotive engineers. Girls who are logical and enjoy debate and public speaking should be allowed to engage in activities such as drama and the debate club. They may become attorneys some day.

If a child's interest moves in a certain direction, but the parent requires perfection—no failure—it may be impossible for the child to become familiar enough to continue in the activity and develop a field of interest.

In these ways, we "train up a child in the way he should go, and when he is old he will not depart from it" (Proverbs 22:6). We help build healthy emotional characteristics for the future and promote stability in our children's futures.

Chapter 24

Changing Your Lifestyle

I watched a man come into the office one day, head and shoulders slung forward and a terrible grimace frozen on his face. He was the picture of dejection, blind to hope and deaf to encouragement. He had spoken to me before about his problems with depression but was not open to suggestions I had given for improving his outlook. He came to talk but not to change.

Convinced that he was the victim of a depressive lifestyle deeply rooted in his background and personality, this man pessimistically looked at the years ahead of him. Depression for him was here to stay.

Many who sit in my office for the first time describe themselves as depressives. They sit down, squirm a bit, and finally say, "I'm a melancholic." We learn early to classify ourselves in stereotypes. These rigid descriptions help our minds organize information about ourselves.

But must our feet be set in concrete? Are we unchangeable, bound to serve sentences of gloom and dismay in depressed lives? Can these lifestyles be altered? Can our conditions improve, and can we move to a better place?

I give a resounding yes to those questions. Humans are process-oriented, dynamic beings. It is possible for us to loose ourselves from the shackles of negative lifestyles . . . and be free.

LIFESTYLES—WHAT ARE THEY?

The concept of "lifestyle" was introduced by a man named Alfred Adler. Lifestyle might be defined as "a person's unique and characteristic pattern of relating to his world and environment." Lifestyle means the ways we respond to and interact with the events that happen daily. It involves the ways we overcome problems we face.

Each of us develops his own unique lifestyle.

Lifestyles have an important bearing on mental illness. In spite of evidence citing genetic determinants for certain kinds of emotional difficulties, no person is destined to be a depressive. Environments, lifestyles, and what we bring to life are all important.

In this chapter, we will discuss aspects of healthy lifestyles.

Although we might feel that our lives have been characterized by gloom, we can reach a place of joy and happiness. We can be optimistic and enthusiastic about meeting each day. We can awaken refreshed. Excitement about the prospect of the day before us can prevail. But for these things to characterize our mood levels, we must often alter the way we respond to and interact with the world about us.

Through the years I've monitored my own lifestyle and those of my clients. I have observed definite characteristics of healthy lifestyles. These characteristics include the following:

1. Firm commitments
2. An adequate philosophy of life
3. A willingness to be human
4. An inner sense of direction
5. The ability to see myself as unique
6. A model of liberty as a Christian

FIRM COMMITMENTS

Of all the issues involved in personal lifestyles, none is more important than the nature of our personal commitments. Healthy, stable persons must have healthy, stable commitments. Commitment is involved in almost every one of our successes as well as in all our successful functioning.

I see at least four aspects in commitment. *Direction* for our lives is the first.

Commitments have direction. Commitments point toward a person, ideas, causes, or something else that exists. And we move toward whatever we're committed to.

The second aspect of commitment is *total abandonment*.

Such abandonment is demonstrated by one who does not allow danger, disillusionment, or distance to turn him back from his goal. He does not give up when the going gets rough or difficult. Commitment implies never letting go, always hanging on, and being persistent to the end.

Another characteristic of commitment is its *reorganizing aspect*.

Commitment pulls inner aspects of our lives tightly together. Commitment keeps us from disintegrating, from falling apart, from collapsing into a directionless pile of rubble.

Finally, commitment calls forth *appropriate behavior* toward its object and direction. It calls forth responsibility, love, and emotion.

Without commitment, we might indeed become depressives. The nature and directions of our commitments determine whether we will become emotionally healthy persons. The authors of this book believe in making Jesus Christ the object of our supreme commitment.

AN ADEQUATE PHILOSOPHY OF LIFE

The characteristic of firm commitments is closely followed by another characteristic common to adequate lifestyles. And that is the characteristic of a healthy philosophy of life.

If life were no more than a grasshopper dance to oblivion, philosophy of life would be no issue. But life is more! Our lives begin, continue, and move us to eternity. We face conflict, pressure, and loss as the norm of our existence. We aren't like the mayfly that is born and dies the same day. Because of the brevity and simplicity of its life, it has no mouth and no need to eat. Our lives are vastly more complex and need a philosophy for living.

What is a philosophy of life? Three aspects of belief or understanding are involved in its definition. We begin to summarize our own philosophy of life by simply answering this question: "What do we believe is real, true, and good?" As we put the flesh on this skeleton question, we put together our own unique philosophies of life.

How can we answer the question "What is real?"

We know of two basic realities—the seen and the unseen. Some of us may accept what we see as our only reality. The reality of the material world. That which enlivens our senses—sights, sounds, smells, tastes, feeling of touch—is the seen reality. This reality includes money, sunshine, other people, the world in which we live.

Some of us also accept unseen reality. Never having seen God who is Spirit, we know there is reality in Him. We believe in a world that is not seen, made up of spiritual, not physical, forces.

We must also answer questions regarding what we believe about truth.

What is truth? What is it like? Where does it come from? How is truth revealed? Is it revealed in nature? What about Scripture and its claims? Are there other written sources of truth, like the Hindu Vedas or Islam's Koran? Can we create truth? Is it relative or absolute, or perhaps both?

The third important consideration in our philosophy of life identifies what we consider important in life.

What do we value? What is good? What is the most important? What are we striving for? For some the answer is material wealth. For others, success in rearing a family is most important. In the life of a Christian, pleasing Jesus Christ is high on the list of priorities. Whatever we value or consider important becomes the answer to "What is good?"

The quality of our philosophies of life determines how effectively we deal with our world. To be concerned only with material things will cause us to neglect that which is unseen and eternal. In a similar manner, allowing my life to be governed by my own truth, and feeling that all truth is relative, will eventually lead me down a path of ultimate destruction and dismay. I simply do not have adequate ability to know right and wrong apart from divine revelation. Nor do I really address things of highest value that do not have Jesus and eternity in view.

An inadequate philosophy of life can map a path for the depressive's lifestyle and other types of mental illness. On the other hand, a sound set of principles, grounded in a personal relationship with God and healthy guides for living, can open the road to emotional soundness.

Try to systematize a philosophy of life. See these principles as governing life today. Ask yourself:

What do I believe is

real, true, good?

You may find your answers totally inadequate and wish to renew, rearrange, or perhaps develop something entirely different for your philosophy of life.

A Willingness to Be Human

Christians have often equated humanness with evil. Or with weakness. To be human is to be fallen! If we can deny our humanness, therefore, we deny a part of us that needs rejecting!

Such denial forfeits any appreciation we can have of our development as a person. We shut off characteristics of existence that give meaning to life.

Humanness refers to what is natural for us. It is natural to be hungry, to cry and laugh, to feel things. Humanness spawns feelings of self-preservation. It is human to be weak and to grow old. We are human when we make mistakes. Many of these human characteristics frighten Christians and cause us to try to eliminate them from our lives.

To be healthy, however, we need to see ourselves as truly human and allow ourselves to be just that! Fathers need to see themselves as not always right; mothers as failing their children on occasion; business executives as making wrong decisions; pastors as preaching some sermons poorly, and being too exhausted to do their work as well as they might wish.

Many have observed that as we begin to be the person we truly are, fewer feelings of guilt plague our lives and we experience less depression. When behavior matches feelings, we do not feel so much like failures.

We need to be ourselves without fear! As we begin to live humanly, we set the stage for developing the fourth characteristic of a healthy lifestyle—an inner sense of direction.

AN INNER SENSE OF DIRECTION

People who can make their own decisions, and take responsibility for the same, are people who function most effectively. They are inner-directed.

Being "other-directed" means that we do things because other people believe we should do them. Our lives are governed and managed by the "shoulds" and the "oughts." If this is the chief motivator of our behavior, we set ourselves into a mold or lifestyle that leads to depression.

The apostle Paul is a good biblical example of inner-directed life. In his epistle to the Galatians he recounts confronting Peter for his "two-faced," other-directed approach to fellowship. Peter would not fellowship with Gentiles when Jews were present because of pressure from his believing Jewish friends.

Philip is another example. He followed the inner leadership of the Holy Spirit spontaneously and joined himself to the Ethiopian eunuch in his chariot.

Christians have a unique opportunity to develop inner-directedness. God has chosen to indwell each of us in the person of His Holy Spirit. The Holy Spirit is the true inner Director in each child of God. He is deep in each of our lives. He functions at the seat of our being to control our lives. He is so integrated into our psyches for the purpose of controlling us that we are usually unaware of what He is doing.

As we practice spirituality (living in ways that facilitate the Spirit's control), He guides our movements, our choices, and the directions we take.

"Practicing spirituality" simply means to "walk in the Spirit," be "led by the Spirit," or "be filled with the Spirit." It involves being aware of any sin that has intruded into my life, immediately confessing that sin, and believing that I am again controlled by the Holy Spirit.

In this way, our lives truly become "inner-directed." We do not need people to tell us what we ought to do.

THE ABILITY TO SEE MYSELF AS UNIQUE

Believing and valuing our uniqueness is crucial in the development of a non-depressive lifestyle.

People compare themselves with others. We see someone we admire and realize how far short we fall when comparing ourselves with them. We end up getting depressed! We feel short-changed, ill-equipped, and relegated to second-class citizenship.

The apostle Paul says comparison is not wise.

"For we are not bold to class or compare ourselves with some of those who commend themselves; but when they measure themselves by themselves, and compare themselves with themselves, they are without understanding" (2 Corinthians 10:12).

We also do ourselves a gross disservice when we compare. To desire to be like, to envy the place of, or to compare ourselves with others is to forget the uniqueness granted each of us by our heavenly Father.

We see an example of our individual uniqueness in the face each of us has. Each of our faces has a nose, eyes, a mouth, and two cheeks. There is a forehead and varying amounts of hair on each head. These are certainly similar characteristics. Yet in all the world, except for monozygotic twins, we would be pressed to find two faces just alike.

The same is true for our gifts, our intellects, and our experiences. We are unique individuals.

MODEL LIBERTY AS A CHRISTIAN

The ability to "be free" is a vital part of being one's true self. It is central in the concept of being "inner-directed" and not "other-directed." Let's examine some concepts about "liberty" that free us to live.

1. The only true place of freedom in all the world is that place of being a servant to Jesus Christ. Being a servant and being free appears to be a contradiction. Yet apart from being a servant to Jesus, we are hopelessly bound as slaves to sin.

> "For when you were slaves to sin, you were free in regard to righteousness. But now having been freed from sin and enslaved to God, you derive your benefit, resulting in sanctification, and the outcome, eternal life" (Romans 6:20, 22).

2. As a servant, we are free to regulate our lives and behavior by guiding principles set forth in Scripture. This is particularly true in areas where Scripture gives no direct command.

3. One of the scriptural principles governing behavior alerts us about the responses a weaker brother (one who doesn't understand liberty) can have to our behavior.

> "It is good not to eat meat or to drink wine, or to do anything by which your (particular) brother stumbles" (Romans 14:21).

We should not cause a weaker brother, by our exercise of liberty, to "fall flat on his face" and no longer walk with the Savior.

In the New Testament times, the best USDA grade A beef that could be purchased was found in the idol's temple. A new believer who had previously offered such meat to idols and saw reality in those offerings might be turned away from Christianity by seeing a mature believer eating meat in freedom. He would possibly no longer walk with Jesus.

4. Even though a weak brother has a "conscience" against a behavior, this does not mean that we should become "other-directed" and not practice liberty ourselves. Our love for a weaker

brother may cause us to model liberty and help the brother learn to practice liberty himself.

An almost ridiculous example of how distorted a weaker brother's concept might be is that of a man who once told me he couldn't eat peanut butter and jelly on bread because of a biblical injunction to not "mix seed"—i.e., grain and peanuts.

To never practice liberty because a weak brother has a conscience against a behavior would leave us in an unbiblical position. We would miss the pleasure of peanut butter and jelly, and we would forever be regulating our lives according to noninstructed, wrongly-conditioned consciences. Our behavior under these conditions would continue in a maze of immature thinking with no modeling of the freedom which is truly ours in Christ.

5. Because Christians still fail, we need to talk about feelings of guilt that a condemning conscience stirs up when we do fail.

Many years ago in Los Angeles, I heard a radio minister say, "Conscience is a heavy footprint of God upon a man's heart." That is not necessarily true. In man's original condition, conscience may have been a perfect indicator of right and wrong. Today, however, conscience is more often the "heavy footprint" of man's social conditioning.

We can be conditioned to feel guilty about any type of behavior, even if it isn't sin. A weak brother has been conditioned to feel it's wrong to eat peanut butter and jelly on bread. Certainly this is not sin. Conscience may or may not be consistent with the will and holiness of God.

Guilt is objective. We never feel guilt. It is a condition that exists when I violate the will or holiness of God. "Feelings of guilt" are subjective. It is "feelings of guilt" that hurt. They may or may not be actually related to true guilt.

When I bear false witness, I am guilty. I may or may not experience guilt depending upon my understanding of this behavior as sin and my own sensitivity. This depends upon the nature of my early conditioning and my knowledge of Scripture. The better my understanding of the Word of God, the more appropriate my feelings of guilt will be.

There is a movement in Christian psychology to eliminate

confession as a practice, even when we are aware that we have sinned. Yet confession plays a vital part in behavior related to forgiveness, restoration, and freedom from "feelings of guilt" (which <u>are</u> related to guilt when we have sinned). Only as we learn to confess sin in our lives can we experience the removal of guilt and have freedom from an oppressive, guilty conscience.

This chapter ends with the hope that, using some of the characteristics of healthy lifestyles, we can evaluate, alter, and enter a lifestyle that will be depression-free.

Section 3

The Unmentionables

Chapter 25

Suicide

*E*arly in my pastoral ministry, I shared the anguish of a young husband whose wife took her own life. Having just given birth and apparently suffering from a postpartum depression, this young woman left her home during the night. She was found later face down in a flooded field behind her house. She had drowned herself in about five inches of water from the spring overflow of the small river nearby. The young husband grieved deeply over the loss of his precious wife.

Suicide is a problem among Christians as well as among society in general. Some who read these chapters have lost a loved one or friend in this way. Others will experience suicide, or the threat of suicide, in their families at some future date. Some may even be contemplating suicide as they read this sentence.

THE RELATIONSHIP OF DEPRESSION TO SUICIDE

It is unlikely that suicide will occur in isolation from depression. I have never known an individual who enjoyed an optimistic lifestyle, experienced success, and anticipated the future with happy expectations to terminate his own life.

Suicide is associated with feelings of despair.

The potential suicide victim feels hopeless. As the deeply depressed person assesses his life situation, it is as if there is no way out of the corner. Life is too painful. There seems to be no alternative left for a person but to take his life.

It is not easy to understand fully what happens when suicide, as an alternative action, at last becomes a real and viable choice. The individual has probably been deeply depressed for some time. Suicide has remained in the person's thoughts as a difficult idea to dislodge. Leaving life looks like the only escape route from difficulties. The pain would then be over. Suffering would cease. As the depression begins to ease a bit, and a person gains a little of his strength back, he makes the choice to put his chosen method into action. And he kills himself.

Suicide happens in the context of a depression that lingers and becomes difficult to overcome. It seldom, if ever, is isolated from the gloom of a mood disorder.

COMING TO GRIPS WITH THE ISSUES

Believers face certain issues with respect to suicide. These questions are not always clear, nor are there ever easy answers. The following are just a few of the issues the Christian world struggles with as the rate of suicide in our subculture increases.

1. How can one who is a leader among Christians, one who is set apart by God for ministry, ever consider such a heinous sin? (Both Don and I have had thoughts about suicide!)

2. Can a person who is sane take his own life?

3. Would a true Christian ever contemplate suicide seriously and take his own life?

4. If one is a believer, does he terminate his relationship with God by this act of self-murder, ushering himself from God's presence eternally before being able to ask forgiveness for his sin?

How could Christian leaders have suicide thoughts? How can it be that some actually end up taking their own lives?

We need to remind ourselves that our pastors, teachers, and counselors are clothed in human flesh like other people. In many respects, these individuals are more vulnerable to stress, loss, family difficulties, and even attacks by the enemy, Satan.

For these reasons, the option of suicide can be just as real for the Christian leader as it is for the lay person. The church needs to pray for and support these choice servants of God

Let's consider the matter of Satan's direct involvement in suicide. Surely every attack of depression is not demonic. We have talked about biochemical irregularities, environmental factors, and internal personal dynamics as sufficient cause for a person to be depressed. Even suicide can be free from Satan's direct influence.

On the other hand, special demonic activity can bring about the possibility of losses, hindered or hampered relationships, or other situations which could cause depression. Satan's involvement as the "god of this age" can also create pressures at a time of deep depression which may encourage one to end his life.

The suicide of any child of God—a member of His body, the church—is always a sad loss. This is true not only for the immediate family but also for the church itself. Every believer stands equipped with spiritual gifts that enable him to function within a given body of believers. One may be depressed because of feelings of uselessness associated with not developing these gifts. The suicide of a Christian, however, permanently cripples the functioning of the church on earth because of the loss of the ultimate development and use of those gifts.

Consider next the sanity of the suicide victim.

Are not all who take their lives obviously insane? To believe this would, of course, shelter one from dealing with issues like the eternal destiny of the suicide victim. A plea of insanity for a suicide victim would basically absolve him of responsibility for the act.

How do we define insanity? Insanity usually means that a person is not responsible in any way for his actions. An insane person who commits suicide is beyond the ability to make a choice to live. But is this true about the depressed person who takes his life? Can he no longer choose life?

Some who take their lives are obviously insane. Most professionals would agree with this. It is also apparent that many who take their lives do make rational choices up until the point of self-destruction, and they see suicide as the only alternative for escape from their seemingly hopeless situation.

But many suicidal people see and choose additional alternatives to ending their lives. So we cannot attribute suicide to insanity alone. If this were true, no person who killed himself would ever fully understand the implications of this desperately final act. And yet some do.

Does suicide ever become a reality for a true believer in Jesus Christ? The answer is "of course."

The Christian community is no more immune from this experience than from any other effect of sin in the human race.

When the assaults of depression buffet one, suicidal thoughts are common. In a severe, prolonged depression, in the midst of seemingly hopeless circumstances, many believers have taken their lives. These people wrongly assessed their circumstances. They had not explored all of the alternatives. The depression had distorted their thinking. But they are yet children of God who became ultimate victims of a mental disorder which caused them to consider self-destruction . . . and follow through with it.

And then there is the matter of the suicide victim's eternal destiny. Many feel that suicide is the ultimate sin for which there is no forgiveness. Isn't a person who ends life left in a position of not being able to repent or seek restitution?

This is obviously a misunderstanding of the gospel of God's grace. The only sin that truly keeps one from God's presence is the sin of unbelief—of not trusting the work of Christ personally. The inability to confess suicide as a sin is not a real issue.

God's forgiveness gives me a position as His child and deals with all of my sin—past, present, and future. If salvation depended upon confessing every sin committed as a believer, no one would qualify! We have all sinned in ways we either were not aware of or were not concerned about enough to confess individually.

"Payment God does not twice demand
First at my bleeding Surety's hand
And then again at mine."

The unfortunate and sad ending of an individual's life by his own hand does not nullify the effect of the grace of God in his life. Suicide victims who are children of God are redeemed souls in the presence of their Heavenly Father.

UNDERSTANDING AND ASSESSING RISK IN THE POTENTIAL SUICIDE VICTIM

Before leaving this chapter, I would like to make some observations about suicide's occurrence and the suicide victim.

Most people who take their lives have talked about it to someone. This is a way in which they ask for help. It is important to listen and always view any talk about suicide as important. Serious thinking about suicide formulates some detailed plan in the person's mind for carrying it out. We can inquire about this at some point in our conversation with him.

Even though a person has been a suicide risk at one point in his life, this will not always be true of him. Individuals who have been suicidal can again be enthusiastic about the future. "Once a suicide risk, always a suicide risk" is simply not true.

A person who becomes suicidal really has mixed feelings about death. Most would prefer to work out their problems and live. Because of this, most suicidal people do respond to counseling and other efforts that instill hope. No depressed person who appears on the verge of suicide should be given up as hopeless.

Suicide does not "run in families." It is true that family members can pick it up as a model for the way out of a problem, but there are no specific genetic determinants of suicide. Discount this theory!

Most suicides occur relatively soon after improvement begins. The deeply depressed person rarely has enough strength to take his own life. When the heavy cloud begins to lift, however, the time of greatest risk begins. Those who want to help need to be especially alert to the danger at this time.

In concluding this chapter, there are some special indicators of the high risk of suicide that are worth knowing.

The risk of suicide is always higher when there has been a history of previous attempts. These attempts—even if they lack serious intent—weaken life-preserving responses.

There is higher risk when there are chronic self-destruction patterns in a person's life which include fantasy and preoccupation with suicide. This observation is associated with the previous statement.

I remember a college student majoring in art who was obsessed with suicide. In almost every artistic production of human figures, she would include a splint on a leg or an arm indicating a severe injury to the body of the person in the picture she drew. She herself was at that time constantly dealing with suicide as an alternative in her own life.

If a depressed person has recently suffered a severe loss, or is on the verge of a severe loss, this makes risk higher. The loss of a job for a man in his late fifties can be a severe blow in an economy such as that of the early 1980s. With no hope of ever again being employed and with retirement benefits gone, the individual feels there is little to live for.

Sometimes there are those who are unable or unwilling to accept help. These individuals are always to be considered higher potential suicide risks than those who are willing to work on their problems.

Finally, those people with personal inner resources will be lower risks. Such resources include the ability to relate effectively with others. A person who relates to others does not feel so alone and will find friends to help share his heavy load.

Perhaps the most significant and meaningful resource is a tie to the church and relationship with Jesus Christ as a friend.

Consider these next statements, friends of sufferers and sufferers who are searching. Christ has promised to make every loss a means of personal growth. His friendship is never-ending and closer than that of any brother. He can open alternatives in one's life in most unpredictable ways. And He provides more grace for every trial.

When there is a relationship with Him, there are infinite inner resources. Suicide risk does not have to be as great.

Chapter 26

Hang-Ups of Christians

"The mentally ill are demon-possessed and should be avoided."

"Those who are spiritual do not become mentally ill."

"I would be embarrassed if others learned I have been in counseling."

"It's a sin to be depressed."

"If I truly appropriated the adequacy of Christ, I would not be experiencing emotional difficulties."

"Increased Bible reading and prayer will cure my emotional illness."

"God could never use the experience of depression to conform me to the image of His Son."

Until recent years, the area of mental and emotional illness has been misunderstood and feared by the Christian community. Because of this fear, we feel a stigma if we face mental difficulties in ourselves or in our loved ones. We have developed attitudes that are unrealistic and naive as illustrated in the above statements.

Don talked about some of these attitudes in his narrative. How could a pastor experience what he was going through? Professional counseling really is of little value for the Christian. It is a shameful thing to experience such emotional struggles.

Christians need to be free from this kind of bondage. We need to be free enough to acknowledge our psychological problems and seek appropriate help. As a rule, however, we are too uninformed, too embarrassed, or too fearful to get this help.

In this chapter, we will discuss some of those more common hang-ups that create poor attitudes and prolong emotional difficulties in our lives.

MENTAL ILLNESS AND DEMONIC INVOLVEMENT

People have misunderstood mental illness since the beginning of time. Historically, those suffering in this way have been considered incurable and isolated permanently from society. Care at best was only custodial and in many cases was no better than would be afforded animals. Many were confined in prisons and not a few burned at the stake because of supposed demonic involvement.

During the past 100 years, however, scientific efforts to understand and treat these disorders have greatly increased. These efforts have not gone unrewarded. The public in general more readily understands and accepts the mentally ill. The general populace recognizes psychiatry and psychology as valid healing disciplines.

The overall picture has been somewhat different among Christians, however. We continue to cling to our superstitious fears and distorted thinking in these areas.

Mental illness and demonic activity have been seen by many Christians as synonymous. It would be foolish to deny that mentally distorted thinking and behavior never indicates demonic influence. On rare occasions, Satan himself may attack an individual. He is our enemy. He wishes to disrupt, confuse, and destroy our lives of effectiveness. But when or where there is direct involvement of the enemy would be difficult to judge.

When we attribute the whole scene of mental illness to Satan, we remove personal responsibility for our choices and our behaviors. Satan gets the credit and we get an excuse. The "devil-made-me-do-it" attitude ultimately avoids the real reasons for our condition.

Many of the complex types of mental illness defy human understanding. And so we can easily attribute disorders such as obsessive thinking, compulsive behavior, severe depression, and paranoid delusions to the realm of darkness.

Dean is a high school teacher who hears voices when he lectures. They seem to argue over who will control him as he teaches his classes. They never cease their arguing and Dean is about to go mad. It is easy to label such a condition as demonic rather than the mental disorder of paranoid delusions.

Yet enough imperfection and disorder exists in our world system to create the conditions for a mental problem such as this apart from Satan's direct attacks. We are imperfect creatures. We live in imperfect environments. The "god of this age" could let us alone entirely, and we would yet become mentally ill.

We must face the reality of our imperfect psyches.

We should look at imperfection the way we view physical imperfection. At every period in life, we can develop kidney defects or heart difficulties. This is quite clearly understood by most of us.

Our mental conditions are imperfect as well. Each of us is at least a little bit "neurotic." All of us are capable of developing serious disorders. Understanding this would enable the Christian community to deal more effectively with emotional problems. Certainly we could deal with these problems more effectively when we see their source to be environmental and interpersonal conditions as opposed to demonic or "other-worldly" causes.

"SPIRITUAL CHRISTIANS DO NOT BREAK DOWN"

One event forever dashed to bits this fallacious idea for me. And that was Mary Ann's depression. Mary Ann, my wife, has lived a life of sensitivity, serenity, and spirituality. Yet she suffered an emotional and mental breakdown from which it took five years to recover completely.

If we assert that the spiritual do not become depressed, we heap unbelievable feelings of guilt upon the Christian with a mental disorder. Either he must deny his emotional condition completely or bear the heavy burden of failure in his Christian life. Both of these alternatives are unreasonable. They block healing. The disorder only deepens.

We continue to walk imperfectly in a fallen world. Our perfection awaits our resurrection. Only absolutely perfect spirituality—with never a lapse—could ever make us immune to emotional illness.

In reality, we all fail. We all take control of our lives from time to time. We all sin. Those whose lives are characterized by spirituality do fail. The spiritual do react with aggression. They can rationalize away the truth and lie. The spiritual can become faithless. And the spiritual can experience emotional breakdowns. We can become severely depressed.

In some ways, those who are spiritual may have a sensitivity in their spirits that makes them more vulnerable to depression than the average person. They do not have a "seared conscience" (1 Timothy 4:2). The spiritual are sensitive to sin.

Personal Embarrassment

Jerry was a deacon in a church and a respected leader in his congregation. Unknown to most people, he had a serious problem in his marriage. In order to preserve his anonymity, he urged the counselor to meet him in a bar in a neighboring community where he would be unknown.

One of the most difficult hang-ups Christians face is coming out in the open and admitting there is a problem. We seek professional help with great difficulty.

Christians reveal their timidity about getting help in many ways. Some call for information without giving their names. Others make appointments using names other than their own. The story above shows how some want to meet in neutral places such as a bar, their home, my home, or in the park. Some are even unwilling to use insurance coverage for fear of "being discovered."

Such embarrassment immediately points out how we view an emotional struggle—it is an unreal plague for the weak. We have talked about the need to see emotional illness in the same way that we see physical illness. Then we can see treatment in similar ways. Few are embarrassed to be physically ill. There is no reason to feel differently about mental illness.

Feelings of embarrassment would also diminish if we would see counseling as a "gift of the Spirit" specifically given for needs in the local church. Paul included exhortations as one of the gifts of the Spirit in the book of Romans (12:8). The word "exhort" is from the Greek word *paraclete*—one called alongside to help, one who walks with another. A counselor who is a Christian exercises a spiritual gift when he walks with another member of the family of God.

The church does not fear the benefits of the gifts of pastor-teacher, administrator, or helps. Why should we fear one coming into our lives to encourage us when we experience emotional problems?

"IT'S A SIN TO BE DEPRESSED"

Being depressed is often equated with faithlessness or unbelief.

Let's return to Don's emphatic statement: "It's not a sin to be depressed!" Depression does lower our mood level. It seriously hampers the effectiveness of an individual. It often includes deep feelings of hopelessness and despair. Family and friends will be affected by the pessimism. But these conditions do not indicate a lack of faith. This condition does not place a Christian in an inferior position as a child of God.

It is certainly possible that one can become depressed because of continual failure and sin in his life. Scripture teaches that the one who covers sin will not prosper (Proverbs 28:13). This might be a part of the believer's depression. But depression in this sense is simply a result of sin and not a sin in itself.

A quick summary of depression's dynamics might help here. As a general rule, depression results from loss. We handle loss ineffectively when we have negative self-concepts, less maturity, less autonomy, and thereby do not know how to handle anger. As we experience loss, anger related to that loss is turned inward. We become the object of our own anger. When this takes place, we feel worthless and "down." There may be feelings of hopelessness.

But this chain of events does not mean we have lacked faith or have sinned. Nor does it mean that we have forgotten the promises of God.

"IF I TRULY APPROPRIATED THE ADEQUACY OF CHRIST . . ."

This hang-up is a sister to the idea that if we were only sufficiently spiritual, we would never be depressed.

The adequacy of Christ is ever present as a resource for us in times of difficulty. However, we all appropriate this power in relative ways. We do look to God for support in our struggles. We do remember He has given us eternal life and we are strangers awaiting ultimate transformation. His Spirit does dwell within us and produce spiritual graces. But we do not perfectly appropriate these things.

One might argue in the same way for the end of physical illness. Yet the position that physical illness results from a lack of experiencing Christ's adequacy is unbiblical.

Deliverance from mental and physical illness will ultimately be a part of the healing that Jesus brings through His death and resurrection. Fully experiencing the benefits of this atonement, however, awaits our own resurrection. To argue otherwise only adds to the anguish of a child of God who is in the clutches of a depression or some other mental disorder.

"INCREASED BIBLE READING AND PRAYER WILL CURE ME"

Some believe that increased Bible study and prayer blaze the only path back to emotional health. This is a very common idea among believers who are experiencing emotional difficulties.

This strongly held belief arises out of the zeal with which we instruct people to engage in these practices for their own growth and maturity. And these practices *are* essential if one is to make continual progress in his Christian life.

Mood disorders and other types of emotional illnesses create unique problems of subjectivity, problems that can affect our view of spiritual disciplines like Bible study. A person may feel guilt that is all out of proportion to the behavior which is troubling him. There may be grossly self-centered feelings and thoughts. There may be feelings of deep inadequacy in performance. In this frame of mind, emphasis upon increased Bible study and prayer can actually hinder recovery. One will often move randomly through Scripture and settle in the Psalms where David shares the anguish from one of his own depressive experiences. A depressed person ends up overwhelmed as he experiences firsthand another's depression.

The following are suggested guidelines for Bible study and prayer when the individual is depressed.

1. Try to understand that experiencing depression or another emotional illness usually has little to do with the practice of prayer and Bible study.

2. Though prayer and Bible study are to be encouraged in our daily walk, we should not use them as if they would alleviate the emotional illness we are experiencing. Doing more of these things is not the way out of an emotional wilderness.

3. Continuing planned and well-structured Bible study is good if it does not leave one more depressed and if interest continues naturally. Legalistic Bible study and prayer can impede recovery.

4. We should feel free to discontinue dutiful prayer and Bible study if interest wanes or if one becomes more depressed as a result of such practices. As a child of God, the believer will hunger and thirst both for the Scriptures and for fellowship. In time he will naturally move back to these necessary practices of the Christian life.

EMOTIONAL PROBLEMS AND THE WILL OF GOD

We find depression difficult to integrate into the will of God. Yet Scripture assures us that God deliberately patterns the events in our lives. Each happening becomes purposeful and good. As the pattern unfolds, God moves us toward the ultimate goal of conformity to the image of Jesus Christ.

We incorporate tragedy, loss, physical illness, and other experiences into the will of God for our lives. A large body of believers sees emotional illness as different, however. When deeply depressed, we find it difficult to pause and consider how the Father is fitting this experience into His plan for us. It is hard to see what significant learning or new path in life He is opening. In emotional distress, few of us have any thought of creating meaning from the experience or seeking its positive aspects. We just want freedom—from the pain and from the stigma.

We have read Don Baker's account of deep depression. We have probably sensed that, however painful the experience was, there is in the heart of this man a gratefulness to God for what he has experienced. Because of depression, he has become more open. He is now extremely sensitive. He is able to love his people.

Don has learned through his agonizing experience that man's sufficiency is totally inadequate for the position of a servant. In his struggle and confusion, Don discovered that adequacy is found only in partnership with the Father. And Don never meets a depressed person in his pastoral counseling with whom he cannot identify, as he himself has known the lonely pain of that black hole.

The Don Baker of Hinson Memorial Baptist Church today is not the Don Baker of Hinson Memorial Baptist Church twenty-five years ago. The four years of depression and despair are part of God's conforming him to Christ's image. Through this experience, He has equipped him for an unusual ministry. Don will never be the person he was before his agonizing experience. Nor will any of us, if we can see our experiences as part of the will of God for our lives.

Chapter 27

Do Counselors Get Depressed?

A nd now my own story of depression.
Yes. I, too, have been depressed. As some of my depression experience ironically overlapped with the period of time that I walked with Don Baker, I will complete our story with my own narrative.

I accepted my first position as a psychologist on the faculty of Westmont College in 1967. Certain events during the summer and fall of 1969 left me deeply depressed. Common to these feelings was the thought that I was being used like an object by people I valued.

Of course, I had routinely experienced times of minor depression before. Common experiences for a pastor, these "down times" had always been relatively short in duration.

But not this depression. This time it would not go away! I felt dehumanized. All the feelings of being normal emotionally left me. Self-feelings ruled, and I was really down.

My sleep was disturbed each morning at 1:30 or 2:00 and I would toss fitfully until I had to get up for work. Concentration was difficult, and although I managed my teaching and counseling load, my normal lifestyle was altered—cut back—impaired.

As summer faded, I felt myself slipping more deeply into this depressed condition. No amount of effort to "get up" worked for me.

On the day before Christmas I felt like everything was lost.

My sinking feeling accelerated and I could not control the stepped-up emotional pull downward. I was caught in a giant whirlpool of despair. Swirling round, descending, I was utterly powerless to control what was happening to me.

For the first time—ever—I felt that life was not worth living.

I tried to convince myself of the absurdity of that feeling because rationally I knew it was not true. Earlier in the year I had finished my doctorate and experienced an all-time high. But my efforts to convince myself failed. Life seemed empty and meaningless.

On that day, I faced a startling fact—I needed professional help.

Christmas Eve is not the best time to call a therapist. But I called every psychiatrist listed in the yellow pages. (Except the ones I knew.)

Each doctor instructed me to simply check into the county hospital. After all, it was Christmas Eve, and everyone wanted to be with their families.

When I finally realized that no one would see me on an emergency basis, I became very angry with psychiatry as a helping profession. "Where is their commitment?" I asked myself. "What do they really feel about persons in need?" Had I not made an earlier commitment to be available to anyone who really needed me, regardless of the hour or day?

Two significant things happened that evening.

First, I was deeply angered toward psychiatry and the individuals I called. Those feelings of anger somehow lessened my feelings of depression. As I have said, "felt" anger and depression have a difficult time coexisting.

Second, I made a decision that night. I decided to use my depression for learning more about it . . . and myself. I would overcome depression using resources within myself. This depression had to be in the plan of God for me as a learning experience. I decided to try to learn how to make that a reality.

I began reading and rereading everything on depression in my library. I became intrigued with my personal dynamics, my anger, my self-centeredness, and my manipulative efforts that were deeply imbedded in the depression.

I reached a place where it mattered as much to learn as it mattered to not be depressed.

Then one Saturday evening in April I received a call from Arthur Lynip, dean of the college. Dr. Lynip said, "Emery, I'm teaching a class of forty depressed adults at Grace Church. Could you come and speak to them on the subject of depression?"

My response was immediate. "Could I? . . . There is nothing I could do more easily."

In half an hour I had organized my thoughts about what I had experienced during the preceding seven or eight months. The next morning I shared myself and my depression with these people.

While I talked, I felt the cloud of despair lifting. As a cork pops to the top of the water, I felt myself springing out of the gloom that had engulfed me.

When I finished speaking, I was free. I was no longer "down." The hurt was gone. Finding meaning for myself in this difficult experience helped to release me.

Today it's difficult to think that I could have been so depressed.

I began walking with Don during the last five months of my depression. Because our depressions coincided, I could understand his experience and feeling more fully. And my walk with him gave me the meaning I sorely needed at that time.

Now we have written of these experiences with the desire that you who suffer in depression or walk with a sufferer might find hope and be helped. In the plan of God, it could not have been otherwise.

Subject Index

Abiding, 66-68
Abiding in Christ, 66
Abilities and goals, 56
Activities, new, 147-48
Activity, 66-68
Alcoholism, 72-73
Amnesia, 138
Anger
  and depression, 155, 187-88
  as source of guilt, 19, 61
  turned inward, 158-59
Argumentation, 61
Authentic Christianity, 57

Bible
  study of, 188-89
  value of, 108

Child rearing, 157-63
Commitments, 166-67
Communication problems, 62
Comparison, 171
Confession, 174
Confrontation, 61
Conscience, 172-74
Counseling
  as a process, 154
  as spiritual gift, 187
  See also Group therapy
Counselor
  need for, 35-38
  qualifications of, 149-50
Custis, M. L., 29

Decision-making difficulties, 19
Defenses, 138-39
Demoniac. *See* Satanist

Demonic influence, 99-100, 184-85.
  See also Satan
Denial, 138
Depressed person, the
  and Bible study and prayer,
    44-45, 108, 188-89
  and family, 42-45, 145-49
  manipulation by, 145-46
  responses to, 42-45
  responsibility of, 144
Depression
  and anger, 155, 187-88
  causes of, 16, 27-28, 54-56, 110,
    122, 189-88
  deliverance from, 101-3
  and demonic involvement,
    99-100, 184-85
  duration and intensity, 25, 43
  and embarrassment, 186-87
  experienced by many, 108
  and family, 143-46
  and job loss, 89-91, 94
  finding meaning in, 154-55,
    192-93
  misunderstandings of, 17, 183-90
  as normal reaction, 110
  prevention of, 157-63
  and spirituality, 185-86, 188
  and suicide, 47, 177-78
  types of, 121-26
  and will of God, 189-90
Devil. *See* Satan
Diet, 18, 153. *See also* Weight
Direction, inner, 170-71
Discipline, 160-62
Divorce, threat of, 77-81

195

Pain's Hidden Purpose

Finding Perspective in the Midst of Suffering

Contents

The story of Job is the story of a man
who suffers without a reason and loses
without a cause—and survives.

Preface

I've never seen a man whose blackened and crusty body was covered with massive, draining sores, rocking back and forth in the ashes of a garbage dump. I've never heard the unending wailing or watched as the person scraped the crusted scabs from his body.

I've never known a man who lost all his wealth, possessions, and children in just one day.

I've seen other kinds of derelicts
    along the skid row
        under the bridges
            beside the railroad tracks.

I've seen them scavenging garbage cans, struggling against restraints in mental institutions, wasting away in hospital beds, or begging in their poverty.

I've seen the rich become poor—
I've seen the strong become weak—
I've watched the mighty fall and shatter like Humpty-Dumpties.

But I've never witnessed a spectacle quite like that of a man from Uz whose name was Job.[1]

Job's story is a real-life, time and space biographical sketch.

It's not a myth, a fantasy, or a legend. Simply because it's old doesn't mean it's not contemporary. It's as up-to-date as today.

It's the story of a man who lost everything.

It's not just a theological treatise. Although it is filled with theology. More time has been spent discussing the philosophical and theological implications of Job than any other book of the Bible.

One of my favorite Peanuts cartoons shows Charlie Brown in his favorite role—that of pitcher for his sandlot baseball team.

In the first cartoon frame we see him on the pitcher's mound in deep trouble. He looks toward the team at bat and exclaims, "Nine runs in a row—good grief!"

Then he opens his mouth and begins to wail, "What can I do?"

Schroeder walks out to the mound, dressed in his catcher's mask and chest protector, as Charlie Brown says, "We're getting slaughtered again, Schroeder . . . I don't know what to do . . .

"Why do we have to suffer like this?"

Schroeder just stands there and very philosophically answers:

"Man is born to suffer as the sparks fly upward."

Charlie Brown looks puzzled and says, "What did you say, Schroeder?"

Then Linus comes up from behind and says, "He's quoting from the Book of Job, Charlie Brown . . . seventh verse, fifth chapter." Linus continues with, "Actually, the problem of suffering is a very profound one, and . . ."

Before he can get another word out of his mouth, he is interrupted as Lucy chimes in. ". . . If a person has bad luck, it's because he's done something wrong, that's what I always say!!!"

Schroeder moves back into the little cluster of people surrounding Charlie Brown.

"That's what Job's friends told him, but I doubt it . . ."

Again Schroeder is interrupted by Lucy, who shouts, "What about Job's wife? I don't think she gets enough credit."

Schroeder continues: "I think a person who never suffers, never matures. . . . Suffering is actually very important . . ."

Lucy interrupts again and screams, "Who wants to suffer? Don't be ridiculous!!!"

By this time the whole team is gathered around Charlie Brown, including a wide-eyed Snoopy, who is listening to every word.

One player says, "But pain is a part of life, and . . ."

Another interrupts and says, "A person who speaks only of the patience of Job reveals that he knows very little of the book! Now the way I see it . . ."

Disgustedly Charlie Brown walks back to the pitcher's mound, looks at his ball team, one by one, and says, "I don't have a baseball team—I have a theological seminary!"[2]

The Book of Job is not just a theological treatise:

It does show God at His best, and
it does show Satan at his worst.
It is a revelation of God's sovereignty, and
it is a revelation of man's helplessness.

But . . . it is first and foremost
the story of a real man,
living in a real country,
suffering a real calamity.

It's the story of
one man's wealth
one man's family
one man's health
one man's reputation, and
one man's spirit

that is lost, destroyed, broken, and crushed beneath an intolerable load of pain and suffering.

It's the story of
one man's God
one man's faith
one man's enemy

one man's friends, and
one man's bewilderment,

as all the traditional values and traditional roles are thrown out of focus.

It's the story of a man who suffers without a cause and loses without a reason—and survives.

It's different from most personal tragedies, however. It's one of the few that tells the whole story, unlike an autobiography where a person tells his own story—as he sees it; or a biography, where a person tells another's story—as he sees it. This story adds another dimension. It's the story of a man's life as he saw it and as others saw it, but it's the story as Satan and God saw it also. It's the whole story.

It addresses the ofttimes unanswerables, like:

How did it happen?
 and
Why did it happen?

It's one man's story, but it's every man's story, for in Job we have the "full picture" of calamity and suffering. And the "full picture" of Job's calamity and suffering is the "full picture" of your sufferings and mine.

Don Baker

Preface, Notes

1. Job 1:1
2. Text from PEANUTS by Charles M. Schulz; © 1967 United Feature Syndicate, Inc.

PART
1

LOOKING AT
SUFFERING

Little did Job realize that, after the loss
of his wealth and the death of his children,
a new pain would replace the old,
and the new pain would be so intense
that even the loss of his children would be forgotten.

Chapter 1

Death—Disease— Desertion

*J*ob slept fitfully during that endless night following the burial of his ten children. The images of each of his seven wonderful sons and three beautiful daughters constantly filtered through a tortured memory. He saw their faces, heard their voices, listened to their laughter, recalled their words, and painfully remembered each of those cherished moments that began on the days they were born.

Seven sons and three daughters really doesn't say much, and yet that's all that's recorded for us in the opening chapters of Job's chronicle of tragedy. It reminds me of the brief, cryptic, sterile obituary notices one reads in a newspaper, or the meaningless list of facts that a minister might recall during a funeral service.

"Seven sons and three daughters"—such a statement of fact is grossly inadequate in describing the joy, the warmth, the oneness of a close-knit family that shared every meaningful moment of their lives together.

But now they were dead—all of them in one day. In one shattering moment ten vibrant, happy, hopeful, promising lives ceased to be—and Job's world ended.

There was no release from the grief that held his smitten

soul in bondage. Job and his wife found no comfort in themselves or in each other. The sorrow that gripped them refused to let go.

Yesterday was a nightmare. Today promised to be no better.

As the morning light first appeared over the mountains of the east, Job must have thought that no man anywhere had ever suffered such pain and such loss. No man anywhere could ever experience anything worse.

Little did he know what God was about to allow. Little did he realize that his own suffering had just begun. Little did he know that before this new day ended, a new pain would replace the old, and the new pain would be so intense that even the loss of his children would be forgotten.

The new pain began with an itch. As Job awoke from restless sleep he soon became aware that his body was inflamed with a sore and angry swelling. The red spots that covered his flesh were hot and tender to the touch.

They spread quickly over his entire body until he was covered with one universal boil that stretched from his head to his feet.

His bones ached.
His legs began to thicken.
His hair fell out.
His face swelled, and
his voice became hoarse.

His entire appearance changed until his face became grim and distorted. His skin was encrusted and constantly running with pus. (See Albert Barnes, *Job*, vol. 1 [Grand Rapids: Baker Book House, 1949], p. 116).

To simply state that Job was smitten with sore boils from head to foot[1] does not begin to explain the extent of his sufferings. To add the words, "he scraped himself with a piece of broken pottery,"[2] suggests more, but still not enough.

To state that due to the chronic and contagious nature of his disease and the hideousness of his appearance, he was banished to the local garbage dump to sit in the ashes,[3] suggests the ultimate isolation but still fails to say it all.

Job describes the enormity of his immense and interminable suffering by stating that—

> He could not sleep—he continually tossed until dawn.[4]
> He used dirt clods to cover his running sores.[5]
> Worms crawled in his flesh.[6]
> The thought of food made him sick.[7]
> His pain was so intense that he was forced to bite his own flesh to tear out the boils.[8]
> His flesh rotted before his very eyes.[9]
> The itching never ceased.[10]
>
> He was flushed and red from weeping.
> His eyes were dark and recessed from lack of sleep.[11]
> His body was shriveled and wrinkled.[12]
>
> Job was exhausted and alone.[13]
> His breath was foul.[14]
> He could barely breathe.[15]
> His soul was bathed in bitterness.[16]
>
> He was emaciated to the point that his bones clung to his skin.[17]
> His flesh turned black.[18]
> He was constantly burning with fever.[19]
> And the pain never ceased.[20]
>
> The only place he could find to rest was in the ashes and dung and garbage outside the city among
> > the beggars
> > > the outcasts
> > > > the lepers and
> > > > > the dogs.
> He was deserted by his friends and mocked by his enemies.[21]

He describes himself as a rag doll, grabbed by the neck and shaken to pieces.[22]

He was as a target set up and shot through with arrows.[23]

His condition was so desperate,
  his appearance so contemptible,
    his pain so continual,
      his shame so complete,
that his wife finally suggested that he kill himself.

Chapter 1, Notes

1. Job 2:7	7. Job 3:24	13. Job 16:7	19. Job 30:30
2. Job 2:8	8. Job 13:14	14. Job 19:17	20. Job 30:17
3. Job 2:8	9. Job 13:28	15. Job 9:18	21. Job 16:9, 10
4. Job 7:4	10. Job 2:8	16. Job 9:18	22. Job 16:12
5. Job 7:5	11. Job 16:16	17. Job 19:20	23. Job 16:13
6. Job 7:5	12. Job 16:8	18. Job 30:30	

Job, the most honored man in the East, began experiencing a long, uninterrupted series of calamities that led him to the very brink of self-destruction.

Chapter 2

Even the Godly Suffer

*J*ob's calamity had been sudden and complete. Just a few days before, one could find Job walking from his house each morning, along the sandswept streets of the Eastern city of Uz to its outer gate.[1] There he spent the day with his friends.

Job was an honored judge[2] in his hometown—noted for his fairness,[3] his integrity,[4] his compassion,[5] and his strong and compelling sense of justice.[6]

The young men of the city of Uz deferred to him, and the old ones stood in his honor whenever he entered the room.[7]

His advice was sought by all. Everyone listened when he spoke[8]—in fact it was generally agreed by all in Uz that when Job spoke, there was nothing more to be said.[9]

Everyone spoke well of Job.[10]

The widows in their loneliness were clothed and fed by his generosity.[11]

The blind often felt the gentle touch of his strong hands as he led them in their darkness.[12]

The lame were never left to their helplessness when Job was present.[13]

Even the strangers were welcomed by the greatness of this gracious gentleman.[14]

On numerous occasions Job received the Man-of-the-Year award in the city of Uz.[15]

His personality exuded a strength that even lightened the spirits of the discouraged.[16]

With firmness he corrected those in error—with wisdom he instructed the confused, and with great compassion he comforted those who mourned.[17]

There was no man on all the earth like Job.[18]

He was a man of immense wealth. His was the largest spread in all the East.[19] In a day when a man's wealth was measured by the size of his family, the size of his herds, the size of his flocks, the size of his staff, and the greatness of his reputation, Job exceeded them all.

It is said that everything he touched turned to gold—that even the rocks poured out streams of olive oil to him.[20]

He had a family that was unusually close—they did everything together—even after they were grown, married, and had left home.

They loved birthday parties. Whenever any one of the ten children had a birthday, it was a total family affair.

The sons and daughters with their children would gather together in one of their homes to celebrate. Sometimes these celebrations would last for as long as a week.[21]

Job was a good father, and as a good father in a patriarchal system, he was also a good priest to his family—long before the world knew anything of an official priesthood.

After each of the family birthday parties, Job would go over to his own little worship center and offer a special sacrifice to Jehovah God, just in case one of his children had said or done something that was offensive to God.[22]

The friendship of God was constantly felt in his home.[23]

There was no hint of discord among his children—no foolish talk of divorce or remarriage—no restlessness among his servants—just prosperity and peace—the longing of all—to be full and to be happy.

Job not only enjoyed a good reputation among his peers but, of even greater importance, he had a good reputation with God. God lovingly spoke of Job as one-of-a-kind, the only one like him on earth—one who was genuine and honest and without blame. Job had a vital, satisfying, and personal relationship that was above and beyond anyone in his generation.[24]

It was a beautiful picture of one man's family, one man's wealth, one man's God, delightfully situated in one man's community where this one man, Job, had all that a person could ever need—and more. He had all that a person could ever want.

Job felt the joy of the immense security that was his and even noted later that he honestly believed he would someday die quietly in his own little nest after a long and good life.[25]

And then, swiftly and without warning, tragedy struck, and all of Job's joy turned sour. Job's life changed, Job's world changed, and Job began experiencing a long, uninterrupted series of calamities that led him to the very brink of self-destruction.

Chapter 2, Notes

1. Job 29:7 TLB*
2. Job 29:12 TLB
3. Job 29:16 TLB
4. Job 29:14 TLB
5. Job 29:13 TLB
6. Job 29:17 TLB
7. Job 29:8 TLB
8. Job 29:21 TLB
9. Job 29:22 TLB
*The Living Bible

10. Job 29:11 TLB
11. Job 29:13 TLB
12. Job 29:15 TLB
13. Job 29:15 TLB
14. Job 29:16 TLB
15. Job 29:20 TLB
16. Job 29:24 TLB
17. Job 29:25 TLB
18. Job 1:8 TLB

19. Job 1:2, 3 TLB
20. Job 29:6 TLB
21. Job 1:4
22. Job 1:5 TLB
23. Job 29:4 TLB
24. Job 1:8
25. Job 29:18 TLB

Job was slowly, methodically, being stripped to the very nakedness of his spiritual being.

Chapter 3

Joy Turned Sour

Job lost it all—in just one day.

It was during one of those happy family celebrations that disaster struck.

All of the children were gathered in Job's eldest son's house, celebrating a birthday,[1] when Job received word from one of his servants that a group of terrorists from the south had suddenly and without warning plundered his herds and slain one of his work crews. Five hundred oxen and five hundred valuable female donkeys were gone, and all but one of his farm hands had been slain.[2]

At the same time that the sole survivor of the massacre was breathlessly describing the horrible event, another servant appeared and described the destruction of Job's 7,000 sheep and all but one of his shepherds.

"It was lightning," he said. "The fire of God fell down and burned the sheep and the servants and consumed them."[3]

"The camels are gone," shouted another. "All 3000 of them."

Those wonderful beasts of burden, invaluable to the desert community, were gone, stolen by another group of terrorists—this time from the north. Again, all but one of his servants were slain—and all of this in one day—his son's birthday.[4]

Suddenly, the rich man had become poor.

His stock market had collapsed.
His business had failed.
His creditors had foreclosed.
His lenders had refused to extend his line of credit.
He had lost his job.

However we might wish to describe it, Job had lost it all.
The richest man in the East was broke.

It was probably at this time that Job turned to his wife and said, "Well, Honey, we may have lost all of our herds and all of our flocks and most of our servants, but at least we have our family."

Without warning, tragedy struck again. Another messenger appeared, bearing the worst news a parent can hear—

"Your children are dead, all of them. They were celebrating your son's birthday when a tornado struck. The whole house collapsed and fell in on them, and all of the young people are dead."[5]

There is no easy way to share that devastating news with a parent. I have been forced to do it many times. I've tried to find just the right series of words and phrases appropriately designed to soften the blow, but with no success. Those words fall with the force of a hammer on the tender heart of an unsuspecting parent, and something fragile is crushed forever.

Job was devastated. In great grief he ripped his robe from his body, shaved the hair from his head to tell the world that all his glory was gone, then fell to the ground and sobbed.[6]

I've often wondered just how long it took for those sobs to subside before he called out to God. And I've wondered if the recorded words were his first ones.[7]

Although the Scriptures say Job did not sin or revile against God with his lips,[8] I'm sure he did question, and like all of us, as he lay there on the ground sobbing in his grief, I'm sure he asked, "Why?" "Why?" "Why?"

Martha and I have stood on a wind-swept hillside, transfixed by the sight of a little white casket in which lay the lifeless form of our only child.

Occasionally the sun would break through the clouds and shine like a spotlight on that little wooden box. And then it would drift back into hiding, and the gray gloom of an early spring day would again fall down around us.

Friends were there
family was there
beloved pastor was there—

and yet we remember nothing but the awesome feelings of emptiness, as if all life, all joy, all hope, all laughter had been squeezed from our very souls—forever.

The memory of that little white casket silhouetted against the green hillside is just as vivid today, thirty years later, as it was on that May afternoon.

The pain has eased, and yet occasionally I'll catch sight of a single tear as it rolls down Martha's cheek, and I'll know that something has stirred the memory of a little life that was loaned to us for such a short time.

It hurts—deeply—to lose someone we love.

To multiply that loss by ten and to be forced to stand beside the caskets of seven sons and three daughters—all you have—is beyond comprehension.

Job's world had ended. Job's life was over.

All the plans for the future suddenly ceased to exist— there was no future—only a past. And even the memories of the past were now no longer pleasant, but haunting—as Job slowly, painfully watched his children, one by one, lowered out of sight, into the sand, beyond his reach—forever.

Job did manage to worship—without benefit of any divine manuscript or printed revelation. Long before even the words of Moses were transcribed, Job worshiped. And he worshiped Jehovah God—the same God worshiped by Adam and Noah and Abraham.

He didn't know much, but he knew enough to bow in

simple,
   spontaneous,
      unstructured,
         genuine worship,

and say:

"Naked I came from my mother's womb,
And naked I shall return there.
The Lord gave and the Lord has taken away.
Blessed be the name of the Lord.[8]

These were profound words dropping from the lips of a man whose revelation of God was yet incomplete—and these were possibly premature words since the greater pain was yet to follow.

These worshipful phrases bore little resemblance to the words which flew outward and upward in response to the greater torment that wracked his body as he lay writhing in pain and torment among the garbage and ashes.

Many have speculated as to just what Job's wife may have meant when she looked at that emaciated and blackened body and suggested that he end his suffering.

Some see Job's wife at this point as hardened and bitter—unconcerned for his relationship with God. I see her as a sensitive, caring, concerned woman who loved Job and honored her commitment. No family could have enjoyed the oneness Job's family shared if their mother had been calloused or cruel.

But she was stretched. Weeks of suffering had passed without relief. Each morning she'd wake to the same pain, only to find it intensified. Each night she'd pray for her husband's healing, but it never came—and there was no medication—

no Tylenol #3
  no Percodan
    no Demarol
      no morphine to ease the pain
        no Seconal
          no Valium
            not even aspirin to help him sleep.

His suffering was so intense, his looks so hideous, his condition so infectious that he was forced to move out.

She could stand it no longer. In a moment of deep and frustrated anguish she suggested, "Job, why don't you curse God and die?"

"Tell God you've had enough."
"He's not able to heal you."
"He's gone back on His promise."
"He's not even aware of your problem."
"I'd rather see you dead than like this—"
"Maybe we could die together."

Again, Job's response was profoundly worshipful—simple, yet filled with deep insights; he said, "Woman, you're talking like one of those foolish ones—one of those unbelievers. Shall we accept good from God and not accept adversity?"[10] And he rejected her suggestion.

Besides the physical pain, the emotional and spiritual anguish was immense.

He was a man with a broken body and a broken spirit.

Occasionally he'd have flashbacks to the good old days—"the years gone by,"[11] he called them—the days

when God took care of him,[12]
when God's friendship was felt in his home,[13]
when all his children were around him,[14]
when his life prospered,[15]
when the elders honored him,[16] and
the young men stepped aside and revered him,[17]

when even the highest officials in the city stood in
    respect for him.[18]

But that was long ago—that's gone. In place of honor
and prosperity, now—

The young men made fun of him.[19]
He was a joke to them.[20]
They'd spit in his face.[21]
They'd lay traps for his path.[22]
They'd come at him from all directions.[23]
He lived in terror—with no one to help.[24]
Depression haunted his days.[25]
He'd cry to God but get no answer.[26]
His voice of joy and gladness had turned to mourn-
    ing.[27]

Job's state was so horrible that even his wife finally
deserted him.[28]

Job was slowly, methodically, being stripped to the very
nakedness of his spiritual being.

All the things that clothe the spirit of man were being
ripped from him.

All that man leans upon for help and strength was taken
from him until all that was left was a soul that was forced to
stand naked and alone in the universe of God.

Chapter 3, Notes

1. Job 1:18	8. Job 1:22 TLB	15. Job 29:6 TLB	22. Job 30:13 TLB
2. Job 1:14-15	9. Job 1:21	16. Job 29:8 TLB	23. Job 30:14 TLB
3. Job 1:16	10. Job 2:10 TLB	17. Job 29:8 TLB	24. Job 30:15 TLB
4. Job 1:17	11. Job 29:2 TLB	18. Job 29:9 TLB	25. Job 30:16 TLB
5. Job 1:18, 19	12. Job 29:2 TLB	19. Job 30:1 TLB	26. Job 30:20 TLB
6. Job 1:20	13. Job 29:4 TLB	20. Job 30:9 TLB	27. Job 30:31 TLB
7. Job 1:20-22	14. Job 29:5 TLB	21. Job 30:10 TLB	28. Job 19:17 TLB

"Job, you have sinned."

Chapter 4

Good Friends— Bad Counsel

Bad news travels fast. Eliphaz, Bildad, and Zophar, long-time friends of Job, soon heard of his dreadful condition. They made an appointment to meet in Uz.[1] They'd heard the rumors and listened to the stories, but they were totally unprepared for what they saw.

Job's great pastures were vacant—his servants' quarters empty—his house deserted. The shutters banged in the wind, the yard was overgrown, the magnificent ranch of the once-mighty Job, richest man in all of the East, was desolate.

Neighbors finally directed them to the local garbage dump.

At first they failed to recognize him.[2] His black, ema-ciated, pus-encrusted body, covered with ashes, bore no re-semblance to that of the honored judge of the city of Uz.

With a startled cry they saw him. These three were so overwhelmed by the sight of Job's condition—

they screamed—
they tore their clothes—
they threw ashes over their heads—
then—they became silent.

For seven days and seven nights[3] they sat alongside this friend whose body now bore little resemblance to that of a human being.[4]

For seven days and seven nights they watched him writhing in pain.[5]

For seven days and seven nights they listened to his soul as it poured out unutterable words of torment.

For seven days and seven nights no one spoke.[6] They simply tried to comprehend the incomprehensible—to understand the magnitude of this tragedy—to answer, in their own minds, the one elusive, evasive, tormenting question—WHY?

Job could restrain himself no longer. After seven days of silence he said:[7]

> I wish God would erase my birthday from His calendar.
> I wish I had never been conceived.
> Why didn't I die at birth?
> Why didn't my mother have a miscarriage?
> Why can't I die now?
> If only I could rest in death.
> If only I could be at ease in the grave.
> If only I could be free from this slavery.
> Why has God done this to me?

Sixteen times Job hurled that word "why" into the heavens. Sixteen times it flew outwards and upwards. And each time he cried for an answer, the heavens were silent. But his friends were not.

Eliphaz, Bildad, and Zophar attempted to answer the unanswerable. That's always a mistake—at least it's always a mistake to answer that question with the air of finality displayed by Job's counselors.

Not only did they claim the ability to comprehend the incomprehensible, they did it with an alarming display of arrogance and with a complete absence of compassion.

Notice how these three "comforters" spoke to Job—

"Will you let me say a word," said Eliphaz.[8]

"In the past you have told many a troubled soul to trust in God and have encouraged those who are weak or falling, or lie crushed upon the ground or tempted to despair.

"But now, when trouble strikes, you faint and are broken."

Eliphaz heaped guilt on top of Job's pain.

Bildad began his speech by saying, "How long will you go on like this, Job, blowing words around like the wind?"[9]

Bildad piled criticism on top of Job's suffering.

Zophar interrupted by saying, "Shouldn't someone stem this torrent of words? Is a man proved right by all this talk?"[10]

Zophar stacked sarcasm on top of Job's agony.

The insensitivity of these three is awesome.

Their main premise, and their only premise, in these interminable arguments with Job was that Job's suffering was the result of his sin.

Eliphaz said, "Stop and think! Have you ever known a truly good and innocent person who was punished?"[11]

Bildad said, "If you were pure and good, God would hear your prayer and answer you and bless you with a happy home."[12]

Zophar said, "You claim you are pure in the eyes of God! Oh, that God would tell you what He thinks! Oh, that He would make you truly see yourself, for He knows everything you have done. Listen! God is doubtless punishing you far less than you deserve!"[13]

These three had but one message to give Job, and they repeated it over and over again. Their unchanging word was:

"Job, you have sinned."
"Your suffering is due to your sin."
"Repent and be healed."

And Job's response never varied:[14]

"I know the difference between right and wrong."
"My one comfort is that I have not denied the words
    of God, and now, when you should be kind to a
    fainthearted friend, you have accused me without
    the slightest fear of God."
"Tell me, what have I done wrong?"
"O God, please tell me why You're doing this to
    me."[15]
"Did You create me just for the purpose of destroy-
    ing me?"

Finally their accusations became specific. They said:[16]

"Job, your sins are endless."
"You must have refused to loan money to needy
    friends unless they gave you all their clothing as a
    pledge."
        or
"You must have refused water to the thirsty and
    bread to the starving."
"You sent widows away without helping them, and
    broke the arms of orphans."

Job replied:[17]

"I have not looked with lust upon a girl."
"I have not lied."
"I have not longed for another man's wife."
"I have not been unfair to my servants."
"I have not hurt the widows or orphans"
        or
"refused food to the hungry"
        or
"harmed an enemy."
"I have never even turned away a stranger."
"Look," he says, "I'll even sign an affidavit claiming
    my innocence."

"But let Almighty God answer me and show me
where I am wrong."

Nine times Job's friends called him into account for his
sins.

Nine times they told him that he was suffering because
he had sinned—and that his suffering continued because he
refused to repent.

Nine times Job denied their accusations.

For twenty-eight chapters they engaged in a running
argument that increased in volume to a virtual shouting
match—

"You sinned," they said.
"I did not," Job answered.
"You did"
"I didn't"
"You did too"
"I did not"

until finally three would-be comforters, turned accusers, had
nothing more to say.

Job sat still in his loneliness and in his pain, and Eliphaz,
Bildad, and Zophar became quiet in their frustration and
bewilderment. Nothing had been accomplished—

no comfort delivered—
no pain relieved—
no insights gained.

Job still hurt, and his one dominant question, "Why?", still
remained unanswered.

Chapter 4, Notes

1. Job 2:11	7. Job 3:1-23	13. Job 11:6 TLB
2. Job 2:12	8. Job 4:1-5 TLB	14. Job 6:10–30 TLB
3. Job 2:13	9. Job 8:2 TLB	15. Job 10:1–8 TLB
4. Job 2:12	10. Job 11:1.2 TLB	16. Job 22:5–9 TLB
5. Job 2:13	11. Job 4:7 TLB	17. Job 31:1–35 TLB
6. Job 2:13	12. Job 8:6 TLB	

Pain speaks a strange language—it plays funny tricks on us.
It makes us think and say things and
even believe things that are not true.

Chapter 5

The Strange Language of Pain

Sitting quietly in the ashes was another—one who until now had been quiet and restrained. He was a shy young man[1] who hardly felt competent to become a part of the illustrious team of theological debaters. He had listened to every word. He had heard every argument—among them words that he personally felt lowered the dignity of Almighty God.

He didn't seem to be overly impressed with the long list of accusations and their vehement denials, but he was angry—angry that Job had continued to maintain his innocence when some of his statements bordered on blasphemy, and angry with his three friends because they had condemned Job without a reason.[2]

"I feel like a new wineskin that's about to burst," he began. "I can contain myself no longer. I must speak to get relief."[3] "Job, please listen to me. You are wrong in what you say about God."[4]

To be told that he was wrong was nothing new. That had been his friends' theme song for days. They had repeatedly told him he was wrong, but that was different. They had said over and over again that he was wrong in what he had said about himself—that he was wrong about his innocence. But Elihu was saying something totally different. Elihu was claiming that Job was saying something wrong about God.

Job was silent. He listened as Elihu listed the condemning statements that had fallen unthinkingly from Job's lips—statements common to all of us when we're submerged beneath the murky waters of pain.

Pain speaks a strange language—it plays funny tricks on us. It makes us think things and say things and even believe things that are not true. When pain begins to bore its way through human flesh and on into human spirit and then just sits there and hurts and hurts and hurts, the mind becomes clouded and the brain begins to think strange thoughts like—

God is dead
    or
He's gone fishing
    or
He's just plain not interested.

In Job's attempt to find the cause of his suffering, he did what many of us do. He began lowering God from His position of uniqueness and began ascribing motives and thoughts that were more like man's than God's. He then proceeded to attack God verbally, with statements like:

God is fighting me.[5]
God is ignoring me.[6]
I might as well have sinned.[7]

These statements are so human, aren't they? Many times I've heard God's people say, "It seems like God is just sitting up there inventing new ways to make my life miserable." Or,

"It seems like God has turned a deaf ear to me. He has directed His attention elsewhere. He has decided never to listen to my prayer again." Or,

"It seems like my whole life has taken a turn for the worse, since I became a Christian. I sometimes feel I would have been better off without Christ."

Job's complaints against God are not unique to the day in which he lived. I have heard them time and again. I have thought them. Yes, I have even spoken them myself.

In correcting the would-be counselors, Elihu gave a brilliant defense for God (Who really needs no defense) but, at the same time, heaped new pain on the already overburdened Job. He said to Job:[8]

"You have spoken like a fool."
"You should be given the maximum penalty for the wicked way you have talked to God."
"For now you have added rebellion, arrogance, and blasphemy to your other sins."
And then again, "Job, you have spoken like a fool."[9]

I shall always be deeply grateful for a nonjudgmental counselor who loved me, listened to me, and tolerated me during the time of my deep depression. There were times I thought things, said things, and did things for which I justly deserved a rebuke.

My friend handled my very fragile spirit with the tenderest of care. He listened to my nonsense—nonsense that originated somewhere deep within my aching soul. He listened to my incoherence—incoherence that emanated from deep within a bewildered mind. He listened—and listened—and listened—and all the time he was listening, he refused to play God in my life.

He did not know why I was depressed, and he freely admitted it.

He fully expected irrational statements. He heard them and then let them fall—and he let them lie—without even dignifying them with a response.

Those who have ever hurt deeply know the value of a friend who, even though he may think he knows the answer, is willing just to listen to the questions.

Job's friends never really heard Job—oh, yes, they heard the words that dropped from his lips, but they were deaf to the cry of his soul. The one cry that kept coming from the heart of this man who had been completely stripped of all dignity was, "Why? Why is God doing this to me? What have I done? What have I done?" That question can never be answered by a man—or by a woman. Only God knows and only God knows just how much of the answer He can ever share with us.

In addition to his great pain, great guilt was heaped on him. And Job just sat there—in the ashes—in his torment— waiting. Waiting for deliverance—waiting for death—little realizing that he was really waiting for God who was just about to arrive.

Chapter 5, Notes

1. Job 32:4-6
2. Job 32:2, 3
3. Job 32:19, 20
4. Job 33:12 TLB
5. Job 33:13
6. Job 33:13
7. Job 34:9 TLB
8. Job 34:35-37 TLB
9. Job 35:16 TLB

Explanations don't heal people—
but they can certainly change the complexion
of an illness.

Chapter 6

God Appears

*A*ll Job wanted was an explanation. Even the severest pain becomes somewhat tolerable with knowledge.

Many years ago my father began suffering with severe back pain, a pain so intense that it not only affected him physically, but mentally. Unable to work, he became depressed and began to withdraw as doctor after doctor was unable to diagnose the cause of his illness.

I was with him in the hospital on the day they finally discovered the problem. He lay silent in his bed, face turned to the wall, unresponsive and detached.

The doctor called us out into the hall and told us that the problem was cancer—inoperable and terminal. Then he asked, "Should I tell your father?" We all agreed that Dad should know—and quickly.

We listened from outside the door as the doctor, with his best bedside manner, tried to say those terribly difficult words that all of us fear.

"Harry, can you hear me?"

"Yes," Dad answered.

"Harry, I'm sorry to tell you this, but you have cancer."

"Oh?"

"Yes," the doctor went on, "cancer of the prostate—it has spread throughout your whole body. It's in your bones, Harry."

"Will I get better, Doctor?" Dad asked.

"No, Harry."

"How long do I have?"

"Maybe a few weeks, maybe a few months, we don't know," the doctor said.

With those words, Dad pulled himself up on the bed, looked straight into the eyes of his doctor, and said, "Is that all that's wrong with me? Hand me my clothes, please. I've got lots of things to get done."

His pain was no less severe, but Dad went back home, went back to work, and with sheer determination lived for nearly three years, long enough to see me finish school and become pastor of my first church—a church in which he served as a deacon.

Explanations don't heal people—but they can certainly change the complexion of an illness.

An explanation was what Job was asking for—an opportunity to speak to God.[1]

A showdown
    a confrontation
        a high-noon face-off

where he could demand from God a reason for his suffering.

Finally it happened. Elihu was speaking. He was paying a beautiful tribute to God—painting word pictures that described[2]

God's righteousness and
    God's knowledge and
        God's justice.

He pleaded with Job[3] not to seek death and not to turn to evil and to remember that there are some things we just cannot know about God.

Elihu lifted his head and directed his words to the growing storm clouds.

"Look how great God is—we don't begin to know
Him or to understand Him. He draws up the
water vapor and then distills it into rain, which
the skies pour down."[4]

Elihu held out his hands to catch the first of the falling rain drops.

Then he looked again to the darkening skies and said,

"Look, Job—can anyone really understand the way
the clouds are spread out above us?"[5]

The first sounds of distant thunder were heard, and again Elihu spoke.

"Can anyone understand the thunder that rumbles
within the clouds?"[6]

Great bolts of lightning flashed across the sky.

"Look how God spreads the lightning around Him
and even blankets the tops of the mountain with
its flashes. . . . It looks like God fills His hands
with lightning bolts like we might do with little
darts, and then hurls them at His targets."[7]

"Job, this thunder and this lightning are awesome—

so loud
so near
so ominous
so frightening
it's like—it's like—I feel the presence of God in this
thunder."[8]

Elihu continued to give us one of the most graphic

descriptions of an approaching storm to be found anywhere in all of literature—and without knowing it, he was describing the arrival of God. For God is approaching in all the "Pomp & Circumstance" of a grand processional, to the accompaniment of the rolling thunder and the flashing lightning.

Elihu said,[9]

"My heart trembles."
"Listen to the thunder of His voice."
"It rolls across the heavens and His lightning flashes
    out in every direction."
"This is glorious."
"God is doing this, Job."
"Look, Job, man is stopping his work."
"The animals are hiding."
"It may be that God is about to punish you, Job, or
    it may be that He is about to reward you."

Elihu then continued to describe the heavens, darkened with the tempest, dazzled by the lightning, and split apart by the thunder.

Suddenly, to the north, the sky brightened, as in a sunrise, as the illuminating presence of God in His resplendent glory approached.

Elihu said:[10]

"As we cannot look at the sun for its brightness,
    neither can we gaze at the terrible majesty of God
    breaking forth upon us from heaven."
"Look, Job, He's clothed in dazzling splendor."
"His power is incomprehensible."
"It's a wonder He does not destroy us."
"No wonder men everywhere fear Him."

And Elihu finally ran out of words—poetic language failed him. His thoughts became disjointed, punctuated by his feelings as he described the approach of God—and then the sounds of wind and thunder took on coherence and meaning, and the deep rumblings from the clouds and high-pitched whine of a whirling tornado translated itself into meaningful words. As from the midst of an awesome storm, God began to speak.

Chapter 6, Notes

1. Job 9:32-35
2. Job 36:3-6
3. Job 36:20 TLB
4. Job 36:26-28 TLB
5. Job 36:29 TLB
6. Job 36:29 TLB
7. Job 36:30-32 TLB
8. Job 36:33 TLB
9. Job 37:1-13 TLB
10. Job 37:22-24 TLB

**All of our arguments cease
when God makes His appearance.**

Chapter 7

A New and Unexpected Pain

I was returning from a speaking engagement a number of years ago. It was 2:00 in the morning—raining—and I was tired. The streets of Portland were deserted.

I drove through a red light. As soon as I realized what had happened, I skidded to a stop in the middle of the intersection. I looked each way and then inched through the remaining few feet of the intersection and proceeded to drive home.

The only other car within miles was a city police car.

The officer stopped me and gave me a ticket.

As I waited for the day of my court appearance to arrive, I became increasingly hostile—incensed—filled with reasons why I felt the fine was unjust.

For days I rehearsed my speech before the judge.

"I fell asleep," I would say.

"I was tired."

"There was no traffic."

"I did stop—it was a little late, but I did stop and then felt it safer to go forward than backward."

You know—all the regular excuses.

I arrived at the courthouse, convinced that I could "beat this rap."

The moment I entered that courtroom, I felt myself in the grip of

something awesome—
　something frightening
　　something terribly intimidating.

The focal point of the room was a high oak bench, behind which sat a stern-faced, black-robed figure of a man. His steely eyes seemed to penetrate the very depths of my soul.

He spoke with wisdom and with finality. When his gavel banged that desk-top, all argument ceased, judgment had been dispensed, the sentence was fixed, there seemed no recourse.

As I waited for my name to be called, I felt all the hostility seeping out of my pores. My arguments seemed so childishly inadequate. In the presence of the judge, I felt a strange combination of awesome respect and downright terror.

Finally my name was called. The charge was read, the judge lifted his eyes, peered right down into my naked soul, and asked, "How do you plead, guilty or not guilty?"

All of my rehearsed speeches vanished, and in their place I heard a small, timid, distant voice meekly answer, "Guilty, your Honor."

For months Job had been pleading for an audience with God. Time and again he appealed for a hearing.

He had rehearsed his speech.[1]
He had his questions memorized.[2]
He was ready to make his accusations.[3]

And then God appeared.

Job was silent. There was not even the small, timid, distant voice. There was not even a squeak—Job was silent.

Until Job heard the voice of God emerging from the

whirling of the wind—he had seen God as just another man—oh, bigger and greater and stronger and older and wiser, but just another man.

His God had been shrunken in size to fit the limited confines of his own finite mind—but now God appeared—and spoke—and Job was awed—and Job was silent.

Something always happens when God reveals Himself to man.

> Something profound
>   something different
>   something life-changing
>   something that's eternally unforgettable.

The terror, the dismay, the guilt that Job felt and later described seems to be a common response to God's appearance.

> Adam hid.[4]
> Abraham fell prostrate on the ground.[5]
> Moses covered his face.[6]
> Isaiah repented.[7]
> Ezekiel fell.[8]
> Daniel lapsed into a coma.[9]
> Saul of Tarsus fell to the ground—
>   his eyes were blinded
>   his self-righteousness exposed
>   his will was broken, and
>   his spirit surrendered.[10]

All of our arguments cease when God makes His appearance.

All of Job's complaints were forgotten the moment God spoke.

If it had been possible to relive those months of complaining, I'm sure that Job never would have asked for an audience with God. The greatest pain Job felt was the pain of his own spiritual nakedness as he stood exposed to the all-seeing eye, the all-knowing mind, the ever-loving heart of the Almighty God.

For the first time in his life this good man—this just man—this blameless man—this upright man—this holy man of Uz—saw himself as God saw him.

Chapter 7, Notes

1. Job 10:2 TLB
2. Job 10:18 TLB
3. Job 34:5 TLB
4. Genesis 3:8
5. Genesis 17:3
6. Exodus 3:6
7. Isaiah 6:5
8. Ezekiel 1:28
9. Daniel 8:18
10. Acts 9:3-9

**God is not only powerful, but also just—
not only omnipotent, but also right in all that He does.**

Chapter 8

Questions That Answer Questions

I'm amazed at what God said. I am doubly amazed at what He did not say.

There was no rebuke, there was no pity, and there was no explanation.

He never did address Job's question, "Why?"

He never did honor Job's complaints.

Instead, God answered Job's question with some questions of His own[1]—seventy of them, to be exact. And He began with the one question that's designed to end all questions—He thunders the one sentence that puts man in his place—and God in His—

"Who is this that darkens counsel by words without
    knowledge?"
        or
"Who is this that questions My providence?"
        or
"Who is this who claims to know more than I do?"

Job questioned God's wisdom, so now God questioned Job's wisdom. Then God threw out a challenge to Job—"You wanted a confrontation, you wanted a face-off—you've got it."

"Stand on your feet."
"Hitch up your belt."
"Roll up your sleeves."
"Let's fight."

Job, who questioned God, was now being forced to answer—or rather forced to admit he could not answer —questions that were basic and fundamental to God; questions to which God not only knew the answers, but questions formed by God before answers were available; questions uniquely designed to reveal to Job that he was but a man and that the One addressing him was truly God.

> "Where were you when I laid the foundation of the Earth? Tell me if you know so much."
>
> "Do you know how its dimensions were determined?"
>
> "Do you know who did the surveying?"
>
> "Do you know what supports its foundations and who laid its cornerstone during that time when the morning stars sang together and all the angels shouted for joy?"
>
> "Do you know who decided the boundaries of the seas when they gushed up from the depths?"
>
> "Do you know who clothed them with the clouds?"
>
> "Have you ever commanded the sun to rise in the morning?"
>
> "Have you ever robed the dawn in red?"
>
> "Can you locate the gates of death?"
>
> "Can you tell Me where the light comes from—or the darkness?"
>
> "But of course you know all of this, don't you? For you were born before it was all created, weren't you?"
>
> "Job, have you ever explored the treasures of the snow or the hail?"

"Where does the light come from? Where does the
   wind come from?"

"Who dug the valley for the torrents of rain?"

"Who laid the path for the lightning?"

"Who causes the rain to fall on the barren deserts,
   so that the parched and barren ground is satisfied
   with water?"

"Has the rain a father? Where does the dew come
   from?"

"Whose mother is the ice and frost?"

"Can you hold back the stars? Can you restrain the
   constellations of Orion and the Pleiades?"

"Can you control the seasons?"

"Do you know how mountain goats give birth?"

"Will the wild ox be your happy servant?"

"Do you know why an ostrich has no true motherly
   love?"

"Have you given the horse strength, or clothed his
   neck with quivering mane?"

"Do you know how a hawk soars . . . and is able to
   spread her wings to the south?"

"Do you still want to argue with me, Job? Or will
   you yield? Do you—God's critic—have the
   answer?"[2]

God has just taken a quick swing through all of creation—the earth, the heavens, and then a fleeting glimpse of
His creative handiwork with some of His living creatures. He
asked only the most basic questions. Job was still speechless.

Finally, the one who had attempted to bring God down
to the size of man found himself shrinking and was forced to
admit—

"I am nothing"

"I have no answers"

"I have said too much already."[3]

Restlessly, like a tiger pursuing its prey, God began again—

"Stand up and brace yourself for battle.
Let me ask you a question and you give Me the answer."[4]

God proceeded to ask moral questions of Job—questions that require a level of discernment found only in God Himself.[5]

"Are you going to discredit My justice and condemn Me, so that you can say that you are right?" Or, Job, do you wish to continue to maintain that I have allowed your pain without a reason in mind?
"Are you as strong as God, and can you shout as loudly as He?" Or, Job, do you think you can out-shout Me in maintaining that your suffering is unreasonable?
"Do you really have greater moral discernment than I?"

God then invited Job to put on the robes of royalty, ascend the throne, and make some routine judgments.[6]

"How would you handle the proud? How does one determine who is truly proud? What sort of correction would you design in order to make them humble? Could you do it with a glance?"
"How about the wicked? How would you determine who is truly wicked? What punishment would you uniquely design for each one?"

God then drew Job's attention to two animals—Behemoth,[7] a land animal, and Leviathan,[8] a sea animal.

Some commentators think that Behemoth is a hippopotamus and that Leviathan is a crocodile. Some think they are real, others think they are mythical. Some say they are symbolic. Whatever they are, it appears that Job knew about them and God described them as

awesome,
  frightening, and
    formidable.

Of Behemoth, God said, "No one can catch him off guard—no one can put a ring in his nose and lead him away." Of Leviathan, God said,

"It's useless to try to capture him."
"No one dares stir him up."
"When he stands up, the strongest are afraid. Terror grips them."
"There is nothing so fearless anywhere on earth. Of all the beasts, he is the proudest—the monarch of all that he sees."

What God was saying with such clarity and such devastating forcefulness to Job is this:

"No one can stand up to Me,"[9] and Job—
  if you can't handle Behemoth—
  if you can't handle Leviathan—
  if you can't solve the moral problems of humanity—
  if you can't even answer the most basic questions about creation—about life—
How can you stand up to Me?
How dare you challenge me?

Job is devastated.
Job is ashamed.
Job is finally ready to admit that he's no match for God—that even if God did answer his questions, he probably would be unable to understand.
He had only asked, "Why."
But even God's answers, as well as His questions, are beyond human comprehension.
Job said, "I know that You can do anything and that no one can stop you."[10]

God is not only powerful, but also just; not only omnipotent, but also right in all that He does; beyond dispute; beyond complaint. Job has finally eliminated the distortion and placed God in clear and sharp focus.

And then he finally answered one of God's questions—the only one God really wanted him to answer—the only one he was qualified to answer.[11] He said, "You ask who it is who has so foolishly denied Your providence. It is I. I was talking about things I knew nothing about and did not understand—things far too wonderful for me."

> "I do not even know enough to question God," said Job.
>
> "I'm too ignorant to even complain intelligently."
>
> "I thought I knew God—but it was only hearsay. All of my information was gleaned from others—but now," said Job, "I have seen You."
>
> "And I have seen myself, and I loathe myself and repent in dust and ashes."

I find it difficult to even comment on this scene. For God is taking a good man, a man worthy of His highest commendation, and making him better. God is taking one of His chosen ones and perfecting him. He's taking Job through that very private and very wonderful experience of purging and purifying. He is gently lifting him in and out of the fire, burning away the dross, and preparing to display him as one perfected through suffering.

Job is enduring the experience that most of us need and all of us fear: the painful but glorious experience of truly getting to know ourselves and truly getting to know our God.

Chapter 8, Notes

1. Job 38:2 TLB	5. Job 40:8, 9 TLB	9. Job 41:10 TLB
2. Job 38:4-40:2 TLB	6. Job 40:10-12 TLB	10. Job 42:1-2 TLB
3. Job 40:4-5 TLB	7. Job 40:15-24 TLB	11. Job 42:3-6 TLB
4. Job 40:7 TLB	8. Job 41:1-34 TLB	

**The only thing God withheld from Job
was an answer to the perplexing question, "Why?"**

Chapter 9

The Unanswered Question

*J*ob never did get his answer. He still didn't know why he had lost his herds, his flocks, his servants, his children, and his health.

But he did get them all back and more.

As God began to vindicate Job, He started with Job's accusers. He charged them with gross misrepresentation, declared His anger, and demanded a sacrifice for sin. He even denied them the privilege of offering their own sacrifice. The privilege was reserved for Job.

Job accepted their seven bulls and seven rams and then offered them to God, at the same time praying for their forgiveness. They were forgiven for the incorrect things they had said about God and the unjust things they had said concerning Job.[1]

At that precise moment, the moment of repentance and forgiveness, the miracles of restoration began.[2] Job's brothers, sisters, former friends, and even Job's wife returned. Job's health was restored. Job's wealth was replaced. Each of his visitors brought him a gift of money and a gold ring.

This godly man—

who had lost all of his 7,000 sheep . . . received
14,000 in return.

who had lost all of his 3,000 camels . . . received
6,000 in return.

who had lost all of his 500 oxen . . . received 1,000
in return.

who had lost all of his 500 female donkeys . . .
received 1,000 in return.

Job's happiness was regained.

This proud father who had lost all of his ten children
received ten more in return—again seven sons and three
daughters—twenty in all—ten in heaven and ten on earth.

A double portion—freely given and joyfully received.

God even doubled his life span. We don't know for sure,
but it is generally believed that Job was 70 years of age when
tragedy struck. God graciously gave him 140 more, so that
he was able to watch his children and his children's children
to four generations.[3]

"Then at last he died, an old, old man, after living a
long, good life."[4]

God had given Job all that he'd lost and all that he'd
wanted. He vindicated him before all of his family and
friends. He even gave him time out of His busy schedule for
a private audience with Himself. He addressed him personally and face to face.

The only thing God withheld from Job—the only thing
He refused to give him—was an answer to the perplexing
question, "Why?"

Chapter 9, Notes

1. Job 42:8, 9 TLB
2. Job 42:10, 11 TLB
3. Job 42:16 TLB
4. Job 42:17 TLB

PART
2

LEARNING FROM SUFFERING

There are times when it's necessary for God
to appear to be the "loser" on earth
in order to be the "winner" of unseen battles
taking place in the heavens.

Chapter 10

The View from the Top

But we know why, don't we? We had a look behind the scenes. We were given a view from the top. Early in his story we had a privileged "peek" over the shoulder of life's Script writer as He inserted a scene in the life of Job that explained it all.

I enjoy reading Paul Harvey's *The Rest of the Story.* Each time I read about those seldom-known facts in the lives of well-known people, I feel like I'm one of a privileged few who is being told intimate secrets known only to a select group.

God told us the rest of the story when He described the two times that He and Satan discussed the destiny of Job—the two times Satan questioned God's sovereignty and Job's integrity—the two times Satan claimed to be holding a trump card—the two times that God called his bluff and won.

It happened sometime in Eternity past. God was having one of His routine staff meetings in Heaven, discussing the conditions of His worlds, when Satan, the god of this world, appeared.[1]

Satan was taking a break from his routine supervision of earth[2] when God asked: "Have you noticed my servant, Job?

He is the finest man in all the earth—a good man who fears God and will have nothing to do with evil."[3]

With characteristic cynicism Satan replied, "Why shouldn't he, when You pay him so well? You have always protected him and his home and his property from all harm. You have prospered everything he does—look how rich he is! No wonder he worships you. But just take away his wealth, and he will curse You to Your face."[4]

God called Satan's bluff. He said, "You may do anything you like with his wealth, but don't harm him physically."[5]

It was then that tragedy struck the first time. It was then that all of his herds and all of his flocks were lost—that most of his servants were slain—and all of his children died.

It was then that Job said,

"Naked I came from my mother's womb, and naked
    I shall return there.
The Lord gave and the Lord has taken away.
Blessed be the name of the Lord."[6]

It was then that it was said of Job, "Through all this Job did not sin nor did he blame God."[7]

Satan never learns, nor do his children. A second time he approached the throne of Heaven. God, with characteristic pride and delight in His children, said to Satan, "Well, have you noticed my servant Job? He is the finest man in all the earth—a good man who fears God and turns away from all evil. And he has kept his faith in Me despite the fact that you persuaded Me to harm him without a cause."[8]

Again Satan threw down a challenge. "Skin for skin," he replied, "a man will give anything to save his life. Touch his body with sickness, and he will curse You to Your face."[9]

Satan was convinced that Job's whole life was a lie: his faithful service for God, his unimpeachable character, his meaningful community involvement were all for selfish reasons. If only he could get through that "facade of holiness," he could then reveal the true Job as nothing but a fraud.

Again God called his bluff. "Do with him as you please," the Lord replied, "only spare his life."[10]

Now that Satan had permission to afflict his body, he began searching for the most effective method of human torture at his disposal:

> If he could just hurt him, endlessly—
>   if he could just isolate him, permanently—
>   if he could just brainwash him, incessantly—

he was convinced that he could extract a confession that would expose Job and dishonor God.

I can imagine that his decision was explored with great care. This was a rare opportunity, and he must not fail. I'm sure he convened his trusted demons, and together they probably considered every possibility—the Chinese water-torture, the bamboo slips beneath the fingernails, and all of the other hideous and inhumane methods that man has invented to hurt man. Finally they chose one that they all felt was most appropriate—one designed

> to hurt
>   to separate
>   to confuse
>   to humiliate
>   to shame and . . .
>   to linger,

one ultimately designed to destroy Job's spirit without destroying his body. It would be a torture that combined deep spiritual depression with an interminable excruciating physical pain—a torture that appeared to offer no possible hope of relief and that forced one to endure alone.

It was then that the itching began. It was then that his body became inflamed with a sore and angry swelling. It was then that red spots covered his flesh—

his bones ached
  his legs began to thicken
    his hair fell out
      his face swelled, and
        his voice became hoarse.

It was then that his entire appearance changed until his face became grim and distorted, and his skin was encrusted and constantly running with pus.

It was then that his wife left him—his friends deserted him, and he was banished to the local garbage dump like refuse from under the kitchen sink, to begin his long journey into the living hell that refused to release him.

But Job didn't know that part of the story. There's no indication that Job ever heard of that heavenly confrontation.

He asked God repeatedly for a reason behind his pain, but God never answered that question. He never described the challenge thrown down by Satan.

He never explained the greater contest being run in full view of the spiritual world. He never discussed the "high stakes" that had been laid on Heaven's table as God "put his money on Job."

Job never knew—before, during, or after—the full reason for his suffering.

He was forced to suffer just as we are forced to sometimes suffer—without an explanation.

He knew, as we know, that suffering is a part of the human experience.

He knew, as we know, that suffering is tied to sin.

He knew, as we know, that suffering is part of God's corrective discipline—part of the purifying process.

He knew, as we know, that suffering in this world is unavoidable.

But when he had fully examined his life and his ways, and even after he had taken whatever corrective measures he felt necessary, the suffering persisted. It was then that he not only pled for his own sake, but also for the sake of God. He believed that God's honor was at stake. God was being forced to sit in the ashes, and that was no place for his God.

Little did he realize that there are times when it's necessary for God to appear to be the loser on earth in order to be the winner of unseen battles taking place in the heavens.

Job didn't know the story of a crucifixion that bore all the marks of defeat. All Job knew was that something unexplainable was happening. And there are times when that is all we are privileged to know.

Chapter 10, Notes

1. Job 1:6
2. Job 1:7; 1 Peter 5:8
3. Job 1:8 TLB
4. Job 1:9-11 TLB
5. Job 1:12 TLB
6. Job 1:21
7. Job 1:22
8. Job 2:3 TLB
9. Job 2:4, 5 TLB
10. Job 2:6 TLB

The battle was not between Satan and Job,
but between Satan and God.

Chapter 11

Who Is Fighting This War?

Satan's goal was not to destroy Job, it was to discredit God.

This brief glimpse into the heavenly war was but a small part of the continuing conflict between Satan and God.

Job meant nothing to Satan. Job was merely an object— a target—a means to an end.

Job assumes the impersonal stature of a foot soldier in the front lines, a prisoner in a concentration camp. He is seen only as an impediment to the larger goal of gaining a strategic victory. In this instance Satan wanted to discredit God by causing one of His trusted servants to renounce Him completely.

That was the meaning of the words, "to curse God."[1]

To curse is not to swear or to use profane or even obscene language.

It does not mean to complain, or even criticize. It does not mean to question. It does not mean to get angry.

Screaming "ouch" when you stub your toe is not cursing God.

One of the tragic interpretations of Job has encouraged people to suffer in silence. It has heaped guilt upon them when they dared to ask God a question or to suggest to God that they would like some relief.

I resent the phrase, "don't cry," and its companion phrase, "don't talk."

Tears are therapeutic and talk is therapeutic. God has given us tear ducts and tongues, and they become a very real part of the relief process when we hurt. And Job employed both.

So many feel some sort of sadistic heroism when they can suppress their true feelings as they're suffering, only to find that those bottled emotions eventually explode in all directions later on in life.

To curse God means to accuse God of unfaithfulness. It means to accuse God of not keeping His word—of being untruthful. But it means more. It means not only to accuse Him of unfaithfulness, but to turn away from Him in search of another god who might be more worthy of our confidence.

This was a typical heathen practice in Job's day—and in ours. Whenever a worshiper made expensive offerings to his god, he expected something from his god in return. He expected that god to prosper him and to protect him. If that god failed, he would then destroy that god or reject that god—or curse that god.

Cursing god meant to exchange one god for another as we might fire our stockbroker if he fails to make a wise investment, or our realtor if he's unable to sell our house.

Satan has never been noted for his high and lofty thoughts about God. He has always felt that he is God's superior or at least His equal. He's always been convinced that he knows the mind of God and even what the limitations of God are.

One great mistake that Satan has always made has been in his assumption that God is limited like himself. Another has been in assuming that God's servants are just like his own: opportunists that can be bought, hypocrites that live their lives only on the surface, proud people that can never condone being humbled.

Satan measured God and His children by his own standards and found himself horribly mistaken.

The more he crushed Job, the more Job emitted a fragrance that both startled Satan and pleased God; the more he stretched Job and squeezed Job, the louder Job cried his allegiance to his God—until, when it was all finished, Satan fled from God's presence like a whipped puppy. Cowering in the corner of the universe, Satan was forced to watch a vindicated man and a glorified God as they continued to walk together in a totally satisfying relationship.

In case you're worried that when your turn comes, you won't be able to "hang on" like Job, let me remind you—the battle was not between Satan and Job; it was between Satan and God.

Job gets a lot of credit, but that's because God chose to give it to him. It's interesting that this is always God's way.

God does the work—but man gets the credit.

That's just like our God, isn't it?

Jesus said, "Without me, you can do nothing."[2] And then He promised the faithful sufferer that "your reward is great in heaven. . . ."[3] If God is the enabler and Christ is the strengthener, it would seem Theirs should be the reward. But no, God does the work, and He gives us the credit.

I can remember when I was teaching my son John to play golf. He could barely hold the club. I would reach my arms around him, take his hands in mine—grip the club, address the ball, and then swing. Whenever we would hit that ball, and it would sail through the air for any significant distance, I would always clap and cheer and pat him on the back, and say, "John, look what *you* did. Great work, Son!"

Now we both knew the truth, and you know the truth. God knows the truth about any spiritual achievements we accomplish in this life. God does the work, but He still chooses to give us the credit.

Job did not curse God, because of the unfailing grace of God in his life; because of the undeserting presence of God in his life; because of the unyielding power of God in his life.

The tribute belongs to God—not to Job; because the war was God's, not Job's, just as it is in our lives.

The outcome was God's, too. And whenever the ultimate purpose and goal is determined by God, the outcome is always predictable.

Satan is a loser—God is a winner. And God has already predicted the outcome for us all. Why? Because we're strong? Because we're faithful? No! Because He is strong and He is faithful and He is able to "keep that which is committed to Him."[4]

Martha and I were talking about God's grace one day when she said, "I don't think that I have dying grace, and it worries me." I said, "We don't need dying grace when we're living. When it comes time to die, the grace will be there."

Many of us worry that we don't have suffering grace. We don't need suffering grace when we're rejoicing. But when it becomes time to suffer, the grace will be there—just as it was when it was Job's time to suffer.

Don't fret. God will hold you up, too, just as He did Job.

Chapter 11, Notes

1. Job 1:11; 2:5
2. John 15:5
3. Luke 6:23
4. 2 Timothy 1:12

No suffering can touch the believer
without having first received the permission of God.

Chapter 12

How to Prepare for Suffering

*I*f you're planning to suffer any time in the near future—and none of us is, though most of us will—then you'd better be sure that your theology is correct.

Our response to suffering is determined by our understanding of God.

What we think about God will influence how we respond to trials in this lifetime.

If you feel like many, that Job's great loss in life was something that Satan slipped by God while He was busy elsewhere, or that Job's suffering was something unavoidable—something God could not help—then you could easily give up in despair.

But if you see God as the God of the Bible—

> supreme
> > sovereign, and
> > > sensitive,

not allowing trials except by Divine permission, then you can see purpose, even if you do not know what that purpose is. The Christian life is kept fine-tuned by biblical theology.

We should always interpret experience by truth—we should always filter every pain through the lens of deity. When God is in sharp focus, then life is also undistorted.

Harold S. Kushner wrote a book, *When Bad Things Happen to Good People*, published by Avon books in 1981, that very quickly became an acclaimed national bestseller. Rabbi Kushner explores the question, "Why?" as he relives the painful experience of his son Aaron's suffering and death. The book is well-written, extremely interesting, and easy to read. The only problem is its theology.

It presents God as a reactive force in the universe, not always in complete control. It describes a god, unlike the God of the Bible, who really doesn't always know what's happening.

He asks the question, "Could it be that God does not cause the bad things to happen to us?"[1]

He then explores the Book of Job for the answer to his own question. In what he considers to be the "Job-fable,"[2] he concludes that "bad things do happen to good people in this world, but it is not God who wills it. God would like people to get what they deserve in life, but He cannot always arrange it."[3]

He suggests that "God wants the righteous to live peaceful, happy lives, but sometimes even He can't bring that about. It is too difficult even for God to keep cruelty and chaos from claiming their innocent victims."[4]

He concludes by encouraging us to "forgive God despite His limitation, as Job does, and as we once learned to forgive and love our parents even though they were not as wise, as strong, and as perfect as we needed them to be."[5]

I recently saw an ad for the movie "The Incredible Shrinking Woman." It's the story of a woman who, for some reason, begins to shrink.

In fact, the woman shrinks until she becomes so small that climbing up onto her bed becomes an impossible task.

Chair legs and table legs appear like skyscrapers to her.

Her great fear is that she will be captured and eaten by her pet kitten.

She finally falls into the kitchen sink and is sucked into the garbage disposal.

Harold Kushner, like many today who cannot comprehend the incomprehensible, tends to shrink God down and down and down to man's size and then attempts to describe Him in terms of man's understanding.

The result is that the Bible's God is eventually and completely lost to the very people to whom it was addressed.

Job had a low view of God.

Job thought God treated His servants as men do—that simply because he couldn't understand the reason for his suffering, God was having one of His capricious, unpredictable mood-swings and punishing him without a reason.[6]

Job needed to fully understand the uniqueness of God.

Elihu reminded Job of his foolishness by saying, "God is greater than man . . . He does not give an account of His doings."[7] But Job did not understand that.

Job also thought that because God was silent, it meant that He was absent.[8] Job needed David's perspective on the abiding presence of God. David said,

> "Where can I go from Thy Spirit? Or where can I
> flee from Thy presence?
>
> If I ascend to heaven, Thou art there;
> If I make my bed in Sheol, behold, Thou art there.
>
> If I take the wings of the dawn,
> If I dwell in the remotest part of the sea,
>
> Even there Thy hand will lead me."[9]

Job could have added one more verse to David's beautiful Psalm. He could have said,

> "Even if I am forced from my home to lie in the dust
> and ashes of the local garbage dump of Uz—
> Thou art there."

God *was* there—hearing—watching—waiting for the right moment to move in on the wings of the wind and restore Job.

I'll never forget how God transformed a miserable little cubicle in the psychiatric ward of a Veteran's Hospital into a sanctuary by simply giving to me a sense of His presence.

Spending Easter Sunday in a foxhole in New Guinea became a rich and rewarding experience simply by enjoying a sense of divine presence.

Brother Lawrence teaches us that the most miserable or the most mundane experiences of life can be transformed by "Practicing the Presence of God."

Job thought that since there was no understandable reason for his sufferings, there must be no purpose.[10]

Job failed to comprehend the sovereignty of God—at first. When God finally revealed Himself, Job's declaration became one of the grandest definitions for sovereignty to be found anywhere. He stated,

> "I know that You can do anything and that no one
>   can stop you."[11]

Job acknowledged active divine involvement in his pain—without knowing why. He finally conceded that God, for some unknown reason, was in charge and in control.

The Book of Job presents a view of very active divine involvement in human suffering. That involvement, as we review the challenge thrown down by Satan, was in the form of divine approval.

Before Satan could lift a finger to touch Job, or his possessions, it was first necessary to gain God's permission.

This means that God allowed Job to suffer. He did not will it to happen, any more than He did not forbid it to happen, any more than He forbade Adam and Eve to eat the forbidden fruit—He allowed it to happen.

God allows us to suffer. This may be the only solution to the problem that we will ever receive.

Nothing can touch the Christian without having first

received the permission of God. If I do not accept that statement, then I really do not believe that God is sovereign—and if I do not believe in His sovereignty, then I am helpless before all the forces of heaven and hell. I am subject to the capricious whims of anyone or anything that might desire to harm me.

When Jesus was about to be crucified, Pilate said to Him, "Do you not know that I have the authority to release you, and I have the authority to crucify you?"

Jesus answered, "You have no authority over Me, unless it has been given to you from above. . . ."[12]

Pilate could not lift a finger against the life of Jesus Christ without first having gained permission from God.

When Jesus was predicting Peter's denial, He said, "Simon, Simon, behold, Satan has demanded permission to sift you like wheat."[13]

Satan could not lift a finger against Peter without first having gained permission from God.

One summer Martha and I planned what we thought was the perfect vacation. We secured the lovely vacation home of a dear friend in central Oregon and planned to spend three uninterrupted weeks of resting, studying, bicycling, and entertaining our children. We both laid out our books, carefully placed the deck chairs, turned down the bed, flipped on the television, and began to enjoy some much needed rest.

The first evening we climbed on two bicycles and proceeded to explore Black Butte Ranch. Before the evening's ride was finished, I had broken three ribs, suffered a mild concussion and numerous abrasions on my arms and legs—I was a mess. I spent five days in a hospital.

Just before my release from the hospital, I developed a severe case of shingles.

There were times during the next few months that I was convinced that Job's boils were really the shingles in disguise.

Needless to say—our vacation plans were somewhat altered. There was no vacation as far as I was concerned. What had promised to be weeks of rest turned into months of torment.

Why? I haven't the slightest idea.

The only thing that I know for sure is that for some reason, unknown to me, God allowed both the accident and the shingles. That knowledge wasn't quite enough then; it took other things like doctors and medication and an attentive wife, but it's enough now.

God allows us to suffer, for nothing can touch the life of a Christian without first having received permission from the Father.

That knowledge of God may not lessen the pain, but it will ease considerably the anxiety that sometimes intensifies pain to the point where it is unbearable.

Let me repeat, if you're planning any experience of suffering in the near future, you'd better be sure that your theology is correct.

Chapter 12, Notes

1. Harold S. Kushner, *When Bad Things Happen to Good People* (New York: Avon Books, 1981), p. 30.
2. Ibid., p. 34.
3. Ibid., p. 43.
4. Ibid.
5. Ibid., p. 148.
6. Job 33:8-13
7. Job 33:12-13
8. Job 33:13-16
9. Psalm 139:7-10
10. Job 34:7-13
11. Job 42:2 TLB
12. John 19:10, 11
13. Luke 22:31

No one can fully explain God's actions but God.

Chapter 13

Why?

What was wrong with the theology of Job's friends?

Eliphaz, Bildad, and Zophar made God angry. He said, "My wrath is kindled against you . . . because you have not spoken of Me what is right as my servant Job has."[1]

These three who had traveled so far, whose intentions were so honorable, whose desires were to comfort and to heal, were almost slain by God. They were accused of outright sin. They had not spoken correctly about God.[2]

First—they claimed to know the mind of God. Has anyone ever said to you, "I know why God allowed that to happen to you . . ." I've heard it many times.

When our son, Jimmy, died, one woman said, "God took your little boy because you did not have the faith to believe he would be healed. . . ."

When I broke out with the shingles, one man said, "This is God telling you to slow down."

While preaching in the Philippines, I became ill. A friend said, "God is trying to tell you to stop taking trips to foreign countries."

The only time I felt that one of these "interpreters of the divine" might be right was when I had my bicycle accident.

My brother said, "I think God is telling you to stop riding bicycles." I agreed with him and have not climbed on one since.

No one knows the mind of God but God.

No one can fully explain God's actions but God.

The only certain understanding any of us has is what God has recorded of His thinking for us in the Scripture.

God has unique and wonderful ways of revealing His will to the body of believers and even to individual believers. But comprehending the divine reasons behind every divine action is reserved for God Himself.

Eliphaz, Bildad, and Zophar had it all figured out. They agreed—they sustained their argument—they never backed down, they said it over and over again—"God is punishing you because you have sinned!"

Everything that follows that opening remark is repetitious—just the same words over again—like a broken record —amplified and intensified—but nothing new and nothing different.

It is sheer human arrogance to claim this kind of knowledge.

It is the ultimate in human pride.

It is effrontery to God and causes embarrassment to the body of Christ.

Only God knows the mind of God.

When people continue to ask me Why? Why? Why?—

Why did God allow my child to die?

Why did God allow me to lose my job?

Why did God permit my business to go bankrupt?

The most God-honoring thing I can answer is . . . "I do not know." There may be human explanations, but as for God's reasons behind God's actions, they are a mystery to me, for . . .

"His understanding is infinite."[3]
          and

"There is no searching of His understanding . . ."[4]
    and says the Apostle Paul,
"Oh, the depth of the riches both of the wisdom and
    knowledge of God! How unsearchable are His
    judgments and unfathomable His ways."[5]

Eliphaz, Bildad, and Zophar did not and could not
know, for sure, what God was doing in Job's life and why.

Second—they handcuffed God and stuffed Him into
their own little man-made theological box.

They had one simple thesis—and no more. Their theology stated that

"Prosperity is God's reward for righteousness,"
    and
"Suffering is God's judgment for sin."
"If you live right you will be blessed.
If you sin you will be cursed."

The word sovereign suggests freedom. It teaches that
God is free to do as He pleases and when He pleases. The
only limitations of that freedom come from those restrictions
that God's very nature has placed upon Himself.

To suggest that God must act and react in exactly the
same way to everyone, everywhere, is to rob God of His
sovereignty.

As I study the Scriptures and recall my own life experiences, I'm convinced that God delights in keeping us off
balance by never employing the same attention-getting device
more than once in a lifetime.

Eliphaz, Bildad, and Zophar portrayed God as inflexi-
ble, with His ways set in concrete. In their view, He was
unable to break from His rigidity long enough to suit a
unique, one-of-a-kind experience and capture the attention of
a unique, one-of-a-kind person. God said,

"For as the heavens are higher than the earth, so are
    My ways higher than your ways and My thoughts
    than your thoughts."[6]

Third—these three men worshiped a God who was a theological cripple, a God who limped along with the leg of His severity much, much longer than the leg of His goodness.

They saw God as some sort of a cosmic judge, ready to "zap" anyone and everyone who took one wrong step.

They saw Him as mean and unforgiving, with

> no compassion,
> > no mercy,
> > > no grace,
> > > > no goodness,
> > > > > no patience, and
> > > > > > no love.

They saw

> only the severity of God,
> > only the righteousness of God,
> > > only the holiness of God,
> > > > only the Law of God,

and completely ignored

> His love,
> > His mercy,
> > > His goodness, and
> > > > His grace.

They were theologically off-balance—as we are most of the time.

Many of us who have grown up in evangelical homes have been overbalanced in the same direction. We call it legalism. We have found it difficult to move from a fear of God to a love for God—to enjoy God rather than be afraid of Him. We have been more obsessed with negatives than positives—with "should nots" rather than "shoulds."

I'm still breaking free of that theological stranglehold and finding freedom in Christ to be a most delightful experience.

The Bible describes God as a God of balance:

Romans 11:22 balances goodness and severity.
Psalm 85:10 describes the balance by saying,
    "Lovingkindness and truth have met together;
    Righteousness and peace have kissed each other."

Theological balance is always difficult.

But theological balance is always necessary if we are going to be able to stand up straight in a crippled world and adequately display our God to a limping civilization.

Eliphaz, Bildad, and Zophar were rebuked because they began talking about God long before they really had gotten to know Him.

Chapter 13, Notes

1. Job 42:7
2. Job 42:7, 8
3. Psalm 147:5
4. Isaiah 40:28
5. Romans 11:33
6. Isaiah 55:9

**If you're thinking about death
as the solution to suffering, be sure that first
you fully understand what death is all about.**

Chapter 14

One Solution That Is No Solution

I have thought seriously of committing suicide. In the book, *Depression*,[1] written by Dr. Emery Nester and myself, I devoted an entire chapter to the subject.

It is always deeply embarrassing for me to recall those low times when I was held in the grip of an unrelenting depression—and found myself considering suicide as a means of escape.

Job wanted to die, too. I've found that at some time in our lives, most of us entertain the same wish.

Job says repeatedly that death is to be preferred to life.[2]

"Why didn't I die at birth?"

"Why did the midwife let me live?"

"Oh, to have been stillborn! To have never breathed or seen the light."

"Oh, why should light and life be given to those in misery and bitterness, who long for death, and it won't come; who search for death as others search for food or money!"

Job not only had a low view of God, he had a low view of death. Job viewed death as the world views death today.

He saw it at times as the end—as a cessation of being—the termination of all—the conclusion of human existence.
He said,

"For if only I had died at birth, then I would be quiet now, asleep and at rest . . ."
"For there in death the wicked cease from troubling, and there the weary are at rest."
"There even prisoners are at ease, with no brutal jailer to curse them."
"Both rich and poor alike are there, and the slave is free at last from his master."
"What blessed relief when at last they die!"[3]

Later he said,

"I'm sick and near death, the grave is about to receive me."
"My hope will go down with me to the grave. We shall rest together in the dust."[4]

He seemed to be unsure, however, of just what death held for him—just like our world today. In one place he said,

"As water evaporates from a lake, as a river disappears in drought, so a man lies down for the last time, and does not rise again until the heavens are no more; he shall not awaken, nor be roused from his sleep."[5]

In another he said,

"If a man dies, surely he won't live again! This thought gives me hope, so that in all my anguish I eagerly await sweet death!"[6]

And yet again his ambivalence—his uncertainty about death—was evident. He said,

"And I know that after this body has decayed, this body shall see God! Then He will be on my side!

Yes, I shall see Him, not as a stranger, but as a friend. What a glorious hope."[7]

He would swing from one conviction to another—confused—not really sure what death would mean to him.

If you're thinking of death, be sure that you know what it's all about before you make any plans to go there.

The church of Jesus Christ is a thoroughly competent travel agency, with plenty of road maps available. There is no need for uncertainty as to what to expect, or just how to get where you want to go.

Two of the speakers responded to Job's lingering wish to die.

Elihu pleaded with great emotion to Job:

"Do not long for the night, when people vanish in their place."[8]

Please, Job, do not wish to die, he said.

God asked a question of Job:

"Have the gates of death been revealed to you?
Or have you seen the gates of deep darkness?"[9]

We have such a sterile, unrealistic view of death today.

We view make-believe death on the screen, and it looks so harmless.

We see death in the funeral home, and it looks so life-like. I like to take members of my staff to funerals with me—not only to watch the service, the interaction with family members, and to listen to the words of comfort—but also with the hope that I might take them from the viewing room to the embalming room and show them the unbelievable and marked contrast between real death and make-believe death.

The lifeless form of a dead person is a hideous, empty, unforgettable sight. Many have never seen real death—death without rouge and lipstick and mascara and skin coloring. It's awesome and frightening.

God asked Job:

"Have the gates of death been revealed to you?
   Or have you seen the gates of deep darkness?"

Do you really know what death is like, Job? As hideous as physical death is, spiritual death is even worse. To be separated from the body is frightening, but to be separated from God is unthinkable.

In sharp contrast to what Job seems to think, the writer of Hebrews tells that death is not the place of rest—not the place of escape—not the place of release, but the place of judgment.

". . . it is appointed for men to die once, and after
   this comes judgment."[10]

Rest, release, and peace are reserved for those who have made arrangements to spend eternity with Christ in Heaven and are willing to wait and willing to allow God to play out His drama in their lives until that precise moment when He chooses to bring down the curtain and call them home.

If you're thinking about death as a solution to suffering, make sure that you fully understand all that God—Who holds the keys of life and death—has to say about it.

Chapter 14, Notes

1. Don Baker and Emery Nester,
   *Depression: Finding Hope and
   Meaning in Life's Darkest
   Shadow* (Portland, Ore.:
   Multnomah Press, 1983).
2. Job 3:11-21 TLB
3. Job 3:13-22 TLB
4. Job 17:1, 16 TLB
5. Job 14:11, 12 TLB
6. Job 14:14 TLB
7. Job 19:26, 27 TLB
8. Job 36:20 TLB
9. Job 38:17 TLB
10. Hebrews 9:27

To complain is to doubt God.
It is the same thing as suggesting that
God really doesn't know what He's doing.

Chapter 15

Job's Sin

Did you ever accuse God of not knowing what He was doing?

Probably not in so many words—but to complain means the same thing. It's far from cursing God, but it is an accusation against God. It questions God's wisdom and God's good judgment.

It's called presumption. A complaint about any uncontrollable circumstance in life presumes that God is either absent or that He is not nearly as smart as we are.

To complain does not mean to discuss—or to explore—or to search for meaning. It does not mean to describe one's feelings or to appeal to others for insight or prayer or compassion.

To complain means that after investigation has been made of any uncontrollable circumstance, a charge is lodged against God. An accusation is hurled heavenward that suggests that God is unfair or unwise or unloving or even unconcerned about our needs.

Job complained—loudly, bitterly, incessantly. In fact, the word "complain" appears more times in the book of Job than in any other book of the Bible. Nearly one-half of the "complaints" in Scripture fall from the lips of Job.

He said:

"I will complain in the bitterness of my soul."[1]
". . . I will give full vent to my complaint."[2]

With one bold stroke of his verbal pen, God brings the sin of Job's complaining into sharp relief when He says:[3]

"Who is this that darkens counsel without knowledge?"
> or

"Why are you using your ignorance to deny My providence?"
> or

"Who is this that doubts My good judgment?"
> or

"Who is this that claims to know more than I do?"
> or

"Who is this that thinks he knows what's better for his life than I do?"
> or

"Who is this that dares to question Me?"
> or

"Who is this that accuses Me of not knowing what I am doing?"

With that one blazing question, God placed His divine finger on the single sin that marred and disfigured Job's whole experience of suffering—the one sin for which Job ultimately was forced to repent.

The enormity of the sin of complaining is described in Psalm 78 as God recounts for us the early experiences of Israel as they traveled from Egypt to Canaan.

They complained when their leader was present.
They complained when their leader was absent.

They complained because they had no water.
They complained because they had no food.
　　When God provided food,
They complained because they had no meat.
They complained because their journey required
　　time and
　　　　effort and
　　　　　　battles.
They complained because God punished them for
　　their complaining.

Israel's constant complaints angered God, and His wrath was kindled against them—why? Because God has always equated complaining with unbelief. He called it[4] "sin," "rebellion," "unbelief," "deception," and "treachery."

God reacted to their unbelief. He rebuked them, judged them, killed some of them, destroyed their crops, killed their cattle—He loved them, forgave them, was compassionate toward them, and restrained His anger time and again. Why?—because to complain is to doubt God. It's the same as to suggest that God really does not know what He is doing.

Israel loved the prospect of freedom. They loved the promise of a land "that flowed with milk and honey"[5]; they loved the thought of a place of their own, where they could worship Jehovah God—*but* Israel hated the process they were forced to endure in order to get there.

Job was delighted with the prospect of someday dying quietly in his own little nest after a long, good life—but Job hated his experience of suffering.

He loved the promise, but hated the process.

We revel in thoughts of Heaven, but the thought of dying is frightening, and we fight it until we can fight it no longer.

We love the promise, but hate the process.

We rejoice in the hope of perfection, but we struggle with the pain of perfecting.

We love the promise, but hate the process.

If only we could go from the promise to its fulfillment, without the process.

It's during the process of getting to where God has promised that we experience life's bitter complaints. We plod through circumstances that *seem* to have no bearing whatever on the "promise." It's then that we wonder if God has left us or if God really knows what He's doing.

Years ago I was invited to pastor a church in an area where I had never wanted to live. I was restrained from saying no.

One morning as I was reading from the book of Isaiah, a passage reached out, grabbed me, and refused to let me go.

It said some very relevant things to me. It suggested that

1. you will enjoy the land
2. your ministry will flourish and
3. your health will improve.

As I sat there rereading the passage, I wanted to resist the personal implications on good hermeneutical grounds. I knew that the promise was originally made to Israel, and I knew the dangers of tampering with a context—nevertheless, as I read I suddenly became aware that tears were flowing from my eyes.

Martha came in and sat beside me and asked, "Are we going?"

"Yes," I answered, "We're going." When I showed the passage to her, it seemed so appropriate, so right, and so exciting.

Months later I sat alone in my car on the outskirts of that city. It was desert, and I'd always hated desert. I loved green—green grass, green trees, green hills, and green mountains. But in that place everything was brown—brown soil, brown grass, brown houses, brown buildings, and no hills and no mountains.

I used to ride an elevator to the thirteenth floor of the tallest building in town just to see something—it was so flat.

And the ministry was hard. It was only nominally successful.

My health—I experienced more health problems there than anywhere. I spent four years in deep depression, ten weeks in a psychiatric ward. I was forced to resign because of continuing poor health.

All the time I was wondering—

Where was God?
Does God really know what He's doing?
    or
Did we misinterpret the signals?
    or
Did we misread the Scriptures?

From our present vantage point, Martha and I rejoice in a promise that we still feel was personally meant for us. The problem was that we didn't understand the process.

Today, many years later, we love the place of our ministry, my health has improved, and the work is flourishing. None of this would have been possible, however, without the process of a desert experience that included all the things we needed but had never expected and certainly never wanted.

I complained while in the desert.

I repented when I became aware of the enormity of my sin.

To complain about any circumstance in life—

my health
    my wealth (or lack of it)
        my success
            my failure
            my job
                my age
                    my place of residence
                        my appearance
                            my parents (or absence of them)
                            my singleness
                                my married state
                                    my children (or lack of them)
                                    even the weather—

is an accusation against God's wisdom and God's good judgment; it presumes that God is either absent or that He is not nearly so smart as we are.

After listening silently to God and finally seeing himself "as nothing"[6] when compared with God, Job forgot his discomfort, fell back down amidst the garbage, and said, "I know that Thou canst do all things, and that no purpose of Thine can be thwarted."[7]

Job admitted that God was smarter, more competent, and far more discerning than he, and in so doing, Job acknowledged that God was far more capable of successfully running his life—even if the process included the experience of painful suffering.

Chapter 15, Notes

1. Job 7:11
2. Job 10:1
3. Job 38:2
4. Psalm 78:17-57
5. Exodus 3:17
6. Job 40:4 TLB
7. Job 42:2

When God appears, man changes.

Chapter 16

Job's Victory

When God appears, man changes.

God's speech to Job, one of the longest Person-to-person visits recorded in Scripture, brought about a dramatic transformation.

Job forgot his pain.
He ceased his wailing.
He dropped his broken shards of pottery.
He stopped the scraping of his pus-encrusted body.
He stopped shouting questions at God and accusations at his counselors.
He forgot the ashes
and the dung
and the garbage
and the lepers
and the dogs—

he was aware of only one thing—God was present—and when God appears man changes.

Man forgets the unimportant and the temporal—man remembers the significant and the eternal. Job saw himself.

For the first time in Job's life he saw himself. He said, "I am nothing."[1]

For a man of Job's stature to admit that he is nothing—was something.

On the surface one might question Job's self-concept and even argue with him. But it would be futile—for when one sees God and compares himself with God, the only conclusion is the one Job came to—"I am nothing."

Job saw God. For the first time in his life he saw God. His prior knowledge was all second-hand—somebody else's information or revelation, but not his own. It was hearsay—it was like most of the things we know about God; but now his information was his own—his understanding of God was unblurred, undistorted, and clearly focused.

He said, "I know You can do anything and that no one can stop You."[2] For the first time in his life,

> he saw God as completely sovereign
> he saw God as the gracious controller of all things
> he saw God as free—free to do
>> whatever He pleased
>> whenever He pleased—and without explanation.
> He saw God
>> behind all the events on earth and
>> above all supernatural powers in Heaven.
> He saw
>> the sovereign will and
>>> the sovereign power and
>>>> the sovereign purpose
>>>>> of the sovereign God, and

Job was no longer interested in answers; he was only interested in a relationship.

Whenever I leave home for any length of time, I always phone or write. My calls or letters are filled with questions and requests for information.

How's the weather?
How are the kids?
Is the dog all right?
How do you feel?
Is everything OK at the church?

Just routine—even somewhat mundane.

But when I come home and walk through that door and take Martha in my arms, I don't waste time asking about the weather, or the kids, or the dog, or even the church.

I'm not interested in answers, I'm interested only in a relationship—and a relationship was what Job was enjoying.

He assumed the proper position—down, down again to the garbage and ashes.

The custom of dirt and ashes is somewhat like our custom of wearing black when we're in mourning. The ancients tried to appear on the outside the same way they felt on the inside.

So Job sat in the ashes again and then lifted handful after handful over his head and let it fall like rain down over his body until his flesh was the color of his soul—gray—the color of the ground beneath him.

God's ultimate intention for Job was not only repentance—it was also restoration. The restoration of Job's wealth and of Job's health was really no problem. That could have been accomplished as quickly as was his loss—in just one day.

To restore family and friends to a vindicated and healed Job posed no real problem.

As soon as Job's health returned—
as soon as his blemishes faded—
as soon as the fear of infection was gone—
as soon as he had shaved and showered

they would all come back.
Job's place in his community could be restored. He could

fight his way back to the top. He could start over, and with the natural abilities God had heaped upon him, he could be successful again. But for one thing!

> Job had been offended
>> he had been deserted
>>> he had been ridiculed
>>>> he had been humiliated
>>>>> he had been wounded deeply—
>>>>>> permanently.

Could he forgive—

> His friends?
>> His family?
>> His wife?

The healing process could have been stopped right there.

The bitterness that was smoldering in the mind of Job could have continued and could have ignited into a full-scale fire that would have consumed him.

Can a man forgive a wife who deserts him in the time of his greatest need?

Can a man forgive relatives who will just stand back and allow tragedy to run its full course?

Can a man forgive would-be counselors who offer only criticism without compassion?

Can a man forgive such words as: "hypocrite," "arrogant," "wicked," "rebel," "blasphemer"?

In a previous pastorate of mine, a young man returned home from Vietnam minus one leg and one wife.

His leg had been blown off by a land mine, and his wife had deserted him when she heard of the severity of his wounds.

He hobbled into my office one day, threw his crutches against the wall, and said, "Pastor, I'm mad! I've never been so mad. I'm mad clear down to my bones! Everything I've ever wanted is gone—my wife, my career, my home, my future, even my self-respect. And I want to fight the whole world, or die—and I'm not sure which.

"I'm so tired of people looking on me with pity—thinking I'm helpless. Do you want to know how helpless I am? Come on, I'll show you."

He never gave me time to answer. He just picked up his crutches and began swinging that leg—and that stump—down the hall, out the door, and to the parking lot.

"Get in," he said. I climbed in, buckled my seat belt (firmly), and watched as he struggled in behind his automatic controls; and then he took off—50, 60, 70, 80, 90, 100 miles per hour. Down the back streets, through stop signs, blind intersections, unpaved alleys, completely ignoring danger.

He drove like a madman. Once he looked over at me and said, "Scared, preacher?" I wasn't scared—I was terrified. But I'd never admit it. "Am I supposed to be?" I asked.

Finally he stopped, laid his head on the steering wheel, and began to cry. Between the sobs he would look over at me and with hate-filled eyes said, "Don't talk to me about God—about love—about honor—about faith! Don't talk to me about forgiveness! Don't ask me to forgive my wife. I'll never forgive her for what she did to me!"

And, as far as I know, he never did.

As far as I know, he's still living with the fire of hate burning in his soul.

Job had that option.

Job could have reacted with great glee when God said to Eliphaz, "I am angry with you and with your two friends . . ."[3]

He could have said, "Go for it, God!—Tell him off! Give him what he deserves. Zap him." But he didn't.

Job could have refused when God instructed him to help offer sacrifices for their sins.[4]

Eliphaz, Bildad, and Zophar went to Job, they offered their sacrifices and Job offered his prayer—and the Lord accepted Job's prayer.[5]

What do you suppose Job prayed? The same thing Jesus prayed in His great suffering—"Father forgive them. . . ."

That was the only prayer that God could have accepted. That was the prayer that cooled His anger—and Job could not have asked God to forgive them unless he had forgiven them himself.

It's impossible to ask God to forgive someone we will not forgive.

We never pray, "Father, please forgive so and so for what he's done to me—but don't expect me to. . . ."

No one asks God to be nice to someone when we plan not to be.

Job prayed for them—
   that means
Job forgave them.

There is great freedom in forgiveness.
There is great release in being forgiven.
But, there is even a greater freedom—
That is the freedom of forgiving. That seems to be so hard for so many of us.

We can forgive most people once, twice, maybe three times, if the sin isn't too great. But after that—forgiveness becomes terribly difficult.

Our response to requests for forgiveness are so unlike God's—

"I'll forgive you, but—"
"I'll forgive you—just give me a little time."
"I'll forgive you this time, but don't let it ever
   happen again!"
"I'll forgive you—I'm not sure I'll ever forget this,
   but I'll forgive you."

Job had just seen God—
Job had just been forgiven the sin of questioning God's providence—
Job's heart was full.
Job's anger was emptied, and

Job forgave—

    his wife
      his friends
        his relatives
          his counselors—

Job forgave them all.

And then—Job was restored. Not a moment before. "Then when Job prayed for his friends, the Lord restored his wealth and his happiness! In fact, the Lord gave him twice as much as before!"[6]

Chapter 16, Notes

1. Job 40:4 TLB   4. Job 42:8 TLB
2. Job 42:2 TLB   5. Job 42:9 TLB
3. Job 42:7 TLB   6. Job 42:10 TLB

If there is anything a sufferer needs,
it is not an explanation, but a fresh, new look at God.

Chapter 17

Job's Satisfaction

Does God really owe us an explanation for what He does? Job thought so.

Martha and I thought so when Jimmy died. The only word that seemed to fall from our lips during those bewildering days was the word, "Why?" We asked it of God, of ourselves, of each other, and we asked it of anyone who took the time to listen to us speak from our grief.

Like Mary and Martha we instinctively questioned God—not for long—but we did question God. Do you remember Martha's first words to Jesus after her brother Lazarus had died? John 11:21 records them. "Lord, if You had been here, my brother would not have died."[1] Mary said the same thing a few moments later. "Lord, if You had been here, my brother would not have died."[2]

Those stinging words of accusation, directed at the very heart of God, really didn't catch Jesus by surprise. Human reactions to any circumstance have always been predictable to God.

And yet, when those two sisters—close friends of Jesus—charged Him with gross negligence, unnecessary delay, and unexplained absence to the point of actually con-

311

tributing to the death of their brother, it must have taken
some toll on the sensitive, loving nature of the Son of God.

We all question God when tragedy strikes.

It's inbred—
  it's innate—
    it's normal—
      it's natural.

A question, in its spontaneous, unrehearsed form com-
prises a temporary tribute to God.

It says that we believe there is a God.
It says that we believe He knows.
It says that we believe He cares.
It says that we believe He controls.
It says many things that we often forget to say to
  Him or about Him in the normal course of every-
  day life.

In the temporary insanity that deep grief causes, we lash
out at everyone and everything in a vain attempt to find
answers and, if possible, to change circumstances.

Did you notice in John 11 how Jesus responded to their
words?

He made no reference to them: No rebuke, no shame, no
charge—just silence—and then He proceeded to teach them
something far more important about life and death.[3]

We even blame ourselves.

When Jimmy died, we often pointed the finger of blame
at ourselves. "If only we had prayed harder," or "if only we
had taken him to a doctor sooner," or "if," "if," "if," and yet
we were told that his death was unavoidable.

I became irritated with Jimmy's constant crying the
night before his death. I spoke sharply to him. Imagine, a
grown man rebuking a three-month old son for crying when
he hurt—nevertheless, I did it. I often look back upon that
moment with regret and guilt and shame and wish I could

recall those words. I even wonder if maybe—but no, neither of us can take the blame for the unavoidable.

We blame others—doctors, nurses, hospitals, emergency personnel, anyone who comes to mind—anyone who in any way could have contributed to our grief.

It's normal—and it passes. It only becomes a concern when that blame sinks deeper and deeper into the human spirit and resides there to take on the form of bitterness. It's then that help is needed to bring blame and bitterness into sharp focus. There are sixteen "Why's" in the book of Job.

Why was I born?[4]
Why can't I die?[5]
Why is God doing this to me?[6]
Why doesn't God forgive me?[7]

Sixteen times Job asks, "Why?"

Sixteen times he hurls this question heavenward—and never gets a response.

When God does speak, He never addresses Job's questions.

He never describes the challenge thrown down by Satan, recorded in the early chapters.

He never explains the greater contest being run in full view of the spiritual world.

He never discusses the "high stakes" that have been laid on heaven's table as God had "put His money on Job" and won. He never explains "Why."

I have long since quit seeking the answer to that question in my own life. I really don't know why God does things the way He does, and I'm not sure that I'll ever know. I have a hunch that heaven is going to be so spectacular that I'll not even want to take time out then to seek the answers to so many of life's unanswerables.

God owes me no explanation. He has the right to do what He wants, when He wants, and how He wants. *Why?* Because He's God.

It's interesting to note in Job that, in response to sixteen "Why's," there are fifty-nine "Who's" in the book.

Martha's aunt visited us shortly after Jimmy's death and listened to our "Why's" until she found an appropriate moment. Then she said, "It might help if you changed the spelling of that word. Try spelling it with an 'o' instead of a 'y'. Change the word from 'Why' to 'Who'."

That's what God does in His speech to Job.

Job didn't need to know why these things happened as they did—he just needed to know Who was responsible and Who was in control. He just needed to know God.

When he said in chapter 42, verse 2, "I know that Thou canst do all things, and that no purpose of Thine can be thwarted," he was finally changing his "Why" to "Who."

He was finally letting God be God in his life.

If there is anything that we need during any of life's baffling or bewildering experiences, it is not an explanation, but just a fresh, new look at God.

Chapter 17, Notes

1. John 11:21   5. Job 3:12 TLB
2. John 11:32   6. Job 7:20 TLB
3. John 11:25, 26   7. Job 7:21 TLB
4. Job 3:11 TLB

Bibliography

Archer, Gleason L., Jr. *The Book of Job: God's Answer to the Problem of Understanding Suffering.* Grand Rapids: Baker Book House, 1982.

Barnes, Albert. *Notes on the Old Testament: Job, vols. 1 and 2.* Grand Rapids: Baker Book House, 1949.

Cambridge Bible for Schools and Colleges. *The Book of Job.* Cambridge: University Press, New ed., 1918.

Epp, Theodore H. *Why Do Christians Suffer?* Lincoln, Neb.: Back to the Bible, 1970.

McGee, J. Vernon. *Job.* Pasadena: Thru the Bible Books, 1981.

Scammon, John H. *If I Could Find God: Anguish and Faith in the Book of Job.* Valley Forge, Pa.: Judson Press, 1974.

Stedman, Ray C. *Expository Studies in Job: Behind Suffering.* Waco, Tex.: Word Books, 1981.

Zuck, Roy B. *Job.* Chicago: Moody Press, 1978.

Acceptance

Loosing the Webs of Personal Insecurity

To Martha
My wife, who inspired
the writing of this book, and
who has accepted me.

Contents

"I am still trying to gain that complete freedom
that has eluded me for so long."

Chapter 1

The Cocoon

I received a most unusual gift the other day—small, boxed, and beautifully wrapped. I opened it with excitement, carefully removing ribbon, wrapping, and finally lifting the lid.

What was this? Some sort of joke?

The box contained a small twig of wood about six inches in length. Attached to the twig was the ugliest little "whatever" I think I have ever seen. At first glance it appeared to be the color and texture of a long-since dead mouse. I laughed—nervously—all the time realizing that my friend was not sharing my humor.

I touched it—lightly—smelled it, examined it, and finally asked, "What in the world is it?"

"Don't you know?" my friend asked. "It's something you mention often. You even use it to illustrate the Christian life. It's a *cocoon*. It's the cocoon of a beautiful, multi-colored, giant silk moth. I bought it the other day, thinking you might like to watch the transformation of something ugly into something very beautiful.

"In just a few weeks, without any noticeable outward change, the living organism in that ugly little brown cocoon will free itself and emerge into—well, you'll see."

I was intrigued. After my friend left, I placed the cocoon in a little net cage near the window and began to watch.

Weeks have passed. There has been no noticeable change—no movement of any kind. It's still brown, ugly, and apparently lifeless. And yet, inside that hideous little shell is a living thing—a small caterpillar—actively engaged in the struggling process of gaining its freedom and becoming beautiful.

While still in the larval state, that little living thing spun a web around itself—an endless web of silk and sand and dirt. Finally, when completely hidden in a prison of its own making, it then began the long, slow, painful process of gaining its freedom.

I've read of this metamorphosis, this change from imprisoned caterpillar to colorful butterfly, many times, but I've never watched it. I never realized just how ugly a cocoon could really be. I didn't know it took so long. I'd never heard just how hard that emerging creature would be forced to struggle—and without any outside help. In fact, assistance of any kind would cause it to die. Breaking free of that cocoon is something that must be done. It must be done with great pain, and it must be done all alone.

As I have daily examined my woolly little friend in its ugly brown cocoon, bound so tightly in that web, I have come to realize that I'm not only watching the emergence of a butterfly, I'm watching something far more profound and frighteningly personal. I'm actually watching humanity engaged in its constant struggle to free itself of its webs, its hang-ups, its bindings, its prisons. Webs of its own making—webs spun by others—webs that have bound so tightly and so thoroughly that the real occupant in that little house has become completely obscured to the outside world.

I'm watching myself, hidden by external wrappings, imprisoned by internal fears, bound by the trappings of society and confined by the prejudices of people and even some distorted truths of Christianity. I am still trying to gain that complete freedom that has eluded me for so long.

I am watching my own determined struggle to be free of all of the suffocating webs that still hide me from myself and from those who would wish to love me.

"It seems, at times, that life's greatest struggle
may not be that of loving, but rather that of accepting love."

Chapter 2

In Hiding

I really don't know when I went into hiding. I do know that at some time and for some reason not completely known to me, I began spinning a web—a web consisting of the strangest notions—neurotic little notions of

    inferiority
      inadequacy
        guilt
          rejection
            unworthiness
              insecurity
                tentativeness
                  ambivalence—

notions that caused me to be guarded and withdrawn, to feel unloving and unloved.

It's awfully hard for me to receive love. That admission would be difficult if I didn't believe that so many others, like myself, have the same problem. I'm one of a vast army of internally frightened and lonely people who have built an impenetrable web about themselves. This web makes it impossible for others to move in close and to love and to affirm and to assure and to accept.

At the same time, I genuinely doubt that there are many people who are more loved than I. God loves me, my family loves me, my church loves me, my friends love me, my dog loves me. Thousands of friends each year send affirming messages of love. Hardly a day goes by without a love note from someone who has been touched by my ministry.

My internal responses to such gestures of love are often baffling. Outwardly, I appear grateful, pleased, secure, and believing. Inwardly, I question motives, suspect manipulation, doubt another's integrity, or more commonly, hope that those who say they love me will never discover how truly unworthy I am of their love.

It seems at times that life's greatest struggle may not be that of loving, but rather that of accepting love. Somewhere in life I, along with others, have picked up the mistaken notion that love and acceptance are marketable commodities, to be dispensed only to purchase something felt to be of value. People who feel no worth or value within themselves could never expect to enjoy unqualified love or acceptance.

I sat with two friends recently discussing "acceptance." Both are happily married Christians, students of the Scriptures, and outwardly secure and happy. I asked them, "Do you feel accepted by God?" They both answered, "Certainly we have been accepted by God. Ephesians 1:6 says that part of the total experience of becoming a Christian means that we have been 'accepted in the beloved'" (KJV). "That's not what I asked," I said. "Do you *feel* accepted by God?" They both thought for a moment and answered, "No." One went on to say, 'I don't even feel forgiven by God—I believe I am, but I don't feel like it."

I then asked, "Do you feel accepted by your wives?" Again there was a pause, and both answered, "No, not completely."

"I don't even feel accepted by myself," one of them offered. Finally, with hesitancy, we all agreed to feeling exactly the same way.

As I walked away from that conversation, I thought to

myself, "Where did all those suffocating webs come from that make it so difficult for us to feel comfortable with ourselves? Why is it so impossible to feel comfortable with God? Why do we struggle so to feel comfortable with others?" And really, that's all acceptance is and that's all acceptance says— it's just the experience of being totally comfortable with others.

I have no difficulty explaining those feelings of discomfort in the lives of those who have never experienced the love and forgiveness of God. My problem is that so many of my Christian friends, including myself, seem to still be imprisoned in that stifling little cocoon, living only partial lives and longing for that elusive freedom that seems so distant—so impossible.

"My difficulty in accepting myself has made it extremely hard to accept others."

Chapter 3

Spinning the Webs

I have always had difficulty accepting myself.

I think I must have begun spinning my own web when I first began hearing ugly statements about myself—statements that were meant to be harmless, yet have remained ingrained in my memory. Statements like:

"You sure do have a big nose."

"You're so fat I can't even see your collar."

"Your legs are awfully short."

"Why are your hands so stubby?"

"You have more freckles than anyone I've ever seen."

"Did you know you have a slight lisp?"

"Boy, you've got a lot of moles on your back."

"You're so barrel-chested you should wear a bra."

"Why do you hold your mouth like that?"

"Can't you find clothes that fit you?"

"I wish you weren't so sensitive."

"Man, you're stupid."

"And you call yourself a Christian?"

None of these many statements was designed to be destructive, and had I been less sensitive, none of them would probably have even been remembered. But they were spoken, and I am sensitive, and they are remembered. When I combine them with the many other negative comments I have picked up through the years, they seem to paint a picture of an ugly self that wants to go into permanent hiding.

Now, please don't misunderstand me—not all the things that have been said to me or about me are negative. I suppose for each negative comment I have received, I've heard a thousand heart-warming, gracious, generous, loving compliments.

For some strange reason, though, my memory seems to be warped in the direction of the negative—it dwells on the negative—it remembers the negative—it believes the negative, and as it does, it sees an image of self that is negative and totally unacceptable.

When I first began hearing God describe me in the Scriptures, again all I heard was the negative. He said:

> I am filled with all
>   unrighteousness,
>   wickedness,
>   greed, and
>   malice,
> I am full of
>   envy,
>   murder,
>   strife, and
>   deceit,
> I am a gossip,
>   a slanderer.
> I hate God.
> I am insolent,
>   arrogant,
>   boastful.
> I actually invent evil.
> I am disobedient to my parents.
> I am without understanding,
>   untrustworthy,
>   unloving, and
>   unmerciful.

And not only am I guilty of such things, I actually encourage others to do the same.[1]

A biblical passage like that is anything but complimentary. It certainly did very little for my self-image except to cause me to start spinning webs—fast. If that's the real me—I wasn't quite sure how God found it out—I was determined that it must be hid at all costs.

There was nothing in that list of characteristics that was acceptable to me or to anyone else.

How could I accept myself—be comfortable with myself—if that was the real me?

I have not only had difficulty accepting myself, I have also had a problem accepting God, and even greater problems feeling accepted by him.

My first impressions of God were those of some sort of cosmic judge, just waiting to bang down the gavel of his cosmic justice whenever my performance failed to measure up to his heavenly standards.

Like most Christians my age, and even younger, I was weaned on little songs like:

> Be careful, little eyes, what you see,
> Be careful, little eyes, what you see,
> For the Father up above
> Is looking down in love, so
> Be careful, little eyes, what you see.

Again, what could have been a very positive, reassuring message of hope—a graphic word-picture set to music that described an ever-present, watchful, attendant, loving God—spoke just the opposite to me.

The little song spoke warnings, not only to my eyes but also to my lips, my ears, my hands, even my feet, until God took on the appearance of some sort of "Big Brother" in the sky, spying on my every move, just waiting to pounce on me whenever I did or said something that displeased him.

I can remember, years after I had received Christ, sitting in church through long, intense, persuasive invitations to "sinners to come to Christ," feeling that the preacher was talking directly to me.

Why couldn't I feel the love and forgiveness of God even though I had already accepted it?

I was afraid of God. I tried to hide from him—knowing all the time it was impossible, but nevertheless trying anyway.

> God's promises seemed to always have impossible strings attached.
> God's invitations seemed always to be selective and exclude me.
> God's love seemed always to be conditional, and I never quite measured up.
> God's presence seemed always to be elusive, unattainable and beyond reach.

Was my early theological training unbalanced?

Words like *grace*, *love*, *forgiveness*, and *acceptance* were either seldom mentioned or I failed to hear them.

But words like *law*, *fear*, *shame*, and *rejection* . . . those were the terms that sifted through my hearing into my uneasy heart.

It seems that most of my early training consisted of "Thou shalt not's." I felt imprisoned by a system ingeniously designed to create constant feelings of fear and bondage.

I can remember at age nine standing by the front door of my church one Sunday morning, waiting until everyone had finally shaken my pastor's hand and then walking over to him and fearfully asking his permission to go roller-skating. Permission was denied.

A friend of mine went swimming one Sunday—dived into shallow water and fractured his neck. My first reaction was, "He should have known better than to go swimming on Sunday."

My father repaired a broken padlock one Sunday following church. The family later went for a drive. Upon returning home we were involved in an accident. Dad's first words were, "I knew I shouldn't have worked on that lock today."

Whenever I spent any time reflecting on myself, all I could see was an overweight, stoop-shouldered, freckled-faced kid whose mind always wanted to drift off into a world of happy, exciting, adventurous fantasy because the real world and the real me always looked and felt so grim.

The fact that my body, with its blemishes and imperfections, was never counterbalanced with the dynamic and freeing truth that God made me just as I am and had a divine reason for shaping every part of my being just as he did, was never brought to my attention.

I remember the first time I realized just how much divine involvement there had been in the process of my birth. I read Psalm 139:13-16 over and over again. I searched its every meaning in the various translations that were available. And something wonderful happened. At that very moment I stopped praying for someone to invent Porcelana and began thanking God for every single freckle on my body.

The fact that I was totally depraved, unrighteous and unholy, was never counterbalanced with the awesome truth that I was fearfully and wonderfully made, in the very image of Almighty God, presently as precious to God as his own dear Son and ultimately destined to be just like Jesus.

People never told me how truly wonderful I really was in God's eyes—or if they did, the contrary voices were so loud I couldn't hear them.

At age twelve, I was unexpectedly called into the principal's office. I was terrified. I was certain that doomsday had arrived. I didn't know why, but then who needed a reason?

Miss Plank was the most frightening principal I can recall. She was short, grossly fat, and was never known to smile. I never saw her without a heavy twelve-inch ruler in her hand and often heard the heavy "smack" as that piece of wood landed on unsuspecting flesh.

I crept into her office, crouched down on the bench in front of her desk, and looked at that forbidding creature as she continued to pore over the papers on her desk.

After what seemed to be an interminable period of time,

she looked up, trained her eyes on me, looked deep into my naked soul, and said, "Donald Baker?"

I heard a squeaky "Yes, Miss Plank," in response.

"I was just looking over your records," she said in a deep and threatening voice, "and I noticed that today is your birthday. Today is my birthday, too," she said, "and I thought it would be nice if we could just wish each other a 'Happy Birthday!'"

With that she lumbered from behind her desk, enveloped me with her mammoth arms, and then pushed me out her door to go back to class.

Why was I so frightened?

Why was I so stunned?

Why do tears come to my eyes even now when I recall that memorable moment?

Who is the culprit responsible for making me feel so uncomfortable with myself and so clumsy around others?

Could it be that someone neglected to tell me the whole truth—or was it that my mind was just unable to comprehend it?

Half-truths, untruths, or subtle innuendos, whispered from without and within, made me feel not only uncomfortable with myself, but uncomfortable with my God.

To accept myself as I truly am and to accept my heavenly Father as he truly is and then to *feel* accepted by myself and to *feel* accepted by my Father has come with difficulty—and oftentimes with great pain.

My reluctance to accept myself has made accepting others an uphill struggle. David Seamands has said, "Some of the most powerful weapons in Satan's arsenal are psychological," and, "The most powerful psychological weapon that Satan uses against us is low self-esteem."[2]

This low self-esteem, or inability to feel comfortable with myself, makes me uncomfortable with others. My cocoon not only isolates me, but it also distorts the images of others until I begin seeing them in the same way I view myself.

Some of the hardest people to live with in all the world

are the people who don't like themselves. No one knows this better than I. I have worked with people most of my life. Much of this time was spent while struggling with a strong dislike for myself. Someone asked me once, "Why are you so angry?" I never was able to tell him until I later realized that my anger was self-directed. I was angry because I could not be what I wanted to be or feel toward myself as I wanted to feel. I didn't like myself—I didn't accept myself—I was terribly uncomfortable with *me*. Too often this anger erupted and spilled over on unsuspecting victims such as wife or children or friends who never fully understood the cause of my wrath.

I have viewed others as hostile, frightening, suspicious, or deceitful. I have viewed their differences as threatening. I often developed an authoritarian and rigid stance toward many, simply as a defense mechanism that allowed me to feel freedom from questions or complaints. At times my pulpit was regarded as the impenetrable wall from which I could fire my verbal volleys with impunity. No one dared argue publicly with the preacher.

My view of myself colored my view of others, and the worst accusation I could think of—but never stated—was that another person was just as phony and evil as I.

I must admit to bigotry, to intolerance, even to chauvinism, not because I was trained in such thinking, but because my inability to accept myself made it impossible to accept others.

Someone has said the kingdom of God is a kingdom of right relationships. Christ came to make things right, not only between ourselves, but within ourselves.

An inability to accept myself made it impossible to feel comfortable with others—and the word *others* includes all the "others" who inhabit my total world. That includes God. That includes individuals. That includes a whole world that is at times outright hostile toward me.

To feel comfortable in and with this world has also posed some real problems for me. I am told not to love the world, yet God did. I am told not to be like it, yet not to withdraw from it. I am told not to seek its acclaim, yet to seek its approval. I am expected to experience its hatred, yet never to run away or retaliate.

Right relationships include all of the above—the ability to feel comfortable with myself, comfortable with my God, comfortable with others, and even comfortable with this world in which I live.

That's the meaning of the word "acceptance"—to feel comfortable with another. It's somewhat like the emerging life of a beautiful and gigantic silk-moth that has painfully freed itself from its isolation, to fly with freedom and to light gracefully with admired beauty wherever it wishes to go. It moves from one sphere of its world to another with beauty and with grace and with ease—to be admired by all.

But, you may ask, who could ever live a life like that?

Chapter 3, Notes

1. Romans 1:29-32

2. David A. Seamands, *Healing for Damaged Emotions* (Wheaton, Ill.: Victor Books, 1981), pp. 48–49.

"Jesus was the most perfect and intriguing example of psychological balance that ever lived."

Chapter 4

The Model

*J*ESUS DID!

Jesus was the most perfect and intriguing example of psychological balance that ever lived. Whenever I read the gospels, I never cease to be impressed with his complete comfort with himself and others—never a hint of feeling threatened internally or externally.

One of the greater miracles in the earthly life of the God-man—a miracle seldom, if ever, mentioned—was the unbelievable manner in which he adapted to his new environment.

Jesus was a good candidate for a mammoth culture shock. No one has crossed cultures as he did. Coming from heaven to earth was the farthest distance physically, socially, spiritually, and psychologically that anyone could ever travel. The contrasts were unimaginable, and yet he accepted his displacement, along with his new and vastly different role, with incredible ease.

Jesus was demoted as no other being in all of history. He was lowered in rank, forced to give up his prestigious position, relinquish his wealth, change his name, even limit his energies. Yet he always appeared to be at peace with himself, his Father, his people, and even with a frighteningly hostile world.

If there was ever one who had reason to go into hiding, if there was ever an individual who could have felt justified in spinning an endless web about himself, it was Jesus. He had good reason to display all those neurotic little notions I have often struggled with, and yet there was never a moment that he even suggested a hint of such feelings.

He came as a servant, yet never displayed inferiority.

He limited his own powers, yet never suggested inadequacy.

He was sent down from heaven, yet never complained of rejection.

He disrobed himself of all his majesty, yet never appeared unworthy.

He owned no property and possessed no home, yet never complained of feeling insecure.

His days, from the very beginning, were numbered, yet he never felt tentative.

He placed himself completely at the mercy of man, yet knew every moment exactly what was happening.

He possessed infinite wisdom, yet was able to be completely comfortable chatting with the world's most ignorant.

He was supremely holy, yet he could comfortably sit with the world's great sinners.

He was Jewish, yet he had no difficulty crossing racial barriers to talk with a Samaritan.

He was a man, yet he was comfortable any time and at all times with God.

He was the world's Savior, yet he could move with ease even in the presence of hostile threats of murder.

Jesus accepted himself. He knew who he was and why he was here. He could accept compliments or insults without clumsy responses.

On the occasion of his baptism, his Father made a dramatic, if not somewhat embarrassing public announcement about his Son. He spoke from the heavens for all to hear that Jesus was very special to him. "Beloved" was the word he used. He even stated that his was the perfect Son and that he was truly delighted in him. That sort of parental exclamation of pride is often met with embarrassment. And yet Jesus let his Father brag about him without blushing or even responding. He knew the truth about himself, accepted it, and was totally comfortable with the facts as they stood.

Whenever he was accused of evil, even the worst of all sins, blasphemy, he met the challenge with a simple request: "Prove it. Search as hard and long as you like," he would say, "but prove it."

He even stated that Satan could find no fault in him.

Jesus never went into hiding. He never spun a web around himself or withdrew into his cocoon. His was a totally transparent life.

When asked where he lived, he gave no evasive answer. He didn't even hand out business cards with a printed address. He said simply, "Come and see." Nothing to hide, nothing to fear.

When our daughter, Kathy, was small, the first place she would always take her friends would be her bedroom. That bedroom was not only where she slept, it was a representation of herself. The most intimate declarations she could make about her person were in that one little room. All of her interests, likes, and dislikes were on display for anyone who was interested to see. That act was always the ultimate in childlike transparency.

Jesus did the same. "Come and see," he said. He didn't even run ahead to tidy things up.

For three and a half years he peeled off layer after layer of divine mystery and exposed his being to any who really wished to know him.

He hid nothing.
He knew himself.
He accepted himself.
Jesus was totally comfortable with himself.

He was also comfortable with God.

He could speak of him in the most lofty terms with
total knowledge.
He could also speak of him in the most intimate
language with absolute comfort.
He had no fear of God.
He experienced no separation from God.
He could spontaneously pray in public without any
exaggerated preparations.
He could move into seclusion and begin talking to
his Father with no feelings of guilt or requests for
forgiveness.
He knew his Father always heard him.
He fully expected his Father to give him whatever
he requested.
He understood his Father's heart.
He knew his Father's purpose.
He recognized his Father's wisdom.
He trusted his Father's power.
He expected his Father's full approval.
He looked forward to his Father's presence.
He even knew, and declared publicly, the fact that
there was an extraordinary and quite intimate
union between himself and his Father.
Jesus was totally comfortable with God.

Jesus was comfortable with people.

He accepted people.
He accepted them right where they were and for
what they were.
He knew why he was with them.
He knew their need of him.

He even knew why they did what they did.
He was equally at home with—
a scoundrel like Zacchaeus,
a tyrant like Pilate,
an adultress in Samaria,
a worshiper like Mary,
a religious leader like Nicodemus,
a fisherman like Peter,
a turncoat like Judas,
a Roman soldier, or even
a Jewish high priest.
He could listen to the charges of his worst enemies.
He could even accept the accusations of his dearest
friends.
When Mary and Martha blamed him for their
brother's death, he responded without a hint of
defensiveness.
He could accept the rebuke of Peter without rejection.
He could receive the doubts of Thomas without
feeling threatened.
He could mingle with all classes, all ages, and all races.
Jesus was totally comfortable with people.

Jesus was comfortable even with a hostile world.

He accepted those who rejected him.
He knew who was responsible for their hostility.
He knew the source of their unholy energies.
He knew why they hated him.
He met their accusations with silence.
He ignored their taunts.
He could rebuke Satan with authority.
He could cast out demons with power.
He could identify hypocrisy.
He could walk away from repeated threats on his life.
He could walk right into his most horrible hour
without hesitation. His confident stride carried
him toward, not away from, a cruel death.

He allowed men to flog him in silence.
He permitted them to beat him without response.
He let them place him on a cross.
He willingly permitted them to kill him.
He even allowed them to lay the "Light of the
World" in the total darkness of the tomb—and
through it all he asked but one thing—that they
be forgiven.
Jesus accepted even those who hated him.
Jesus was comfortable with a hostile world.

Jesus displayed acceptance and enjoyed acceptance. He
was totally comfortable in what was potentially history's
most uncomfortable position.

I have often looked at the life of my Lord with not only
spiritual, mental, and physical admiration, but with psychological admiration as well.

His life of balanced relationships—
His characteristic transparency—
His genuineness—
His ease with people—
His peace with himself—
What a model to emulate.
What a life to copy.
What an example to cherish and seek after.
Could I ever experience that sort of freedom?
Could I ever display that degree of acceptance?
Could I ever be that spiritually beautiful?

"I wanted to be so genuine that I could
feel absolute and total comfort with myself,
with God, and with others.
I wanted to be REAL."

Chapter 5

"I Want to Be REAL"

I first started taking a long, hard look at myself when I was stuck in a deep, black hole of depression. From that position everything about myself was obscured, blurred, or completely invisible. Nothing looked good. Nothing looked real.

All of my neurotic little notions were magnified. They all appeared so big, so overpowering, that I was finding life with this ugly self becoming intolerable. I liked nothing about me and of course felt that everyone else shared the same opinion.

At about this time, a new message began coming from pulpits across the land. It was foreign; it was also suspect. The message was telling me to love myself.

At first it sounded good—especially to a person so engulfed by self-hate as I was. Yet I remember filtering that little four-letter word, self, through my mental concordance every time I had the opportunity. I had often taught that the flesh was nothing more than self spelled backwards with an added letter for emphasis, and that flesh, when used of man in his non-spiritual state, was an ugly word.

I began reading all I could find on the subject of self: Huxley, Niebuhr, Oppenheimer, John Dewey, Skinner, Maslow, Jourard, Jung, and of course Carl Rogers.

The whole theory of Carl Rogers is based on the need for self-acceptance. Rogers teaches that man's basic challenge is to understand himself and to accept himself. He states emphatically that no one can understand and accept himself until another has first understood him and accepted him as he is. Once we are understood and accepted by another, Rogers states, most of the neurotic little notions that bind us can be discarded and we can be comfortable with ourselves.

I became intrigued with all the ego defense mechanisms employed to protect myself from the frightening monsters of anxiety and guilt and inferiority. It seemed that Carl Rogers was talking about me.

As I read Rogers I agreed with him. I did not trust or accept myself to even be myself—that it was impossible for me to be what he calls "real" because I refused to allow myself the privilege of even owning my own feelings.

I was especially impressed with his many statements that suggest that no one can grow until he first accepts himself as he is.

Abraham Maslow states similarly that a lack of self-acceptance hinders growth, blocks knowledge, and stifles maturity.

It began to make sense to me that my obsession with self was a self-limiting problem. I spent so much time concentrating on thoughts of self that growth was impossible.

But "self-love" continued to bother me. Paul's letter to Timothy[1] describes self-love as one of the negative characteristics of man in the last days.

How could self-love be a spiritual goal when at the same time it is described as such an evil characteristic?

As I continued to pursue my own problem, the church's bookshelves began to fill up with books on self-image—self-esteem—self-acceptance—and even self-love. It soon became listed as humanity's number one need.

Dr. Nathaniel Branden, in his book, *The Psychology of Self-Esteem*, underscores its significance by stating that the desire for self-esteem is an urgent imperative. He insists that it is the single most significant key to a person's behavior.[2]

Dr. Robert Schuller, senior pastor of Garden Grove Community Church in Southern California, proposed the idea that the desire to achieve self-esteem is man's "ultimate will" and that what we want more than anything else in all the world is the awareness that we are worthy persons. He says, "Man is a primate driven by a hunger for self-esteem." He argues that "God made the human being to be great, glorious and proud."[3]

But did he? I wanted to understand myself, know myself, and ultimately be comfortable with myself, but the project still seemed to either be blown out of proportion or misdirected. And wasn't there more? Is it only self that needs acceptance? I seemed to be rejecting others nearly as much as myself. Where did they enter this complex picture?

It was during one of these bewildering times that Martha gave me a little book entitled, *The Velveteen Rabbit.*[4] Many have read this intriguing children's story—a fairy tale with all sorts of adult implications. I hadn't—I had not even heard of this delightful little book.

I looked for a long time at the illustrated cover—a cover that displayed the picture of a rabbit—a stuffed rabbit that was tattered and frayed—worn and torn from what appeared to be years of playful loving from an adoring child.

I opened the book with interest. Fairy tales were really not my style, and yet each word seemed to jump from the page with increasing fascination. I realized that somehow a stranger by the name of Margery Williams seemed to be writing a story about me.

The Rabbit with its velveteen covering had been a Christmas gift to a boy who had long since stopped playing with it. It was shy, inferior, and neglected in favor of the more superior and expensive toys that belonged to its owner. It could not claim any uniqueness and felt itself quite out-of-date. It was constantly plagued with feelings of insignificance and loneliness. Its only friend was Skin Horse, grown old and bald from years of constant attention. Skin Horse was considered wisest of all the toys in the nursery.

One day as the Velveteen Rabbit was examining its skin of cloth and insides of sawdust and feeling very sorry for itself, it found itself lying near enough to Skin Horse to ask a question. "What is REAL? Does it mean having things that buzz inside you and a stick-out handle?"

I was stunned as I read that paragraph. From within the covers of a little child's fairy tale, a sawdust-stuffed rabbit had asked a question that to me was *the* question. The question whose time had come. The question that seemed to sum up all of the baffling and bewildering struggles that I had been internalizing for so long. When that make-believe rabbit in that children's fairy tale asked, "What is REAL?" this grown man suddenly felt large, moist tears coursing their way down his cheeks and spattering those clean white pages.

Skin Horse responded that REAL isn't how you are made—it's something that happens to you. It's something that happens when someone loves you for a long, long time—really loves you. It's something that happens slowly and sometimes painfully. It's something that seldom happens to fragile, insensitive people—it's something one becomes, but not before many years of constant use have taken place. Usually REAL doesn't happen until most of your hair has been loved off and your eyes have dropped out. By then, however, it really doesn't matter how you look—for when you are REAL you can't be ugly, except to people who don't understand.

Skin Horse proceeded to tell Velveteen Rabbit how years of loving had made him REAL and concluded by saying "Once you're REAL you can't become unreal again. It lasts for always."

I read on, my attention riveted to the words before me, stopping only to wipe away the tears that would repeatedly blur the words.

Finally the day came, years later, when Velveteen Rabbit heard his owner say those truly magic words. It came after many long nights of sleeping on Boy's arm. Nights when Boy would snuggle close and talk to him through the long moonlight hours. It came long after his fur had become shabby and his tail unsewn and after all the pink had rubbed off his nose. It came after long days in the garden and rides in the wheelbarrow and picnics on the grass. It came at a most unexpected moment when Nana reached down into the bed one night to grab away the little rabbit, wet and dirty from the long day outside.

Boy resisted and Nana, after wiping the Rabbit off with a corner of her apron said, "Fancy all that fuss for a toy!" Boy sat up and reached for Velveteen Rabbit and said, "Give me my bunny! You mustn't say that. He isn't a toy. He's REAL."

That was all I could take. I stopped reading, closed the book, and began to sob. I felt foolish. Imagine a grown man crying over a child's fairy tale—and yet it was, at that moment, far more than a fairy tale. It was a statement—profound, clear, and powerful. A statement that I had been trying for years to make. A statement that I couldn't even wrap the right words around. It was saying what I wanted to be—what I wanted to feel. I wanted to be REAL. Real without fear of disclosure. I wanted to be so genuine that I could feel absolute and total comfort with myself, with God, and with others. I wanted to be REAL.

I sobbed through the night. Who could have known—who would have guessed that a little child's book, given by my wife, might be used to point straight to the heart of my problem. That little book put into clear, discernable language what it was that I was truly longing to experience. I just wanted to be REAL. That was all.

As I continued to look at the cover of that little children's book, question after question began to pour out of my perplexed soul.

Does being REAL have anything to do with feeling accepted?

Is genuineness a part of feeling totally comfortable with myself, God, and others?

How does it happen?
How long does it take?
Is it really as painful as Skin Horse says?
Is love really the all-important key that unlocks the
    door to my ugly brown prison house?
Is it love that frees me of my cocoon?
If so, whose love? What kind of love?
Where is a love to be found that could ever be that
    freeing?

Chapter 5, Notes

1. 2 Timothy 3:2.

2. Nathaniel Branden, *The Psychology of Self-Esteem* (New York: Bantam Books, 1971), p. 110.

3. Robert H. Schuller, "The Theology of Self-Esteem," *The Saturday Evening Post*, May–June 1980, p. 44.

4. Margery Williams, *The Velveteen Rabbit, or How Toys Become Real* (New York: Doubleday, n.d.).

"It seems that the whole world
is sharing my cocoon with me—
that we're all feeling
the same way about ourselves."

Chapter 6

"Why Do I Feel Inferior?"

*H*ow does one really get to know and understand and accept himself? How does one move from his threatening world of "phony" to the wonderful world of "real"?

Is self-acceptance as important as Carl Jung suggests when he says,

> Accepting of oneself is the essence of the moral problem and the acid test of one's whole outlook on life. That I feed the beggar, that I forgive an insult, that I love my enemy in the name of Christ—all of these are undoubtedly great virtues . . . but what if I should discover that the least among them all, the poorest of all the beggars, the most impudent of all the offenders, yes, the very fiend, himself—that these are in me, and I myself stand in need of the alms of my own kindness, that I, myself, am the enemy who must be loved—what then?[1]

As I continued to read, most psychologists were telling me that man is an enigma to himself—that he lacks the means of comparison for self-knowledge. He can distin-

357

guish himself from other animals but is completely lacking in criteria for self-judgment.

Most were saying that if I really wanted to understand myself, I must find someone who will listen to me, not judge me, but love me in spite of what I tell him. I must verbalize my thoughts, my feelings, my fears, and anxieties to someone I can completely trust.

Dr. Paul Tournier, Swiss psychiatrist and author, says,

> How beautiful, how grand and liberating the experience is when people learn to help each other. It is impossible to overemphasize the need humans have to be really listened to, to be taken seriously, to be understood. . . . No one can develop freely in this world and find a full life without feeling understood by at least one person. . . . He who would see himself clearly must open up to a confidant freely chosen and worthy of such trust.[2]

Rogers and Jourard were telling me the same thing—find a friend whom you can really trust and tell him everything.

I did.

It happened during the time of my deep depression. Dr. Emery Nester, psychologist and long-time friend, offered to listen, and I was finally willing to talk.

Self-disclosure came terribly hard at first. I had suppressed feelings, thoughts, and ideas for so long that to dredge them up and force them to the surface was not only difficult but downright painful.

I called these long hours "my trip to the womb." The process was more one of self-disclosure than psychoanalysis. Emery was very careful, in true Rogerian style, to make no value judgments, draw no conclusions, and offer no criticism. He just listened. Occasionally he would probe with an appropriate question or he would offer a brief but relevant comment, but mostly he just listened.

For the first time in my life, I was hearing myself as I

wrapped intelligible words around unintelligible thoughts and feelings.

I talked about my feelings of anxiety. I learned to describe just how they felt, when they were strongest, how they affected me. We then explored possible reasons for their existence.

An overwhelming sense of inadequacy consumed much of our conversation time together. It was a mystery to both of us how one who had experienced such success in life could continue to feel so inadequate.

We explored feelings of guilt. We found that while there was just cause for some, most of those feelings came from an inability to fully accept forgiveness.

Hostility was a big subject. How can one who professes love feel so hostile? We explored the frustrations and bitternesses that had accumulated through the years into such a large pile of unacceptable disappointments that they finally overpowered my feelings of love with outbursts of unrestrained anger.

I was anxious to know why the cocoon? Why was I so obsessed with the need for a covering to completely hide me from what I felt were the prying eyes of humanity?

Why did I feel so inferior? Was it inherent or acquired? Was it real or imagined? How did it display itself? When was it most evident? When was it least evident? When was it no problem at all?

What was the cause for such low feelings of self-worth? Who had told me directly or implied that I was of such little value? Martha had never implied this. My parents had never suggested it. No one in all my recollections had seriously promoted the idea. Where had such a notion originated?

"Decision-making comes so hard for me," I told Emery. I described how I would vacillate from one position to another, jump from one conclusion to another. I seemed to change my mind too often and for no apparent reason.

Where do the feelings of insecurity come from? I am loved, and yet feel that I could lose that love at any moment. I am respected, but fear that it is only temporary. I am trusted, but fear exposure. Why do I feel that my world is so tentative and my relationships so fragile? Why do I feel that life is one frightful balancing act on a tightrope with the constant, nagging fear of falling always haunting me?

Why do I feel so unloved? I don't know anyone who is more loved than I, and yet it's so difficult for me to feel loved—to enjoy love—to relax in the presence of love.

We explored these questions and more—in depth and in complete confidence—for more than a hundred hours. I talked and Emery listened, usually for no longer than an hour or two at a time. As I reached further and further back in time and deeper and deeper into that deep pile of suppressed feelings, some remarkable things happened.

I learned first of all that many of my feelings and thoughts and fears were quite common to all. I was not the only person confined to a cocoon. Many people spin webs. As a matter of fact, most of us hide in the very same cocoon, so absorbed with ourselves that we don't even notice each other.

I remember being deeply impressed with a fellow-member of a group therapy session during my stay in the Veterans Hospital. Bob was one of the most "all-together" people I had ever met. He was always impeccably dressed, poised, and confident. His deep, resonant voice sounded so magnificent—especially compared with what I felt was my own squeaky, high pitched vocal quality. He was successful in business, liked by others. When he spoke, everyone listened. When I spoke, it seemed that suddenly the whole world lost interest. He was tall and handsome. Alongside him I felt squat and ugly. I *felt* genuinely and totally inferior to him.

Following an extensive group therapy session one day, I finally summoned up all the courage I could muster, turned to Bob, and said, "Bob, how do I come through to you?" He looked down at me and asked in his authoritative and resonant voice, "What do you mean, how do you come through to me?" I stammered for a moment, rephrased my question and asked again, "Bob, what do you think of me? How do I appear to you? What kind of person do you think I am?"

Bob stopped, looking intently at me for a long time before answering. As he was framing just the right words, I noticed his eyes becoming moist, and finally, in a halting and hesitant manner, he said, "Don, I would give anything to be like you. I don't think I have ever met a man who has got it all together more than you. If ever I would pick a model after whom to pattern my life, you'd be the man."

I was stunned—speechless—bewildered. I suddenly saw beyond myself just long enough to realize that I was not all alone in my cocoon after all. I had company. There was one other person in this world who was struggling with the same feelings of inferiority as I—and he had been willing to admit it!

That one experience of awareness was freeing to me, and as I have opened my eyes even wider in the darkness of my little hiding place, I have become aware of other forms and figures crouched in their little corners, fearful of discovery. In fact, now it seems that the whole world is sharing my cocoon with me—that we're all feeling the same way about ourselves.

I learned something else. I learned that many of my fears were imagined. I have a vivid imagination and an alarming tendency to play mind reader. Often when I'm trying to determine what another person is thinking, I drift about as far away from reality as possible. I ascribe thoughts and motives to others that have no basis in fact whatever.

I am also sensitive. Sensitivity is one of the most important tools in my trade. I use it constantly. I am always looking for hidden signs of pain—seeking for subtle indications of hurts. I listen intently for words or innuendos that will unexpectedly expose another's hidden wounds so that I can move in close to become the healer.

All too often, however, this sensitivity backfires on me, and *I* become the wounded. Grasping a misspoken word or a subtle look, I interpret it as a clever little dart thrown in my direction and designed to inflict pain on me, when that was not intended at all.

Even after all the helpful counseling sessions, though, I was finally forced to admit that this still wasn't enough.

The project had just begun.

I had learned that most of my prison was of my own making. Some of it was even an illusion.

I had learned that I was not the only prisoner. That was comforting, but didn't really set me free.

I had begun to spot some of the webs that bound me and found that some could even be loosened. Still others, however, held me tight.

I needed more than someone to listen to me.

I needed an authoritative, totally trustworthy voice to tell me what was really true about myself—a voice that was clear, concise, honest, and directive.

> If reality is so important—
> If genuineness is so vital—
> If acceptance is so necessary in order to experience a feeling of total comfort with myself, my God, my friends, and even my enemies—
> If this experience is as critical as everyone suggests—

then it *has* to be important to God. And if it's important to God, it must be discussed concisely somewhere in the great depository of Truth—the Scriptures.

Chapter 6, Notes

1. Carl Jung, quoted in Cecil Osborne, *The Art of Understanding Yourself* (Grand Rapids: Zondervan Books, 1967), p. 28.

2. Paul Tournier, quoted in John Powell, *why am i afraid to tell you who i am?* (Allen, Tex.: Argus Communications, 1969), p. 5.

"I was amazed when I first realized just how psychologically precise the Bible really is."

Chapter 7

The Way Out

I came upon the solution quite by accident. I was doing an extensive study on the subject of church growth in Ephesians, when I became intrigued with one paragraph—three verses that for some strange reason I had failed to fully comprehend.

I was surprised to find four words, long overlooked, that when fully understood became the answer to my life's most baffling questions: How can I experience acceptance? How can I feel accepted? How can I be comfortable with myself, God, and others?

Four words provided me with the secret to right relationships—the means by which I could experience total comfort with others—the key to acceptance. Four simple but strategic words, tucked away in one of the Bible's most important chapters, actually described the way out of my cocoon. Those four words pointed me to the single, almost invisible thread that began the long, slow, unraveling process ultimately designed to free me.

The four words provide the explanation for Jesus' totally integrated personality. They are relational terms, spiritual words, and psychological expressions. To the degree that I understand and employ these important concepts, I am able to enjoy the same delightful balance experienced by my Lord.

The problem with these words is that they are what I call "ho-hum" terms: words that are used so often, practiced so seldom, and defined with such vagueness that we're tired of trying to merely understand them—let alone practice them.

Each word, in itself, provides a gold mine of psychological and spiritual insight. Each word is loaded with the sort of verbal dynamic needed to release me from my bondage. Each word relates to the subject of acceptance. When understood and practiced, these words allow for the elusive privilege of being totally comfortable with myself and with others.

These words speak to the disabling problems of low self-esteem, hostility, fear, and rejection—those numbing warps in my personality that make comfortable relationships so difficult.

I was amazed when I first realized just how psychologically precise the Bible really is. The Bible not only describes and defines all those neurotic little notions I spoke of earlier, it also tells where they come from, how they are cultivated, why they continue to exist, and what is required to be relieved of them.

The four words are found in the Book of Ephesians, chapter 4, verse 2. They are a vital part of one of the most important passages on human relationship in Scripture. They describe the relational attitudes that were characteristic of Jesus Christ and are then expressed as the relational attitudes to be displayed by each believer. They are basic to spiritual unity and necessary to make any company of believers irresistibly attractive to the world.

The four life-changing words are—believe it or not—

Humility
Gentleness
Longsuffering
Forbearance

The entire passage reads:

I, therefore, the prisoner of the Lord, entreat you to walk [or live] in a manner worthy of the calling with which you have been called [or worthy of the name Christian],

with all *humility* and *gentleness*, with *patience*, showing *forbearance* to one another in love,

being diligent to preserve the unity of the Spirit in the bond of peace.   Ephesians 4:1-3

Verse 1 states that these four terms characterized the life of Christ.

Verse 2 exhorts us to employ them in our own lives.

Verse 3 makes them indispensable to the experience of spiritual unity or oneness—the experience of feeling totally and wonderfully comfortable with ourselves and others.

These four crucial words, located at the fountainhead of Scripture's most illuminating passage on church growth, describe four relational foundation stones. They are essential to the construction of a company of believers who are comfortable with each other and profoundly attractive to a lonely, withdrawn, isolated, imprisoned population—a population that craves the companionship available in the Christian community.

Do you realize that a company of believers potentially provides the only place on earth where a man can be truly at peace with himself and with others? When this peace is being experienced, it makes the church an irresistible attraction to the outside world.

This peace, this oneness, is dependent upon a full and complete understanding and application of the meaning of only four words. Words that tell us how to be totally comfortable with God, totally comfortable with a hostile world, and totally comfortable with ourselves. Fully accepted and fully acceptable.

The word *humility* or lowliness of mind *addresses the*

problem of low self-esteem and enables me to know myself and accept myself as I really am.

The word *gentleness* or meekness *addresses the problem of hostility, inner rage, floating anger*—those bewildering, negative feelings that lash out at others, oftentimes for no apparent reason.

The word *long-suffering speaks to the fears* that come from living in the midst of a hostile world—a world that is committed to the elimination of the church.

The word *forbearance speaks to the problems of factions, of bigotry and bias, intolerance, impatience, and discrimination.*

In other words, these four life-changing words are basic to our understanding of how to get along with people!

Christianity, remember, is an experience of right relationships. Self-acceptance, self-esteem, is not my only problem. I must learn how to relate not only to myself, but also to God, to others, and to the world about me. These words tell me just how that's done, and they tell it in that order.

Whenever we begin talking about relationships, the strategy of Satan and the strategy of God are immediately brought into sharp focus.

Satan's strategy has always been to divide—to separate—to alienate. Satan is the author of loneliness since his plan has always been a plan of estrangement. He's the one, I'm sure, who coined the phrase, "irreconcilable differences." He invented the word "incompatible." His goal has always been that of division.

He separated himself from God.
He separated the angels from God.
He separated man from God.
He separated man from woman.
He separated nation from nation.
He separated earth from heaven.

He knows how to drive sharp and penetrating wedges between people. That's his program, and he's been uniquely successful.

I sat in the living room of a couple married nearly thirty years and watched and listened as they spat their venom at each other. Their young teenage son sat, white and silent, in a distant corner. Finally in exasperation, the wife said to her husband, "Do you know, John, what I wish you'd do? I wish you'd take your gun, put it to your head, pull the trigger, and kill yourself—only please do it in the garage, so I don't have to clean up the mess."

I've been a member in a local church meeting where a state police officer was called to keep the peace.

The story is told of a small church that wanted to buy an organ. The only problem was that there were those who wanted it and those who didn't. They argued long and bitterly over the purchase. Finally it was bought. They then argued over where to put it. Each week it was moved from one side of the little auditorium to the other. One Sunday, the congregation arrived to find their new organ missing. They searched the building to no avail. They hurled accusations back and forth but still were unable to locate the missing instrument.

Years later and quite by accident it was found—right where it had been all the time—in the church baptistry.

Satan's strategy is to separate, to alienate, and in so doing to totally frustrate the work of Christ in believers' lives.

I'm a peacemaker at heart, and I'm called to sit or stand often between two lonely, frightened people whose world has stopped turning because of their inability to relate properly to each other.

I have felt that same loneliness myself. I have experienced it with my wife, my children, my friends, and my church family. Satan swings his sledgehammer of hate and drives that wedge deep into the heart of a beautiful relationship.

I've often wished I could forget the times that I have spoken ill-timed, ill-advised, cruel, and cutting words to those

I love the most. Words that can never be recalled and that can seldom be forgotten.

Satan's world is a powerful world—but a lonely one. The world is frantically searching for a place where it can be at peace with itself and comfortable with others—a place where it can experience true acceptance.

God's strategy is just the opposite of Satan's. His is a strategy of reconciliation—of unity and peace and oneness. Since sin began, God has been taking broken relationships and putting them back together again. God's program is to

> reconcile man to God,
> man to himself,
> man to woman,
> man to man,
> nation to nation, and
> earth to heaven.

God knows how to blunt Satan's wedges and ultimately force them out of a relationship, restoring the oneness. God is in the business of dispelling loneliness and creating a body of people who are at peace with themselves and with each other.

Four simple words can frustrate the strategy of Satan. Four words can dress believers in a garment so attractive and compelling the world is forced to stop and stare. Four words that can free us from the need and desire to spin any more webs or hide in our sheltering cocoon. The first word, *humility* or *lowliness of mind*, is designed to deal with the perplexing problem of self-acceptance.

"There is Someone who knows me—the Real me—
the complex me—past, present, and future.
He's already done a complete character profile
on me in the Scriptures."

Chapter 8

Someone Who Knows Me

S elf-acceptance simply means to accept what is totally and actually true about myself.

There are varying opinions as to how the truth about self is finally learned.

It is true that man is an enigma to himself; man cannot fully comprehend himself.

I do not know the REAL me.

I, along with the rest of the world's confused, have spent my whole life in front of distorted mirrors as a part of a life-long comedy routine, trying to look either horribly ugly or wonderfully beautiful.

I am told that to fully understand myself I must find someone I trust and verbalize my feelings to that person.

I did that, and was relieved to find some significant relaxation from many of my internal pressures—but not all of them.

We are told to study our past, listen to our friends, seek competent counsel, or check with our family. I also found a great deal of help in reading books related to the subject.

But every human source of understanding was limited.

No one possessed the type of X-ray vision needed to read my mind.

373

No one was capable of feeling the true psychological pulse of my heart.

No one fully knew my past.

No one understood my present.

No one even pretended to comprehend my future.

Self-acceptance can never be achieved while drifting through the foggy, imprecise notions of a baffling secular humanism—a baseless philosophy of life that denies the fact of God, the reality of eternity, the existence of authority, the purpose for being, and the sanctity or indestructibility of human life.

There is only One Source of undistorted, undisputed truth.

There is only One who knows the total truth about me.

There is only One who loves me enough to reveal that truth to me.

The truth, the whole truth, and nothing but the truth can come from God and God alone. As the Hebrew poet asserted in Psalm 139:

It is God who has searched me.

It is God who has known me.

It is God who knows when I sit down.

It is God who knows when I rise up.

It is God who understands my thoughts before I even think them.

It is God who knows my directions before I even walk in them.

It is God who is intimately acquainted with all my ways.

It is God who knows it all.

It is God from whom I cannot hide.

It is God who formed me.

It is God who made me.

It is God who plotted my whole existence before I was even born.

Those twelve statements qualify God to tell me who and what I am.

Just in case more evidence might be required to convince us of God's limitless credentials, the book of Job, chapters 38–41, reveals the infinite distance between man's understanding and God's.

God asks Job seventy questions, none of which Job can answer—all of which are basic knowledge to God.

The God-Man, Jesus, on numerous occasions displayed his ability to tell me the truth about myself.

It is said of Jesus in John 2:25:

"He did not need anyone to bear witness concerning man for He Himself knew what was in man."

No one needed to inform Jesus who would betray him—

"For Jesus knew from the beginning who they were who did not believe, and who it was that would betray Him" (John 6:64).

Do you remember the first time Jesus saw Nathaniel? They had never met. As Nathaniel approached, Jesus did a complete character profile on this total stranger by commenting, "Behold, an Israelite indeed, in whom there is no guile!"

When Jesus spoke to his critics in John 5:42, he spoke to all of humanity. He stated simply, "I know you."

There is Somebody who knows me—the real me—the complex me—past, present, and future. He has already done a complete character profile on me in the Scriptures.

He has painted a multi-dimensional portrait of me—one that displays me as I truly and really am.

And then he flashed a statement for all to see that provides the key to my prison door. He said,

"And you shall know the truth, and the truth shall make you free" (John 8:32).

If I want to know all about me, it's already written, word for word, in the Scriptures.

But if I want to become comfortable with myself, accept myself, learn to live with myself, get acquainted with the

REAL ME, something more is required—and that something more is HUMILITY—genuine humility or "lowliness of mind" as some versions read.

Humility is the act of the will that takes truth, drives it down from the head to the heart, and translates it into experience. It's the means by which I not only get acquainted with the REAL ME, but it's the means by which I even become comfortable with the REAL ME. Humility is the divine path to self-acceptance.

"We cannot change, we cannot move away from what we are, until we thoroughly accept what we are."

Carl Rogers

Chapter 9

Accepting . . . What God Says about Me

"*I*'ll never be remembered for my humility," is a remark I often heard my father-in-law laughingly make in reference to himself. Yet, that's exactly the most outstanding memory I have of this man of God.

Humility is one of those abused little words that carries a different meaning to almost everyone who hears it spoken.

In pagan Greek it suggested someone who was small, slavish, silent, and grovelling.

The phrase "lowliness of mind," which I prefer to *humility*, to some suggests someone who walks around with a bowed head, downcast eyes, and folded hands. I think this is what Dad had in mind when he used the word, and he was right, for this austere, dignified, southern gentleman who preached with the power of an apostle Paul never displayed that sort of demeanor.

Humility is hard to define.

"Lowliness of mind" is far more graphic, and since it is used repeatedly in Scripture to describe such persons as Jesus in Matthew 11:29, the apostle Paul in Acts 20:19, and since it is required of all believers in Ephesians 4:2, it can't be all bad.

The word does not suggest that I make myself small—a suggestion often found in the word humility. It's a word, rather, that teaches me—

Not to bow my head,
     but to bow my mind.

It means that I lower my mind and cause it to bow in full reverence and respect for divine truth.

Lowliness of mind, the first step toward freedom, the first door to self-acceptance, the first move in the direction of total comfort with myself, God, and others, says:

I ACCEPT ALL THAT GOD SAYS ABOUT ME
WITHOUT ARGUMENT.

This was the chief characteristic of Dad's life and ministry.

I counsel a lot. I'm amazed at the number of people who move from pastor to pastor, much like some do with medical doctors. They're seeking a second opinion—a third opinion—or ultimately that one professional opinion that agrees with their own.

Humility or lowliness of mind acknowledges but one opinion, and that's God's. His opinion is first, last, and final. His opinion is right, and humility not only acknowledges the fact, but acts in accordance with that truth.

All of the truth about me is found in Scripture, and humility agrees with all that the Scripture says about me. Humility, then, becomes the biblical imperative that addresses the problem of self-esteem, self-image, self-concept, and self-acceptance.

It's the word that, when understood, tells me how to find the REAL ME.

It's the word that paves the way to ultimately becoming comfortable with myself.

The REAL ME is found in the Scriptures. It's in the Bible that I am fully and correctly described.

God's word addresses the disabling problem of low self-esteem.

David Seamands described low self-esteem as Satan's deadliest weapon—a weapon of the enemy that

paralyzes my potential,
　　destroys my dreams,
　　　　ruins my relationships, and
　　　　　　sabotages my Christian service.[1]

Dr. James Dobson listed ten sources of depression in marriage. Among these ten was low self-esteem. Fifty percent of the respondents rated it as problem number one. Eighty percent of the respondents listed it among the top three on their lists.

Humility speaks to this need. It tells me that if I want an objective, honest answer to who and what I am and why, then I must ACCEPT ALL THAT GOD SAYS ABOUT ME WITHOUT ARGUMENT.

A classic example of humanity's profile is found in the Book of Ephesians, chapter 2, verses 1-7. It explicitly tells the awful and wonderful truth about me, past, present, and future.

It not only tells the truth about me, but also the truth about you. In fact, we're allowed in this passage to look over the shoulder of God into the heart of all humanity—and surprise! We all look alike.

This passage is humanity's great equalizer. It eliminates words like *spiritual advantages* and *spiritual disadvantages.*

It erases words like *inferiority* and *superiority* in the spiritual realm.

It places us all under one great umbrella of Truth as look-alikes, act-alikes, and be-alikes.

These verses tell us that:

WE ALL HAD THE SAME PROBLEM (v. 1)

"And you were dead in your trespasses and sins."

We were *all* "dead in trespasses and sins." The word *dead* means more than just the absence of life; it means more than to be unresponsive and insensitive; it means to be actually and totally separated from the source of all life, which is God himself.

It means not only physical death or even emotional death, but spiritual death.

Humanity's obituary notice is carried in Genesis, chapter 3, and is explained in the Book of Romans:

> Therefore, just as through one man sin entered into the world, and death through sin, and so death spread to all men, because all sinned (5:12).

The infectious disease of death has spread through the entire human race.

This death or separation from God was caused by trespassing or crossing over the boundaries of God's law and by sin, or failing to live up to God's standard.

Since there are no degrees of death—nor degrees of life—one is either alive or dead. That means that no one has any advantage over me in this respect.

> I had no advantage over any other.
> I was dead.
> You were dead.
> Death is the great equalizer.
> We were all bound by the same limitation—
>   infected with the same hideous disease—
>   laid low by the same giant problem.
> We were all dead!

The chief characteristic of death is total helplessness. None of us could move ourselves in any direction, much less the direction of the Source of life.

Spiritual death ultimately invades every part of our being. It displays itself in varying states of emotional death: depression, restlessness, guilt, negativism, hopelessness, fear, and hate.

Just as a dead body has discernible characteristics so does a dead spirit.

Spiritual death is the sole cause of physical death, which is the universal consequence of sin. We were all dead and still are dead, as long as we remain separated from the life-source, which is God himself.

Have you ever noticed how lifelike a mortician can make a dead person appear? There is very little that's repulsive or ugly about a corpse at a funeral.

In our state of spiritual death we do the same.

We try desperately to appear lifelike and alive.

Cocoons are quite popular among the spiritually dead.

Nevertheless, God says that the REAL me—before Jesus Christ entered my life—was dead.

Self-acceptance acknowledges this truth as a fact of life.

Lowliness of mind states that I accept all that God says about me without argument—even if it appears untrue.

WE ALL HAD THE SAME LORD (v. 2)

in which you formerly walked according to the course of this world, according to the prince of the power of the air, of the spirit that is now working in the sons of disobedience.

The second thing God says about me—THE REAL ME—past, is that I was completely under the control and influence of demonic energy.

I was a Satanist.

The energizing spirit that controlled my thoughts as well as my actions was the same energizing spirit that controls the entire world system—the prince who rules over earth—Satan, himself.

My first experience of exorcism was both awesome and frightening. After hours of spiritual struggle I finally witnessed the freeing of a twenty-seven year old man from the domination of Satan.

The long, hard battle wearied and wounded us both.

I was feeling quite proud of what I mistakenly thought

was my accomplishment. I began telling the fascinating story in vivid detail every chance I got.

I took my new friend to Multnomah School of the Bible in Portland, Oregon. As we walked into Dr. John Mitchell's office, I said, with carnal pride, "Dr. Mitchell, I want you to meet my new friend and brother in Christ—he is a former Satanist."

Without a moment's hesitation, Dr. Mitchell responded with, "Weren't we all?" He proceeded to talk to us without any further comment in regard to my friend's former life.

"Weren't we all!" Yes, we were—all of us—Satanists, completely under Satan's power and control.

I was a pawn of Satan, helpless to have any say whatever about how I would live.

Lowliness of mind says I believe all that God says about me without argument—even if it's very uncomplimentary.

WE ALL HAD THE SAME LIFE STYLE (v. 3)

Among them we too all formerly lived in the lusts of our flesh, indulging the desires of the flesh and of the mind, and were by nature children of wrath, even as the rest.

The REAL ME, past, lived to satisfy only one person—me. I was indulgent and sensual—interested in making certain that I had anything and everything I wanted. Greed and selfishness motivated me completely. I had only my interests at heart.

My concern for others was displayed primarily as a means of getting something for myself.

The human tendency to spin webs around ugly reality is at its peak right here. All of us, before coming to Christ, did our best to hide the fact that we were totally selfish and self-centered.

Carl Jung has said that only when a person understands the duality of his nature—his capacity for evil as well as good—can he begin to understand and cope with those who threaten him.

Only when an individual discovers his true inner nature can he accept the gift of meaningful life from God.

Carl Rogers has said that only when a person accepts himself as he really is, does he have the capacity to change.

Verse 3 paints a very unflattering picture of the REAL ME, and I must confess that when I first began taking a long look in that undistorted mirror of self, I wasn't sure that I really wanted to know more.

Lowliness of mind means accepting all that God says about me without argument, even if it's bad.

WE ALL HAVE RECEIVED THE SAME LOVE (v. 4)

But God, being rich in mercy, because of His great love with which He loved us . . .

Of all the insights into self-acceptance, this one may be the most crucial.

Have you noticed how many times I have stated the same concept over and over again?

"No one can accept himself until he is first accepted by another."

I cannot love me unless you do.

The rejected are never able to experience total comfort with themselves or with others.

Do you remember Abraham Maslow's hierarchy of needs?

I was stunned when I first saw them years ago. There was the answer to my perpetual question: Why was professional growth—personal growth—so slow, so difficult?

Maslow states that:

Before there can be growth, there must be self-esteem.
Before there can be self-esteem, there must be love.
Before there can be love, there must be security.
Before there can be security, physical needs must be met.

He outlines them in this order:

Growth

Self-esteem

Love

Security

Physical Need

As long as I'm hungry—I'll never feel secure.
As long as I'm insecure—I'll never feel loved.
As long as I'm unloved—I'll never have self-esteem.
As long as I lack self-esteem—I'll never grow.

My problem focused immediately. My inability to accept love—to feel love—to experience and enjoy love—made it impossible to accept myself.

Notice the critical moment in Scripture where God injects the miracle potion—LOVE.

He has just described us as separated, Satanists, and sensual, and now he pauses to tell us that he loves us anyway.

He describes the heavenly rescue operation, prompted only by love, that was designed to

> bring us to life,
>> snatch us from the clutches of Satan, and
>>> preserve us from the weakness of self.

You'd better read that verse again.

> But God, being rich in mercy, because of His great
> love with which He loved us . . .

I get a catch in my throat every time I read this passage.

I get another catch in my throat every time I hear Bill Gaither's little chorus:

> I am loved. I am loved. I can risk loving you
> For the One who knows me best, loves me most.

All the nasty things God says about me in the first three verses of Ephesians, chapter 2, would tend to make me think that God could not love me—ever.

But he did, and he does.

Lowliness of mind states that I believe all that God says about me without argument—even if it's unbelievable.

Believe it—God loves me, anyway.

WE HAVE ALL RECEIVED THE SAME LIFE (v. 5)

> . . . even when we were dead in our transgressions, made us alive together with Christ (by grace you have been saved) . . .

The REAL ME has been revived, resuscitated, restored—brought back to life. God has devised his own method of cardio-pulmonary resuscitation that reaches beyond the organ of the heart to the human spirit.

The spirit of man that went limp when Adam sinned has been made alive. This aliveness, this new life, is the result of a fusion with the source of eternal life—Jesus Christ.

It's not accomplished by a wand or with a touch.

It's not like the resurrection of a Lazarus who was called out of death or a widow's son who was commanded to live or even a priest's daughter who was lifted out of death by the tender hand of Jesus.

This aliveness is not just a change of mind or a change of direction.

It's not a new-found allegiance or a redefined dedication.

It's the actual merging of two persons—one dead and one alive.

It's the result of the eternal, indestructible life of the ever-living, never-dying Christ, moving right into my being.

It's the result of my never-ending death being drawn right into his never-ending life and being eternally conquered.

My death is swallowed up by his life.

My death is exchanged for his life.

We two, Christ and I, become one.

Christ lives in me and I live in him.

We are so inseparable and so indistinguishable that when God the Father sees us, he sees us not as two but as one.

That's what is meant in verse five when it says, "made us alive together with Christ."

It's interesting to note right here that the same Satan who works overtime to convince spiritually dead people that they are alive also expends a similar amount of demonic energy to convince spiritually alive people that they are still dead.

At age nine it really wasn't difficult for me to accept the fact that I needed to accept Jesus.

What *was* difficult was to accept the fact that Jesus had accepted me.

I struggled with uncertainty for ten frightening years before I was able to believe that I had been brought back to life.

The unmistakable signs of spiritual life were everywhere. The most significant sign of life was my fear of spiritual death. Dead people have no awareness of their state whatsoever. Only the spiritually alive are capable of even expressing concern over their spiritual welfare.

I completely ignored this obvious sign of my aliveness.

The fact of life is just as real as the fact of death.

Since there are no degrees in death or in life, no one is more dead or more alive than anyone else.

Life, like death, is a great equalizer. The passage of time doesn't make me any more alive than I am at the moment of my spiritual birth.

Even the process of maturing contributes nothing to my aliveness.

Outside of Christ, I could not be any more dead than I was.

In Christ, I cannot be any more alive than I am.

The REAL ME is alive with the eternal, indestructible life of Christ—a life that can never again know the kind of death and separation it once knew.

Be sure you don't overlook the little word *grace* in that verse. That little word, big with meaning, makes it clear that the process of becoming alive is something accomplished by

God alone—it's a free, totally undeserved gift given to anyone who is willing to accept the whole truth just as God states it.

Lowliness of mind states that I accept all that God says about me without argument, even if it's astonishingly wonderful.

WE HAVE ALL RECEIVED THE SAME STATUS (v. 6)

. . . and raised us up with Him, and seated us with Him in the heavenly places, in Christ . . .

Since Jesus and I are inseparable and indistinguishable in our spiritual life, I am not only alive, I am already comfortably positioned with Christ in the very same place Jesus is located today. I am already located spiritually where someday I'll be located physically—in the very presence of God the Father. This is in a place beyond the reach of Satan, beyond the possibility of loneliness, and beyond the threat of weakness.

I am already positioned for perpetual peace and everlasting security.

I am located in a spot that is not tentative.

I am assured by a promise that is not ambivalent.

I am surrounded by forces that are indestructible.

I am as secure for all eternity as is Jesus,

    as close to God as is Jesus, and

        as acceptable to God as is Jesus.

Jesus is heaven's status symbol, and since you and I both are located in him and with him, there will never be any class distinction or segregation or discrimination. In Christ we are all on the top rung of the heavenly ladder, and from that perch we'll enjoy forever together.

Lowliness of mind states that I accept all that God says about me without argument, even if it's beyond comprehension.

WE WILL ALL SHARE THE SAME PURPOSE (v. 7)

. . . in order that in the ages to come He might show the surpassing riches of his grace in kindness toward us in Christ Jesus . . .

The REAL ME is in store for something that's both special and spectacular. In the future—the eternal future—God is going to spend his time heaping blessing after blessing upon me and pause only occasionally to show me off to all his creation as a trophy of his mighty power and his wonderful grace.

Eternity will be like one long ticker-tape parade, where we will be the spectacle for all the angelic beings to behold.

We will be the freed hostages that will be displayed as a lasting tribute to the strategy and wisdom of God.

We will be the marvel of the ages to come. Heaven's hottest commodity. God's greatest achievement. Time's most spectacular miracle.

The REAL ME is going to be SOMEBODY forever.

Lowliness of mind states that I accept all that God says about me without argument even if it, excuse the expression, boggles my mind.

The Word of God describes the REAL ME and the REAL YOU.

It gives us a realistic, objective, honest appraisal of ourselves.

It's discouraging at first, but it directs us to the means by which we can be changed.

It describes my wonderful status in Jesus Christ, and promises me that it's going to get even better.

It singles no one out as better or worse—it places us all under the same umbrella of divine truth and enables us to ultimately accept ourselves as we truly are.

If God can accept me—and he does—knowing what he knows, then I can accept me.

If God can love me—and he does—knowing what he knows, then I can love me.

If God esteems me as he esteems his son, Jesus, then I can give myself the esteem I truly deserve.

That esteem is not a haughty arrogance that presumes superiority—it is rather a grateful serenity that has finally found peace and comfort with itself.

The truth of God frees me! It eliminates the need for spinning webs of unreality. It allows me the privilege of breaking free of my cocoon and enables me to fly with ease and grace and magnificent beauty above and beyond all the restraints of an unbelieving heart.

Chapter 9, Notes

1. David A. Seamands, *Healing for Damaged Emotions* (Wheaton, Ill.: Victor Books, 1981), p. 50.

"In order to be comfortable with God,
I must know my God as he really is."

Chapter 10

Accepting . . . How God Deals with Me

I just took another look at my woolly friend. I study him often—in fact, I find myself getting a little anxious, wondering if that moth will ever break free.

From all appearances, nothing has changed. The cocoon shows no sign of life or struggle. There's no indication that soon something beautiful will emerge, no hint that something magnificent and alive will climb out of something that appears so ugly and lifeless.

It took a long time for that little larva to wrap itself so tightly and completely. It takes a long time to break free.

If you're getting discouraged with the bindings that have caused you to go into hiding—be patient. The process of gaining freedom may seem frightfully slow, but that freedom is certain once you've begun your struggle.

Believe me! I know.

Part of the process must include learning to feel comfortable, not only with myself, but also with God. Accepting God for who he is and feeling accepted by God are indispensable to the freedom we crave.

The second word in Ephesians 4:2 addresses this worthy project. In your revised version it reads *gentleness*. In the

King James the word is *meekness*. I prefer the word meekness even though it also has suffered some terrible abuse in translation.

I read a sign on a billboard the other day that said, "Meekness is weakness." Modern society views meekness as a lack of aggressiveness, or assertiveness, and rejects it with contempt.

True meekness, however, *is not weakness*. It is an inner strength that responds positively to all the happenings of life.

Meekness is a grace of soul that produces acceptable responses to even unacceptable circumstances.

Meekness is the spirit's positive response to negative experiences.

As lowliness bows its mind to the truth of God, meekness bows its will to the dealings of God.

It is the gentle, mild, undisputing, unabrasive response to whatever God allows to take place in my life.

Meekness says:

I ACCEPT ALL OF GOD'S DEALINGS WITH ME WITHOUT RESISTANCE OR BITTERNESS.

Jesus, in Matthew 11:29, described himself as meek (KJV).

Paul, in 1 Corinthians 4:21, says, "I came to you in meekness" (KJV).

Timothy, in 1 Timothy 6:11, is instructed to serve in meekness (KJV).

Wives in 1 Peter 3:4 are encouraged to display meekness.

Meekness in Galatians 5:23 is a fruit of the Spirit.

It's obvious from all the biblical emphasis on the word that meekness is a *positive* quality—not weakness, but strength.

One of the classic Old Testament illustrations of meekness is found in the life story of one of history's best-known sufferers, a man by the name of Job.

In one day Job lost everything he owned, 7000 sheep,

3000 camels, 500 yoke of oxen, and 500 female donkeys. In one day this rich man's world collapsed. He lost it all. In addition to his material loss, he was forced to take charge of the funeral arrangements and bury all ten of his children—all in one day (Job 1). All the heartbreaks of a lifetime were compressed into one twenty-four hour period, without even the privilege of time to heal the wounds.

How did he respond? Job 1:20-22 says,

> Then Job arose and tore his robe and shaved his head, and he fell to the ground and worshiped. And he said, "Naked came I from my mother's womb, and naked I shall return there. The Lord gave and the Lord has taken away. Blessed be the name of the Lord." Through all this Job did not sin nor did he blame God.

That's meekness. Job accepted all of God's dealings with him without resistance or bitterness—at first anyway.

As Job's story continues and as the pressures of pain and loss intensify, his display of meekness begins to waver.

> Job complains,
>   questions,
>   criticizes,
>   demands an explanation, and
>   pleads to die.

At the conclusion of his chronicle of suffering, Job confesses that his negative responses to negative experiences were the result of his limited knowledge of God.

Job, like most of us, knew God secondhand. His training had been thorough, his instruction had been complete, but his knowledge was academic.

An academic knowledge of God, one that's complete with all the right answers to all the right questions is fine for the classroom, but it will never suffice in life's living room.

In seminary I completed all of my biblical and systematic theology classes with superior grades, but I still didn't know God.

I knew about God—but I didn't know God.

Like Job, I had heard of him with the hearing of the ear—I had all the hearsay insights that I could handle.

I could define the terms, describe the relationships, and list the attributes. Like Job, however, my understanding of God was pitifully limited. I hadn't seen him with the seeing of my eyes.

Moses had the same problem. He had spent eighty years in a God-culture, knew his Jewish catechism, later even wrote his own Jewish history book, but when he stood beside that burning acacia bush at the base of Mt. Horeb, he suddenly realized that he hadn't even entered theological pre-school.

Moses did not know God.

Neither did Isaiah nor Ezekiel nor Daniel nor Jeremiah. Nor do we, until we encounter him personally in one of life's unexpected moments.

Knowledge of God is forged out of the furnace of life, formed on the anvil of experience, and oftentimes shaped with the hammer of pain.

My knowledge of God has only grown in proportion to my encounters with life—real life—hard life—cruel life—sometimes painful life. The most positive growing times have been amidst the most negative experiences.

As I am writing this, Martha and I are engulfed in another of life's baffling encounters, one that's downright painful.

After ten and a half happy years at Hinson Baptist Church in Portland, we're being asked to leave. Not by the church, but by God. We're being asked to leave our home, our children, our grandchildren, my eighty-six-year-old mother, my brothers and sister, all of our lifelong friends, our security, and this beautiful city, which we dearly love.

Not only that, we're being asked to go to a strange country, a different culture, an unknown people, and even a new denomination.

God is asking us, in these best years of our lives, years that are fast approaching retirement, to do something that feels strangely like starting all over again.

We feel a little like Abraham being asked to leave Ur of the Chaldees. The only difference being that Illinois—from my present vantage point—bears little resemblance to the Promised Land.

Our knowledge of God is being stretched again. We know enough about him to know when it is that he's speaking, and what it is that he is saying. We know enough about him to know our Sovereign God has a sovereign plan—one that we may or may not understand someday.

We know enough about him to realize the importance of obeying him. What we do not know is the exact, unique, wonderful, personalized, tailor-made reason for this bewildering request.

We're displaying meekness—oh, there's a little kicking and screaming going on—some tears and some apprehension—lots of questions—but we are meekly responding to the sovereign call of God.

You see, meekness says I accept all of God's dealings with me without resistance or bitterness.

As lowliness demands that I get to know the truth about myself, meekness requests that I get to know the truth about God.

Meekness sees God in every circumstance of life—not always causing it, but at least allowing it.

Meekness accepts the fact that God is sovereign, in control, and free to act in our behalf in any way he pleases.

Meekness truly believes that nothing can touch the child of God without first having gained the permission of our heavenly Father.

Meekness sees God actively involved in my polio.

Meekness sees God playing a major role in my four-year depression.

Meekness bows before a sovereign God in the death of our son.

Meekness views God as a part of every disappointment as well as appointment.

Meekness sees God in my failures as well as in my successes.

A seminary student stopped by the other day with twelve questions he wanted to ask. Paul had been a successful business man prior to his call to the ministry. He was well on the way to his first million and probably felt, like most of us, that his response to God's call would result in even greater prosperity. Instead, just the opposite had happened. And now he was almost penniless.

So he began asking me his questions:

1. Does following Jesus have to be so hard?
2. Why doesn't God answer prayer?
3. Why is seminary so hard?
4. Why do I have the impression that I'm just beating my head against a wall?
5. Why—

I stopped him right there. "No more questions," I said. "I'm not sure that I can answer even one that you've asked so far. I do know, Paul, that there are times when following Jesus seems awfully hard, and I, too, wonder why God is so slow to answer prayer. Seminary was hard for me, too, and at times I felt that my head was permanently damaged from the beatings it took."

As we talked, we both began to weep, for we were both feeling the struggles of an aggressive self-will against the contrary plans of a sovereign God.

"The problem can't be with God, Paul, it has to be with us. God's will is never hard except to an obstinate, rebellious spirit. When Jesus said, "Take my yoke upon you and learn of me, for my yoke is easy and my burden is light," he was telling us that serving him was never meant to be grievous and hard. Yokes are shaped to provide no discomfort whatever to the shoulders of the oxen. Yokes only hurt when the animal resists."

"That's the way it has always been in my life. The will of God is only unbearably painful when I resist it."

With those words, Paul buried his head in my shoulder and wept. He finally said, "Thanks, Pastor, for telling me like it really is. I think I can handle it now—no more questions."

Meekness says I accept all of God's dealings with me without resistance or bitterness.

Another beautiful display of meekness is found in Philippians, chapter 2. In the passage beginning with verse 5, we are told to:

> Have this attitude in yourselves which was also in Christ Jesus, who, although He existed in the form of God, did not regard equality with God a thing to be grasped, but emptied Himself, taking the form of a bond-servant, and being made in the likeness of men. And being found in appearance as a man, He humbled himself by becoming obedient to the point of death, even death on a cross.

This passage describes Jesus climbing down the ladder of self-interest—that's meekness on display as he volitionally displays commitment and compliance with the sovereign wisdom of his holy Father.

Meekness is heard in the form of singing as Paul and Silas accepted imprisonment in Philippi as a circumstance that is painful but providential.

Meekness is seen on a barren island as John the apostle bows to worship after his banishment to Patmos.

Meekness is the word that challenges the single person who wants to be married or the married person who wants to be single.

Meekness is the word that addresses the disappointment of a missionary who is denied a visa, a student who is declined admission, the businessman whose resumé is rejected, the parents who find themselves childless, the athlete who gets injured, the Christian whose business fails, the investor who loses his life savings. Meekness is being able to say,

"Thank you, Father," when all that's been received has been a disappointment.

Negative responses to divinely permitted pressure situations can be terribly destructive.

One Sunday evening I was called to sit between two members of my church as a peacemaker. I had been struggling with them for months, trying to find an acceptable solution to a very complex problem. I was tired, irritable, and genuinely displeased that this conference was tacked onto the end of a wearying day. I did not display my anger in their presence. I suppressed it—restrained it—sat on it—very successfully. It didn't show—but it was there.

As I was driving home, I passed Martha's Datsun sitting alongside the freeway, empty. I stopped, backed up, and found the doors locked and the parking lights dimmed from a near-dead battery.

I was angry because she had obviously run out of gas. I was doubly angry because the battery had run down. I was uncontrollably angry a few moments later when she drove up with a stranger and a can of gas. I was sure I was going to be "gouged" beyond my ability to pay. It turned out that it cost me nothing.

I poured the gas into the tank, vainly tried to start the engine, and finally decided to get behind her and push the car to a safer location. I explained what we were about to do, where we would turn, and when. I failed to explain that she needed to turn on the key in order to unlock the steering wheel. When I started pushing her, rather than steer toward the frontage road, she began heading for the middle of the freeway, with its concrete divider. We both stopped just in time.

I got out of my car, slammed the door, stormed up to her front window and began delivering a tirade. When I was finished, I asked her, "Why didn't you turn onto the frontage road?" She explained, "I'm sorry, I didn't know to turn on the ignition key. The steering wheel was still locked." Again I dumped my anger on her. After a few moments I saw a worried, embarrassed look in her eyes and heard words I'll never forget, "I'm your wife, remember?"

She forgave me—I've never really forgiven myself.

I've always felt that it was a classic example of misdirected anger. I wasn't really angry at Martha, I was angry at those two men who had consumed so much of my time and energy. But, no, not really. The truth is I was angry at God for allowing that long and tiring conference to take place.

Meekness sees God in every circumstance of life and meekness says I accept all of God's dealings with me without resistance or bitterness.

Had I responded to that pressure experience with meekness, I would have spared my wife from a painful wound and myself from a haunting memory.

One of my close friends has recently lost his wife, his health, his mobility, his physical independence, and his purpose for living. He is in a constant depression.

As I sat with him not long ago, he again expressed his disgust with the nursing home, the food, the staff, with himself, and with God for not answering his prayer to die.

"Are you angry with God?" I asked him.

He laughed with embarrassment. "Of course not," he said, "I would never get angry with God."

"Yes, you would," I replied, "and I think you are. Everything that's happened in your life this past year has been allowed by God and you don't like it. Isn't it possible that you are truly angry with God?"

Hebrews 12:15 warns us of the bitterness that spills over and infects many. I call it "floating anger." It's an anger that we're not even aware of, but every once in a while it erupts, usually inflicting wounds on unsuspecting and innocent victims and leaving piles of clutter and debris in the lives of many.

I can get rid of "floating anger" by acknowledging its presence and asking God's forgiveness for improperly responding to one of life's painful experiences. We really don't grow without pain, you know—in fact, pain is indispensable to growth. Pain, if it produces growth, is worthy of praise. Pain, like it or not, often becomes our best friend. God knows just how much pain we can stand and for how long and he knows just how to use it to cause a gentle spirit to emerge. God calls that gentle spirit meekness.

I was speaking in Denver during the time I was doing the word study in Ephesians, chapter 4. I worked late one night on the word meekness, finally defined it as you see it in this chapter, and then left it lying on the desk in my motel.

When I returned to my room the next day, I was just opening my door when a housekeeper came up from behind, asked me if I was Rev. Baker, and then threw her arms around me and began to cry.

I was stunned—I'd never seen the woman before in my life—until she began to explain.

"I'm married to a preacher," she said, "who has not been walking with God. In fact, he has made my life totally miserable. Last week I left him, and I determined I would never go back to him—until I read your definition for meekness. I knelt down beside your bed and asked God to forgive me for thinking I knew what was best for my life. I've already called my husband, and he's picking me up after work. We're going home."

Meekness seldom comes easily, for life is filled with disappointments. The only way that I have been able to experience any relief from the pain of denied self-interest is by getting better acquainted with God.

In order to be comfortable with God I must know my God—as he really is.

The information can't be secondhand, the evidence can't be hearsay. It must be gained from the depository of truth, the Scriptures, and applied in the crucible of life. To know God requires the marriage of truth to life's experiences.

It's such a freeing feeling to know that nothing can happen in my life without first having gained the permission of God.

A little blind girl was seated on her daddy's lap on the front porch when a long-time friend of the family quietly climbed the front steps, winked at his friend and then grabbed the blind daughter from her daddy's arms, ran down the steps and up the street.

He stopped abruptly, startled because the girl had made no effort to struggle or cry out. "Why aren't you frightened?" he asked. "You didn't know who had you in his arms." "I didn't have to know," she answered. "My daddy knew, and that was enough for me."

Meekness is the act of relaxing with any circumstance—knowing that our Father fully understands.

Meekness accepts all of God's dealings with me without resistance or bitterness and enables me to feel comfortable with God.

Meekness frees me from the cocoon of fear, the bondage of hostility, and the darkness of uncertainty. Meekness frees me to live in an expansive universe with the certainty that God is God of all and that every event of my life is under his sovereign control.

Meekness can be summed up in a single passage of Scripture—one that Martha and I have tried to live by all our lives.

And we know that God causes all things to work together for good to those who love God, to those who are called according to His purpose (Romans 8:28).

"God's most powerful weapon on earth is a Christian who, when threatened or harmed, refuses to retaliate."

Chapter 11

Accepting . . . How Man Deals with Me

*L*owliness of mind allows me to be comfortable with myself.

Meekness enables me to be comfortable with my God.

Longsuffering, the third of this little foursome of divine graces, permits me to find some semblance of serenity in a hostile world—a serenity that's uncharacteristic to us humans.

The world, especially when it's experiencing one of its periodic fits of anger, can be a very intimidating place to live.

For the world is a system that is

    ruled by Satan,
        inhabited by demons,
            built on greed,
                fostered by hate, and
                    bent on destruction.

It's a system whose total environment has been polluted by sin.

Its inhabitants resent the presence of Christians.

Its goal is to eliminate God and good, as it attempted to eliminate Christ,

405

The believer is an unwelcome resident. His very presence is a constant reminder of the vast moral difference between God and man. The resentment is greatest whenever he attempts to influence or even change his environment for Christ.

I collided head-on with the world system a few years ago when I led the evangelical community in an attempt to expose a gay activist takeover of Oregon politics in 1980.

Hinson Church is in the midst of a neighborhood strongly influenced by politics. Many of the residents are homosexuals and lesbians or are sympathetic to them. The homosexual community in Portland claims to be 100,000 strong and has threatened to take control of the city.

I must be careful here to explain that we have an active ministry to homosexuals and their families—and that we do not reject or oppose the individual homosexual. We are, however, opposed to the practice, especially when it attempts to dominate a community.

I authored a letter, signed by seven other influential church leaders, that listed all the local, state, and national candidates that were supported by the gay community. I stated the biblical position on homosexuality and encouraged the evangelical community to study the endorsements carefully before casting their votes.

The letter was distributed state-wide to more than 300,000 persons. The outcome of the election was heartening.

The response of the world-system was frightening.

I was maligned, abused, and threatened. Damage was done to the church buildings and its vehicles. Tires were slashed, graffiti began appearing on the walls. Foul-smelling chemicals were sprayed on the shrubs and sidewalks surrounding the church, permeating the entire building during the Sunday services.

I was intimidated and I withdrew.

The campaign was successful, but I hadn't expected the avalanche of hate that poured down upon me and my church family.

I wanted to turn in the direction of a full-scale retreat or gather my forces for all-out war.

My perplexity over what I had done was heightened as I watched the walls of hostility being erected between me and the very people that I wanted so desperately to help.

I began carefully studying the scriptural incidents that seemed to parallel mine:

John the Baptist's public indictment of King Herod for his immorality;

Jesus' rebuke of religious leaders for their hypocrisy;

Stephen's address to traditional Judaism, shaming them for their lifelessness and unbelief;

Peter's public accusation of a religious system that crucified Christ;

Paul's constant warnings against false doctrine and impurity;

John's scenario of the future that predicted the ultimate collapse of the total world system.

All of these men lived in a hostile world.

All of them addressed the evils of their present age.

All of them suffered persecution or death or both for their views.

None of them retaliated or sought revenge. All of them influenced their generation—and the generations to come— by their passive response to hostility.

I'm a war veteran. I'm not a pacifist, by nature or by doctrine. I'm a member of a generation that has grown up with a John Wayne mentality. I was taught to shoot by members of the National Riflemen's Association, and have studied ways to defend myself and the members of my family.

Friends and even members of my church have joined survivalist organizations and stockpiled food, guns, and ammunition, in preparation for the coming world collapse. I have been urged by many to do the same.

I have strongly resisted and insistently refused, not because of my courage, but because of my convictions—convictions that are still in the formative stage, but growing. Convictions that state that:

Hostility breeds hostility;
the believer's true life can never be terminated; and that
God's most powerful weapon on earth is a Christian who, when threatened or harmed, refuses to retaliate.

That brings us to the third word in Ephesians 4:2: LONGSUFFERING.

Longsuffering speaks to my attitude toward antagonism.

It's a quality of self-restraint in the face of provocation which does not hastily retaliate or promptly punish.

It's the opposite of anger and is associated with mercy.

It's a trait that's characteristic of God (Exodus 34:6).

It's a trait that is characteristic of Christ (Romans 2:4).

It's a trait that is to characterize my attitude and response to the world (Ephesians 4:2).

It's an attitude that, when learned and practiced, can provide some degree of serenity and a maximum amount of positive influence.

LONGSUFFERING means: I ACCEPT ALL OF MAN'S DEALINGS WITH ME WITHOUT RETALIATION.

It deals with the natural inclination to want to get even.

It deals with my problem of hostility.

It restrains me in the face of opposition.

It displays itself in a gentle answer that turns away wrath (Proverbs 15:1) sometimes. Not always, but sometimes.

In an early pastorate I was confronted by a hostile man who genuinely felt he had some valid grievances against me. He wouldn't list them, however. I confronted him one day in the church building and asked him to tell me how I had offended him. He refused. I stood in the doorway of the furnace room and said, "I am not going to move, my friend, until we can settle this. Will you please tell me what I have done so that I can make it right?"

With that, this incredible hulk of a man grabbed me, lifted me off the floor, and flung me against the opposite wall. I rebounded from that wall, fists clenched, and headed straight for an all-out brawl.

I never did know what happened next. Either I was seeing stars or a brilliant divine display of neon lights. Right before my very eyes were the words, NO STRIKER. In my King James Bible that was listed as one of the qualifications of a pastor. It meant that I could not be a brawler, pugnacious, or a fighter of any kind.

It meant that I could not hit him back.

I stopped in my tracks, unclenched my fists, bowed my head, and walked back to my office without a word.

The Lord was especially kind to me that day. He preserved me from a heap of guilt. He protected me from a brutal beating, and he provided me with a friend for life—for within a few minutes, my would-be enemy was in my office, and together on our knees we were asking forgiveness of each other.

LONGSUFFERING means: I ACCEPT ALL OF MAN'S DEALINGS WITH ME WITHOUT RETALIATION.

Stephen's martyrdom provides the backdrop for illustrating the awesome power of longsuffering. He was the church's first full-fledged martyr—the first member of the new-born church to die for his faith in Christ. After preaching one of history's most convincing sermons, he was stoned. The enraged enemy could not dispose of him quickly enough.

> They screamed at him.
> They covered their ears as he spoke.
> They rushed toward him.
> They dragged him out of the city.
> They pummelled him with stones until he was not
>   only dead but buried.

His response was: "Lord, do not hold this sin against them!" (Acts 7:60).

One of the agitators who encouraged the murder of Stephen was a man named Saul of Tarsus—later known as the apostle Paul.

This same Saul of Tarsus went from Stephen's murder to ravage the church, going from house to house identifying the early believers and dragging them off to prison. The early Christians were intimidated, imprisoned, martyred, or forced to leave their homes and communities to flee for their lives.

This same Saul intensified his campaign of terror. He broadened his base and moved north from Jerusalem toward Damascus.

It's at this point that the longsuffering of God comes into sharp focus. It's here that we see the infinite patience of Jesus.

The church had just been born.
It was God's baby in this world.
It was small.
It was young.
It was vulnerable, and at the same time it was God's
      secret weapon.
It was God's hope for earth, and it was supposedly
      indestructible.

And here was one man—Saul—determined to destroy it, to wipe it clean from the face of the earth. Here was Satan's hit man with his devilish contract already in his pocket, in the process of liquidating the baby church.

If I were God, what would I have done at this point?

Human tendency would have been to defend or retaliate.

Human strategy would have been to eliminate the opposition.

Human inclination would have been to destroy Saul before he destroyed the church.

But not God. He is longsuffering and knows that long-suffering is a far more effective weapon than retaliation.

He waited—and waited—and waited until Saul's vehemence had reached its peak. Then God, in one startling movement, with non-threatening words of love, completely and instantly conquered Saul, broke his heart, captured his spirit, and made him his willing servant for the rest of his life.

Later, Saul of Tarsus wrote letters under the pen name of Paul the apostle. In one addressed to Timothy, his young protégé, he said:

> It is a trustworthy statement, deserving full acceptance, that Christ Jesus came into the world to save sinners, among whom I am foremost of all.

> And yet for this reason I found mercy, in order that in me as the foremost, Jesus Christ might demonstrate His perfect patience [longsuffering], as an example for those who would believe in Him for eternal life (1 Timothy 1:15-16).

Paul claims to be the classic illustration of God's longsuffering. If anyone wishes to know how truly patient God is, take a long look at Paul. It was that longsuffering that ultimately claimed Paul as one of God's own.

Jesus' story is even more dramatic than Paul's.

> Jesus resisted death, as is human, but did not reject it.
> Jesus felt pain, as is human, but did not plead for mercy.
> Jesus cried out to his Father, as is human, but did not scream at his attackers.
> Jesus fainted, as is human, but did not renounce his deity.
> Jesus was beaten, spat upon, pierced and ridiculed — eventually crucified—but never retaliated—though, unlike others, he could have halted the entire dying process at any time, had he chosen to do so.

Like Stephen, in place of retaliation he cried: "Father forgive them; for they know not what they are doing" (Luke 23:34).

The end result was the conversion of one of the two criminals hanging nearby. A Roman guard, instrumental in the whole crucifixion process, began praising God and proclaiming Jesus' innocence.

The unbelieving world was awed. The stage was set for a resurrection and the whole world was about to feel the impact of a message of power, a message that proclaims the kind of indestructible life that does not fear death.

Our great fear of death has caused us indestructible ones to weave threads of invisibility about ourselves, retreat into our monastic societies, withdraw into our Christian cultures. This fear has blunted the sharp edge of God's most penetrating and powerful weapon: the life of a fearless believer. Our urges for defense, revenge, or even self-justification have weakened God's tool of long-suffering.

When the recession hit Portland I decided that long-suffering was the only possible weapon that could ease the hostility created by my previous confrontation with the activist community.

We had attacked and we had estranged the very people we were trying to reach.

Longsuffering comes hard for me—and yet if long-suffering can reach a hostile world and at the same time diminish my discomfort level, it deserves maximum attention.

We organized fourteen neighborhood churches into a coalition program for one purpose only: to help the needy. We called it REACH-OUT. It was designed as a pre-evangelism bridge to a hostile neighborhood.

Its genius was in its simplicity.

We recruited volunteers from the local churches with certain skills or interests or those who just had the time and the heart to help needy neighbors.
We advertised our presence and our availability.
We played down any church relationships.
We offered help with no remuneration, no strings attached.

We went into homes with no verbal witness, simply
to meet needs that our neighbors could no longer
afford.

We mowed lawns, repaired roofs, shopped for groc-
eries, baby-sat young ones, assisted the elderly,
provided medical care, dental care, and home
nursing, repaired automobiles, moved furniture,
repaired plumbing, and offered transportation.

We fed, we clothed, and we housed needy neighbors.

In two years the church, by invitation, moved into 1800
neighborhood homes. Ninety-five percent of these were un-
churched families. Since that time, the feelings of hostility
have eased. Many have come to Christ.

One family of Vietnamese refugees established a restaurant across the street from the church. We patronized their
establishment, helped them financially, and even housed and
clothed them when their building was destroyed by fire. They
all received Christ. Before leaving the community the mother
came to me and said, "For years people have been telling me
to find Christ. I did not know where to look for him. When
you and your people came to me to help me, I knew that
finally I had found him and now I have grown to love him."

Longsuffering is not just a term of response—it is a term
that denotes action. It initiates action. It moves toward the
hostile and the frightening with overtures of love and caring.

I am learning longsuffering, not only toward a hostile
world, but also toward some forms of hostility that I have
found in my own world—and it works.

It is freeing me.

Longsuffering draws beauty out of ugliness. It replaces
fear with love and causes one to have a dynamic influence
upon the very people whom it once feared.

I learned an interesting fact about my giant silk moth—
the silk moth that still hasn't emerged from its ugly cocoon.
The moth that remains hidden within its own web will have

but one purpose when it emerges. During its life expectancy of ten days or less, its sole purpose will be to reproduce.

It will have no interest in its own comfort or its own longevity. It will only concentrate on one thing—to reproduce itself.

My purpose is similar. I'm here to reproduce people of like kind, of like faith.

This can never be accomplished from within the confines of a cocoon. This will never be achieved in isolation. It can never be accomplished if I withdraw into hiding.

Longsuffering accepts all that man does to me without retaliation, a definition which presupposes risks, which demands vulnerability, and which means I willingly move out of the trenches into the front lines. With my face to those who would oppose me, I readily display the power and majesty of a patient God through the medium of a serene, non-threatened, and indestructible life.

"The ultimate act of divine strategy is to take unbelieving, alienated, lonely, diverse, hostile humanity and make them into friends."

Chapter 12

Accepting . . . Our Differences

*L*OWLINESS OF MIND says

I ACCEPT ALL THAT GOD SAYS ABOUT ME WITHOUT ARGUMENT—and enables me to accept myself.

MEEKNESS says

I ACCEPT ALL OF GOD'S DEALINGS WITH ME WITHOUT RESISTANCE OR BITTER-NESS—and enables me to accept my God.

LONGSUFFERING says

I ACCEPT ALL OF MAN'S DEALINGS WITH ME WITHOUT RETALIATION—and enables me to accept my enemies.

FORBEARANCE says

I ACCEPT YOU WITH ALL OF YOUR FAULTS OR OUR DIFFERENCES—and enables me to accept even my friends.

A Chinese man and a Jewish man were having dinner

together. During their conversation the Jewish man suddenly became silent. A look of hostility spread over his face. Without a word he doubled his fist, drew back his arm, swung, and hit the Chinese man full in the side of the head.

The Chinese man toppled from his chair, sprawled on the floor and lay still. After a few moments he lifted himself slightly, shook his head, looked at his friend, and said, "Why in the world did you do that?"

The Jewish man answered, "That's for Pearl Harbor!"

"Pearl Harbor?" the Chinese man asked. "Friend," he said, "the Chinese had nothing to do with Pearl Harbor. It was the Japanese air force that bombed Pearl Harbor."

The Chinese man climbed back into his chair and resumed his dinner.

Suddenly a look of hostility spread across his face, and he, without a word, doubled his fist, drew back his arm, swung with all his might, and struck the Jewish man in the side of his head.

The Jewish man toppled from his chair, sprawled on the floor, and lay silent for a moment. He then lifted himself from the floor, shook his head and asked, "Why in the world did you do that?"

"That was for the Titanic!" the Chinese man answered.

"The Titanic?" the Jewish man exclaimed. "The Jews didn't sink the Titanic, that was an iceberg."

"An iceberg," exclaimed the Chinese man, "well—Goldberg, Feinberg, Iceberg—what's the difference?"

The story, of course, is apocryphal, but the lesson is easily applied.

It's a rare conflict of any kind in which anyone is fully aware of the issues involved and an even rarer conflict in which one side holds all the moral turf.

Whether we're considering the war between Iran and Iraq; the never-ending struggle in Beirut between the Druse, Moslems, and the Phalangists; the Irish hostility between Catholics and Protestants; the struggle between the leftist guerrillas and the Sandinista regime in Nicaragua; the Sikhs and the Hindus; the Zulu struggle with their class warfare; the political conflicts between Democrats and Republicans; the theological struggles between Evangelicals and Fundamentalists; the sexist battles between men and women; the racist wars between blacks and whites; the marital turmoil between husband and wife; or the family squabbles between parent and child, the questions of why we are fighting and who is responsible are not always clear.

There are countless soldiers and civilians who have died for causes that were no more clearly defined than those battles between people who butter their bread right side up and those who butter their bread upside down.

Forbearance is in desperately short supply in today's human race—and especially rare in the church of Jesus Christ.

I have watched various local churches and denominations and Christian organizations with bewilderment as they have allowed one crisis after another to sap them of their strength and separate them.

Since I've been a Baptist most of my life, I can tell this story. A speaker was tracing the origin of Baptists. "Many of you trace the history of Baptists back to the sixteenth century," he said. "Some of you trace their beginnings back to the second chapter of the Book of Acts—others to John the Baptist. I think you're all wrong," he said. "I think the Baptist church was founded in Genesis, chapter 13, where Abraham said to Lot, "You go your way, and I'll go mine."

No church in history had greater potential for division than the early New Testament church.

Racial, cultural, ethnic, social, philosophical, and even theological issues were so diverse that any form of union seemed totally impossible.

But God performed the ultimate act of divine strategy on an unbelieving, alienated, hostile, lonely, diverse humanity.

He took the two most antagonistic, impossibly different races of people—the Jews with their long history of traditional religion and the Gentiles with their long history of pagan polytheism. Bringing these two groups together, he broke down "irreconcilable differences," melted their hearts toward each other, wound their arms about each other's bodies, and caused them to plant loving, holy kisses on each other's cheeks.

He made them bow together, pray together, weep together, sing together, share together, preach together, and even die together. The first great miracle after Christ's resurrection was the merging of two totally diverse peoples into one body of believing Christians. The impact of this miracle was so great that the unbelieving world stood back in awe and watched with wonder.

God intended that act to be an ongoing miracle—an ever-present source of wonder. Paul exhorts us in Ephesians 4:3 to be "diligent to preserve the unity of the Spirit . . ."

I doubt that there has been a time in church history when there has been so much diversity of thinking, so much potential difference of opinion, so much opportunity for downright division.

The world of Christians, just like the world of non-Christians, has polarized around so many sensitive issues that it would seem unity or oneness could easily become an elusive dream.

The church has become very political—that's not bad unless it allows politics to divide it.

In 1976 my intense interest in the political campaign was heightened by the fact that the Oregon campaign manager for the Republican presidential nominee was an active member of Hinson Church. The treasurer for the Democratic presidential nominee was also an active member of the Hinson family. These two men and their families were close friends and fellow-Christians.

I watched with great interest and prayed with much fervor for them both. As the campaign increased in its intensity, I marveled at the manner in which these men dealt with their differences. The world was so amazed at this phenomenon it was recorded in a local newspaper.

Is spiritual unity a real life option where there is so much diversity?

Spiritual unity is not the absence of differences—spiritual unity is the absence of division.

Spiritual unity is the merging of humans from different ethnic backgrounds, different social, economic, and cultural experiences, different theological and religious orientations —people of different colors, sizes, and shapes—into one unique Spiritual Body.

The individual never loses his uniqueness or his distinctiveness. He never loses his identity. He does surrender, however, his intolerance toward specific people and ideas.

That brings us to the fourth word in Ephesians 4:2: FORBEARANCE.

Forbearance means to "hold up,"
   "to bear with equanimity,"
   "to sustain,"
   "to endure with patience,"
   "to be tolerant."
It addresses the problems of bigotry and bias.
It speaks to any form of chauvinism or feminism.
It breaks down all the real or imagined barriers that
   separate people.

FORBEARANCE means:
I ACCEPT YOU IN SPITE OF YOUR FAULTS OR OUR DIFFERENCES.

Forbearance solves the very real and very human problems of loneliness and alienation.

It means that I am accepted in spite of what is unacceptable about me.

I am welcomed in spite of what I think.

I am received in spite of how I look.

I am encouraged even in spite of what I believe.

Forbearance accepts, in spite of what it knows.

There's a little song sung by Australian children that goes:

The perfect friend is one who knows the worst about
  you
    and loves you just the same.
There's only one who loves like that, and Jesus is his
    name.

Romans 14:1 commands forbearance: "Now accept the one who is weak in faith, but not for the purpose of passing judgment on his opinions."

The Scriptures plead for high levels of tolerance in such diverse areas as what we eat or what we drink or even when and where we worship. It requires conformity only where the doctrine of Christ is at stake, the plan of salvation is at issue, or where Christian morality is being abused.

I must admit right here to some problems. I'm breaking free—but it's a painful process.

I have been plagued with a somewhat restrained Archie Bunker mentality—a mindset that tolerated more bigotry than it should have. I'm still tempted, at times, to laugh at ethnic jokes. I am still conscious of racial backgrounds and cultural differences.

I still struggle with thoughts of male chauvinism—but God is giving me a new heart in recent days. I'm overwhelmed when I stop to think about it—it's almost too much to write about.

It's a heart that has begun to beat with a compassion for the hurting, a new sensitivity for the fallen, a greater understanding for the weak. It's a heart that seems to be enlarging itself to embrace those unloved, unwanted, unaccepted ones who have been made lonely by the alienation of a judgmental church.

It's a heart that no longer repels or rejects.

It's a heart that has finally come to realize that the power of acceptance is the greatest life-changing force in all the world.

It's a heart that has finally caught the great truth of Scripture that teaches that *love never commands obedience— love produces obedience.*

In Luke, chapter 19, we see a classic illustration of what forbearance will do in a life. Do you remember Zacchaeus? He was that little Jewish rebel who alienated himself from all his friends and neighbors by selling out to the Roman government. He became a chief tax collector—which means he made himself rich by taxing Jews and then gouging them above what they really owed in order to line his own pockets. Zacchaeus, along with other tax collectors, was among the most hated of all Jewish citizens. He was regarded with contempt, he was alienated, he was friendless, he was empty, alone, hostile. An outcast.

When Jesus arrived in Zacchaeus' home town of Jericho, however, the diminutive IRS man was curious—so curious that he climbed into a sycamore tree for a better look at the Savior.

When Jesus came to the place, without warning and without any apparent reason he looked up and began to address Zacchaeus.

It was right here in Jericho, beneath a sycamore tree, in the presence of the city's biggest cheat, that Jesus displayed forbearance. With complete acceptance he looked at Zacchaeus and said, "Zacchaeus, hurry, come down, for today I must stay at your house." Zacchaeus heard it, came down, and received Jesus gladly.

Can you imagine the reaction of the crowd? The Scriptures say they grumbled and criticized Jesus for being the guest of a sinner.

As Jesus and Zacchaeus walked toward that house, something big, something wonderful, happened in that little man's heart. Zacchaeus stopped and said, "Behold, Lord (notice how he called him Lord—something had already happened to convince Zacchaeus that he was in the presence of God), half of my possessions I will give to the poor, and if I've defrauded anyone of anything, I will give back four times as much" (Luke 19:8).

What had happened? Had Jesus preached on stealing— demanded repentance—commanded restoration? No. The accepting, forgiving spirit of Jesus unlocked within Zacchaeus the ability to respond to God.

Jesus accepted him, in spite of his faults, and as a result was able to change him.

The most amazing example of forbearance to me, however, is not Zacchaeus, or others like Judas or Matthew or Thomas or Peter or the Samaritan or the thief on the cross. All of these are overshadowed by Jesus' acceptance of me.

The older I get, the more I am made aware of my sin. It seems that my wicked heart never improves, my flesh never weakens, my carnal nature never subsides. The longer I live, the more I marvel at the forbearance of God—forbearance that accepts me in spite of my faults and loves me in spite of my sin.

I often have opportunity to display forbearance when engaging in various forms of church discipline. My first act when moving in to begin restoring a fallen brother is to take him in my arms and hold him close and long, simply to reassure him that I accept him in spite of his faults.

This single act has done more to ease and to hasten the restoration process than any other thing that I could say or do.

Forbearance is on display every Sunday at Hinson Church. Located in an activist, low-income neighborhood, this cosmopolitan congregation constantly welcomes the poor, the lame, the retarded, the hostile, the old, the young. I'm terribly proud of their forbearance.

One Sunday Bruce Wilkinson of "Walk Thru the Bible" was presenting a dramatic portrayal of the book of Habakkuk. The players were costumed. All attention was directed to the platform when suddenly and quietly one of the student actors slipped through the doors in the back of the auditorium in preparation for a dramatic down-the-aisle entrance.

He was dressed like a Chaldean soldier in a toga, leggings, beard, and headpiece—which was not too different from some of the far-out dress we saw daily in our neighborhood.

I watched as one of our senior members turned around

from his place in the back row. He spotted this strange creature—gave him a startled look—sat there for a few moments in bewilderment and then stood up and walked toward him.

I was certain that he was going to ask him to leave.

Instead, he walked over to the young man, smiled and asked him if he would like to have his seat. In doing so he almost spoiled a dramatic moment, but the action spoke volumes: Hinson was learning forbearance.

Forbearance says, I ACCEPT YOU IN SPITE OF YOUR FAULTS OR OUR DIFFERENCES.

> Forbearance produces unified churches.
> Forbearance creates harmonious marriages.
> Forbearance develops happy families.
> Forbearance, like longsuffering, is the church's evangelistic weapon. It totally disarms the alienated, overwhelming them with a feeling of love that's irresistible.
> Forbearance is the result of getting to know each other.

Hinson has established growth groups, supportive fellowships, and all sorts of small group activities for the purpose of getting acquainted. It's impossible to fully love someone we don't know—to understand and trust someone who is a stranger to us.

William was in his late twenties, a resident of mental institutions and foster homes all his life. When the recession hit Oregon, he was of the many placed in neighborhood homes near the church. He dressed like a character out of Doonesbury—coonskin cap, dark glasses, heavy leather jacket, and high boots. He always came late to church and always walked across the front of the auditorium to sit right below the pulpit.

Every time I gave an invitation, he was the first to come forward. After it had happened so many times I sensed the people fidget and heard their subdued snickers. It began to pose such a problem that people refused to come forward, and I almost stopped extending invitations.

No matter how many times we talked to him, he continued to come.

One Sunday evening he came again. The congregation watched him with disgust.

As we paused in our singing, I walked over to him and asked him publicly, "William, why is it you like to come forward every time we close the service?"

He took the microphone from my hand and said, "Pastor, it's because I know you love me, and I just like to come and stand beside you."

From that moment, that bit of knowledge made him not only acceptable but loved by all the people.

To accept you—I must get to know you.

Forbearance is beautiful—irresistibly beautiful. When visible, it catches the eye of the admirer and holds the attention of the beholder.

Forbearance is the freedom to accept as I have been accepted. It's the awesome joy of performing the unexpected act that causes cocoons to fall away and beautiful creatures to emerge.

It erases hostility.
It eliminates alienation.
It dispels loneliness.

Forbearance can make caterpillars feel accepted—even though they haven't yet emerged—even though they haven't shed their binding webs—even though they haven't been transformed.

In fact, it's this kind of acceptance that *enables* caterpillars to emerge. It's the kind of acceptance that creates butterflies, giving wings to those encased by their own bondage.

"To continue to feel comfortable with ourselves
and others requires periodic maintenance.
Even right relationships can go wrong."

Chapter 13

Maintenance and Repair

*E*ven right relationships can go wrong at times. As I have learned to live comfortably with myself, I still find times of self-doubt when reassurance is needed. I still find that those neurotic little notions creep in and stir some of the old anxieties to life.

When doubts about my relationship with God through Christ emerge, I go to the Scriptures. I let God reassure me from his own Word.

When uncomfortable feelings about one of my friends begin to float through my consciousness—feelings that seem to have no basis in fact—I go to my friend. I let him listen, and as he listens, I listen to myself. What is my subconscious trying to say? Simply verbalizing those feelings usually helps me to sort out what's real from what is only imagined.

When relationships with a brother are disturbed through anger or misunderstanding, I go to my brother.

I served on the staff at Hinson from 1957 to 1960 as an associate pastor. I left that position with ill-feeling toward a deacon who had been a dear friend. Fourteen years later I returned to Hinson as senior pastor. On my first Sunday I went to find him—before I preached. I took him aside, asked forgiveness for my offense, received it, and was free to preach.

Another friend, an officer of a different church, and I broke fellowship over a difference of opinion. For years that was the strongest lingering memory of that seven-year ministry. Every time I thought of that church, Bob's face would come into focus, and I would grieve over that unhappy memory.

He came to Hinson one Sunday night years later. It was communion Sunday. As we gathered for an evening around the Lord's Table, I spotted him, halfway back, center section, and our eyes met.

I proceeded to teach, briefly, and then as I lifted the bread plate to pass it to my deacons, I was forced to stop. I put the plate down and said, "I'm sorry, I can't go on. There's a brother here in this audience whom I offended nearly twelve years ago. I have never asked his forgiveness. He knows who I'm talking about—no one else needs to." I asked the audience to all bow their heads and pray. I looked straight at him, and he looked straight at me, and I said, "My brother, will you forgive me?" A broad smile crossed his face, his head bobbed up and down, and I was free.

After the service he came to me, threw his arms about me and said, "You know—if you hadn't done that tonight, I think I would have. I knew it had to be settled tonight."

To feel comfortable with ourselves and with others requires periodic maintenance. Even right relationships can go wrong.

That delightful relationship we have with God cannot be disturbed, but its enjoyment can certainly be diminished. When I feel uncomfortable with God, it's never his fault. It's always mine, and I go to him. I acknowledge the sin that has disturbed our fellowship, claim his forgiveness, and carry on.

When the world threatens me, I go to my knees as Jesus did in the Garden of Gethsemane. That's the only place where courage and strength can be secured to meet the threats of a hostile world that's determined to destroy me, just as it did Jesus.

To continue to feel comfortable in all of life's relationships demands constant awareness and sometimes minor or major repair. But whatever it takes, it requires immediate attention and is always worth the effort.

"My butterfly broke free this morning."

Chapter 14

Out of Hiding

*M*y butterfly broke free this morning. It shed its trappings, slipped out of its bindings, worked its way out
of its web of silk, and left its prison house behind. The cocoon
is finally empty, the butterfly is finally free.

The final act of freedom really didn't take long. It was so
fast I almost missed it. Quite suddenly I detected a little
movement on the tip of the cocoon next to the twig. An ugly
worm-like creature began to appear. It struggled as it fought
its way out of its bondage until, suddenly free at last, it spread
those two magnificent wings and revealed itself as a new
creation in all of its extraordinary beauty.

You may question my credibility at this point, but let me
assure you—as incidental as it may seem to you—that when I
couldn't get started writing this book, the cocoon arrived,
and as I'm finishing this last chapter, the butterfly appeared.

It's absolutely beautiful. Technically, of course, it's not a
butterfly at all, but a giant silk moth—larger than any I've
ever seen. Its wing span exceeds six inches. Its body is the
thickness and length of a large peanut—but far more colorful. The long, feathery antennae tell me it's a boy.

The symmetrical markings on its wing and the wide

range of colors are stunning. The broad, strong wings are a deep green, ringed with reds and whites, with tips that are almost transparent. Its body is striped red and white. Its head and legs are a deep red. Each dark green wing has a perfectly shaped quarter-moon design in white, right in the center.

What a contrast to the ugly, dull, boring brown which housed it for so long. What a delight to see life, energy, and movement in place of the lifelessness of that cocoon.

And it flies! From the moment of its transformation it has pumped its magnificent wings open and closed in preparation for its flight to complete freedom.

I experienced some similar sensations when I broke free from my deep depression years ago. I have enjoyed repeated experiences of this freeing process each time I've gained some new insight into myself, some new truth about God, some new understanding of others.

And each time I dwell on any or all of these simple, life-changing words and then find opportunity to employ them, I experience a new degree of freedom—actually feel a new freedom.

Notice these four words or phrases one more time:

LOWLINESS OF MIND:

> *I accept all that God says about me without argument.*
> To accept myself, I get to know the Scriptures.
> To feel accepted, I employ "thank you therapy," the simple act of offering repeated thank you's to God for what is true about me, whether it feels true or not.

MEEKNESS:

> *I accept all of God's dealings with me without resistance or bitterness.*
> In order to accept all of life's circumstances, I accept the truths about God—all of them—and again employ "thank you therapy," giving thanks in every-

thing. Believing that everything has been allowed by a sovereign, loving, heavenly Father—whether I like it or not.

LONGSUFFERING:

I accept all of man's dealings with me without retaliation.
To feel accepted or comfortable in a hostile world, I thank God for my indestructibility as an eternal person. I also thank him for the privilege of touching lives with a response that will ultimately bring about change.

FORBEARANCE:

I accept you with all your faults or our differences.
In order to accept another person or feel accepted by another person, I must get to know that person. I must then thank God for him, and even for the differences that will stretch my tolerance and love levels to their limit.

The process in my own life is far from complete. I still find some of the debris from that old cocoon hanging on to me from time to time. At other times I actively resist these truths, and am tempted to go back into hiding.

As I was concluding this chapter, Martha and I were located on the top floor of the Prince Kuhio Hotel near Waikiki Beach in Hawaii, in the middle of a badly needed vacation.

We retired early Saturday evening. The last thing we talked about was which morning worship service we would attend Sunday morning—the early service or the later one.

I said, "You know, I'm so tired, I may not go to church at all in the morning."

We were awakened at 6:30 with the news that the pastor of the church we were going to attend had become suddenly and seriously ill. I was asked to preach both services in his place.

As we were driving to the church, I turned to Martha and said, "I'm sorry, but right now I don't feel the least bit meek, nor do I wish to. I really wanted to rest this morning."

As soon as I had unleashed those feelings, we were able to thank God for an unexpected and unplanned experience and believe that a sovereign God had rearranged our day for reasons known only to him.

To come out of hiding, to open myself up to myself and to my God and to others, has been a wonderfully freeing experience.

I covet it for you.

Remember:

In order to feel comfortable with myself—I must get to know myself as God reveals me in the Scriptures.

In order to feel comfortable with God, I must get to know God as he reveals himself in the Scriptures.

In order to feel comfortable in a hostile world, I must get to know Jesus, and he is revealed as the truly longsuffering One in the Scriptures.

In order to feel comfortable with you, I must get to know you as you slowly (and perhaps fearfully) reveal yourself to me.

And then, in the experience of spiritual unity and peace, we can display the magnificent beauty that is characteristic of the body of Christ, we can pollinate the world with the wonder of Jesus and see our own serene, comfortable, acceptable selves reproduced in the lives of others still struggling to become free.

True acceptance, however, must have a starting point. It can begin at only one place, and that is at the cross of Jesus Christ.

It's there that I acknowledge my bondage to sin, and it is there I admit that the only liberating force in the world is Jesus Christ.

It is there that I confess my helplessness, reach out for his love and grace, and experience the power of his forgiveness.

It is there that the limitless power of God is unleashed in my life . . . a power that makes a life of acceptance possible . . . a power that enables me to reach out in every direction . . . a power that allows me to be comfortable in a most uncomfortable world.